Designing Gifted Education Programs and Services

Programs and Services

From Purpose to Implementation

Designing Gifted Education Programs and Services

From Purpose to Implementation

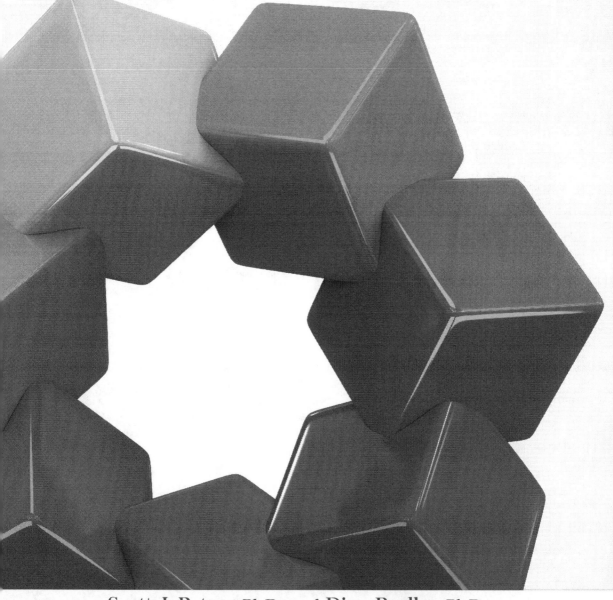

Scott J. Peters, Ph.D., and Dina Brulles, Ph.D.

Library of Congress Cataloging-in-Publication Data

Names: Peters, Scott J., 1983- author. | Brulles, Dina, author.
Title: Designing gifted education programs and services : from purpose to
  implementation / by Scott J. Peters and Dina Brulles,
Description: Waco, Texas : Prufrock Press Inc., [2018] | Includes
  bibliographical references.
Identifiers: LCCN 2017033804| ISBN 9781618216809 (pbk.) | ISBN 9781618216816
  (pdf) | ISBN 9781618216823 (epub)
Subjects: LCSH: Gifted children--Education--United States.
Classification: LCC LC3993.9 .P483 2018 | DDC 371.95--dc23
LC record available at https://lccn.loc.gov/2017033804

Edited by Lacy Compton

Cover design by Raquel Trevino and layout design by Micah Benson

ISBN-13: 978-1-61821-680-9

Printed in the United States of America.

At the time of this book's publication, all facts and figures cited are the most current available; all telephone numbers, addresses, and website URLs are accurate and active; all publications, organizations, websites, and other resources exist as described in this book; and all have been verified. The authors and Prufrock Press make no warranty or guarantee concerning the information and materials given out by organizations or content found at websites, and we are not responsible for any changes that occur after this book's publication. If you find an error or believe that a resource listed here is not as described, please contact Prufrock Press.

Prufrock Press Inc.
P.O. Box 8813
Waco, TX 76714-8813
Phone: (800) 998-2208
Fax: (800) 240-0333
http://www.prufrock.com

TABLE OF CONTENTS

FOREWORD

Like many of us, my journey through gifted land didn't come with directions. I began as a classroom teacher of gifted students—with no prior education in who they were, their social-emotional needs, learning differences, and so on. During my first years of teaching, I took graduate-level courses in all things gifted. It was truly "on-the-job" training, or as I say, "baptism by lava!"

After teaching for 10 years, I felt I knew enough to take on the role of a district coordinator. Again, the expedition was fraught with losing direction, making the wrong turns at the wrong time, and just generally wandering until I found some success. I spent 15 years developing, implementing, and evaluating gifted programs and services, mostly by making a lot of mistakes, going in the wrong direction, and recreating the wheel.

Now, 30 years after I began my travels through gifted land, Scott Peters and Dina Brulles have written the directions I needed so long ago. They have expertly crafted a concise and informative text on the whys, hows, and whats of developing and sustaining quality gifted programs and services. Based on real experiences and substantial research, the authors guide you through the entire process.

Dina Brulles and I became acquainted while attending one of my first National Association for Gifted Children (NAGC) annual conferences. We were both directors of gifted programs in suburbs of large cities. We shared many of the same concerns and issues in making sure we were doing the best for our students. I marveled at Dina's energy and commitment to equity and quality. I knew she was someone who was going to make a mark in the field of gifted education.

The NAGC conference is also where I was introduced to Scott Peters. We met while he was working on his Ph.D., specializing in gifted education. He has matured into a strong voice in the field, challenging old assumptions with evidence. Peters makes a clear case for what needs to be changed in our pursuit of appropriate programming and services. His wealth of knowledge regarding effective-practices comes through in this informative text.

Together, they offer you everything you need to know on your journey. Beginning with developing a quality program philosophy, the authors challenge many of the conventions and myths regarding the educational needs of advanced learners. They demonstrate how to bring diverse groups together to agree upon a philosophy of gifted education, how to seek out resources, and how to define which programs and services will best meet the needs of your students.

Each chapter opens with guiding questions that get you thinking about what's to come. During my reading, I found myself thinking back to my own experiences as a coordinator/director of gifted programs. You are sure to find substantial advice for where you want to take your program. Part II provides authentic examples of various programs and service models. No matter the size of your district, you will be able to replicate what others have created.

The authors' fresh approach "to alleviate unmet academic needs so that every student is appropriately challenged" makes this text the most relevant in programming and services for today's gifted population. As a new coordinator/director, you will find each chapter extremely helpful in where to start and what to do. For seasoned coordinators/directors, this book is a solid reminder of how to maintain the quality and equity within your programs and services.

Make *Designing Gifted Education Programs and Services* your GPS (Gifted Programs and Services) guide. Peters and Brulles offer clear direction in the often-confusing landscape of gifted education. They take much of the guesswork out of the art and science of building, maintaining, and evaluating quality and equitable gifted programs and services.

—Richard M. Cash, Ed.D.
Educator, consultant, author of *Advancing Differentiation* and *Self-Regulation in the Classroom,* and coauthor of *Differentiation for Gifted Learners*

INTRODUCTION

The Importance of a Board-Approved Plan

As of the 2014–2015 school year, 32 states (of the 40 responding to the National Association for Gifted Children's 2015 State of the States report) had some kind of mandate to identify and serve gifted and talented students enrolled in public schools. Of these states, some (21) monitored the compliance of individual school districts, and at least 18 states required local school districts to submit gifted education plans for approval to the state education agency. This means that there is a strong and ongoing need for guidance regarding the creation and structuring of gifted and talented education plans. These plans help lay out what services are provided, which students receive them, and how gifted education aligns with other aspects of the K–12 curriculum. Even for those states where such plans are not required, school districts all around the country are struggling with how to best meet the needs of advanced learners. This issue has become even more prevalent in general education circles as many teachers and schools are beginning to be held accountable for the growth and learning of all students—including those who are already above proficiency. This move toward evaluating educators based on growth has renewed the focus on how to best serve those students who are already proficient. It has also called forth a conversation about how to incorporate gifted and talented education into mainstream education initiatives.

All of this is taking place while the field of gifted education is simultaneously realizing and accepting that what makes for "best practice" in K–12 gifted education can and should look different across different states, districts, and even school buildings. This contemporary view of advanced educational services means that sources of generic "best practices" are not what is needed. Instead, a process is needed for how local school leaders and stakeholders can develop their own plans for advanced educational services to best meet the needs of their students.

As referenced above, the creation and maintenance of a gifted education plan for a local district is required in at least 18 states. Even beyond these states, far more districts maintain some kind of informal plan or policy for how to meet the needs of advanced learners and other students with high potential. Often the creation or revision of such plans is the first job of a tenderfoot gifted education coordinator. Despite this seemingly common requirement, teacher training regarding gifted and talented education is inconsistent at best—only Nevada requires a stand-alone course in gifted education for all preservice teachers. This leaves many districts without experts on staff to help develop or implement services. Because of this lack of consistent training, a book that presents not only a guiding structure and format, but also case study examples from real school districts across the country that have been through the process and lived to tell the tale, has the potential to be of great value. Never has this been truer than in the post-No Child Left Behind age where growth is a major focus—something we will discuss more in Chapter 1. Many districts have seen their funding cut back in recent years, making the task even more daunting. District leaders must now challenge all learners, including those who are already proficient, without expending any additional resources. Because hiring additional staff is rarely an option, many schools need resources at hand in order to accomplish these daunting tasks.

This book is about gifted education plans. By "plans" we mean proactive, thoughtfully derived systems, procedures, and policies regarding how a school or a school district will assure that the needs of advanced learners are met. Although this book will cover many traditional topics (e.g., data use, student identification, programs and services), we chose the topic of gifted education plans for a very important reason. Many people in the field of education can probably reflect back to an outstanding teacher or even a special program that made their school experience especially positive or effective. Eventually, these people will retire, if they haven't already, and all too often the programs retire or move on with them. Effective or otherwise outstanding programs should never have to retire and be created by each generation from the ground up. Likewise, building administrators come and go with their own opinions and ideas about gifted education that might not be in line with the best practices that were put into place by a concerned coordinator. There is also the nonstop questioning from concerned parents who want to know how their child will be challenged. For all of these (and other) reasons, formalized policy is important.

Wisconsin State Statute 121.02(1)(t) states that [Each school board shall] "Provide access to an appropriate program for pupils identified as gifted or talented." In the application of this statute, the Wisconsin Department of Public Instruction required that "Each school district shall establish a plan . . . to coordinate the gifted and talented program" (Wisconsin Administrative Code 8.01(2)(t)2). This is the very first in a list of requirements laid out in this particular Administrative Rule governing gifted education in the state of Wisconsin. But why? Why is one of the most explicit requirements for school districts that a plan must exist and that it is the responsibility of the school board? The answer is likely related to the phenomenon described above that many of us in education have witnessed all too often. Individuals or committees spend countless hours developing plans and procedures just to have many of these plans forgotten with the change of administration or the hiring of a new staff member. Why school board approved plans? We believe that in the contemporary world of K–12 education, where nearly nothing is certain, enshrining gifted education plans and policies in board-approved policy is the best way to leverage support from other stakeholders as well as to assure this particular agenda is taken seriously. Of course, we are not so naïve as to think that this means all one must do is get a policy approved by the board and then it is guaranteed to go off without a hitch. That said, we believe it's a step in the right direction and have seen it help advance advocacy efforts with reluctant teachers and administrators.

This leads us to our very first recommendation: Whatever you take away from this book and decide to implement as a gifted education or advanced academic plan or system in your district, make sure that your procedures and policies are thoroughly reviewed and then placed into a comprehensive plan, which is then approved by your school board. As if the reasons we've already outlined are not enough, many states either require that district plans be developed and then submitted to the states on an annual or semiannual basis, or that they be available in case of a state review or a formal complaint. Because just under half of the states in the nation require districts to have gifted education plans on file with the state, we were surprised to realize that no publication existed on this topic until now. Some of these states are: Alabama, Arizona, Arkansas, Colorado, Georgia, Iowa, Louisiana, Maine, Maryland, Mississippi, Nebraska, North Carolina, Ohio, Oklahoma, Oregon, Rhode Island, South Carolina, Tennessee, Utah, Virginia, and Washington. Of course, this changes all of the time. To see if your state requires such plans, check the National Association for Gifted Children's State of the States website (http://www.nagc.org/resources-publications/gifted-state).

Much of this book is about process. There is no such thing as a canned gifted education program or a one-size-fits-all policy for identification or services, yet volumes abound to provide exactly this kind of information. In this book we hope to guide the concerned school or district through the process of developing its own plan and procedures for assuring that those students who have already mastered grade-level materials remain challenged. Note that we will focus on a much larger population than that which is commonly discussed in "gifted education" circles. Our goal with the gifted education plans that we describe in this book is to assure that any student with an unmet advanced need will have that need met through an appropriate intervention or service. The plans in this book will not tell you what to do with the kids who "are" gifted because of some "happenstance of nature or nurture" (Lohman, 2006, p. 7). Rather, they will assist the concerned school or district in how to plan for what will happen once students have already mastered grade-level content or require support in a domain that cannot be elsewhere provided. Through this process, the end goal is assuring that as many students remain challenged as much of the time as possible while engaged in compulsory education.

STRUCTURE

The book is organized into two parts. Part I provides a structure with which schools or districts can develop their own plans. With this as a goal, we proceed through first understanding who your students are, what they can currently do and already know, and what content would best help them move forward. Much of this involves diving into data (of all types) to determine what it is that students already know and how that compares to what they will be taught. However, every state has its own laws and regulations for gifted education and every district is different. For better or worse, state regulations are often vague at best. Even best practice handbooks can be too theoretical for staff in schools to implement easily. Because of this, Part II includes links to real gifted education plans from districts around the country, coupled with written commentaries from district personnel who were either involved in their development or had to live with their implementation. Rather than reprint all of the district materials, we compiled them all onto our publisher's website (see http://www.prufrock.com/Assets/ClientPages/DesigningGiftedPrograms.aspx). As you read the commentary chapters in Part II of this book, you can follow along with the district materials to see what they actually said about what they put into practice. Our goal here is to show what "real-world" gifted education plans look like and what their rationale was when they were created. Not all practices are ideal and, in some cases, the authors of the commentaries note things they'd like to see changed. In this fashion, this book includes a structure for how to create your own plan as well as in-depth, annotated examples for what such plans look like in practice. We hope that the combination of the "best practices" with the "real-world practices" helps you better meet the needs of advanced learners. If nothing else, hopefully the collective experience of the Part II chapter authors helps you move a little further and a little faster than if you had to start from scratch.

PART I
BEST PRACTICES

CHAPTER 1

Essential Elements of Gifted Education

GUIDING QUESTIONS

- Why have gifted education?
- Why devote funds and resources to kids who are already proficient when so many kids are not?
- Why devote additional funds and services to kids who are already privileged?
- Won't gifted education exacerbate achievement gaps and make inequality even worse?

If you're in gifted education and you haven't had to address these questions yet, be assured that you will at some time! Although many in gifted education tire of them, it's important to have reasoned, rational answers to these and a host of other questions. In an ideal world, it's even better if these kinds of questions can be headed off before they are asked by having in place a comprehensive gifted education plan and communicating it effectively.

Something that continues to shock practitioners and researchers in gifted education is just how rare it is that a program or intervention for advanced learners has an explicit goal for its reason for being. If a parent or school board member can walk up to you, ask you what the goal is for the local gifted program, and you don't have an answer at the ready, then your program may not be around for long. Many definitions of "giftedness" exist, and we will discuss some later on, but the actual "why" of gifted education is rarely made explicit. In this book we will proceed as if the general purpose of any gifted education program, service, or intervention is to more appropriately challenge those who have unmet academic needs. Implied in this goal is that the unmet need is at the advanced end of the spectrum, although as we will discuss, the process should be the same in developing services for those who have unmet needs for remediation or those who have needs related to language development or a disability. Our goal for everyone is to better personalize learning and align educational interventions to student needs.

In conversations with educators who have long experience in gifted education, we have heard concerns about the use of the term *academic* when talking about the purpose of gifted education. It is important we make clear that the term academic does not simply refer to math and reading, nor does it only include the more traditional school subjects of science, social studies, and language arts. Our definition of academic is more liberal and includes any subject area or domain for which the broader school community has decided to provide services. For example, in rural Wisconsin, many schools have strong agriculture programs and credit-bearing courses, while others in urban areas have begun expanding computer science offerings. Such courses are part of their academic offerings. These schools will have some students who are just beginning their exposure to these domains, while others have long history with them, thus necessitating a range of service levels. For these reasons, gifted education does not carry specific domains. Rather, the domains of service are locally determined based on the philosophical, cultural, and practical values of the school and community.

With all of that out of the way, there are a few golden rules that will guide Part I of this book that we recommend any gifted coordinator also keep in mind while drafting a gifted education plan.

1. The primary purpose of any service provided under the label of "gifted education" should be to alleviate an otherwise unmet advanced academic need. These needs are and should be locally defined and continually, proactively evaluated.

2. Any gifted education plan should make it clear how student needs will be assessed and how programs to be provided are in line with and would help alleviate student needs.

3. Any gifted education plan should be explicit in how its implementation would place the school or district in compliance with state rules, regulations, or laws. Ideally, GT plans would also outline how they align to the National Association for Gifted Children's Pre-K–Grade 12 Gifted Programming Standards (2010; see Appendix A).

One of the first things we will discuss in the next chapter is how to understand and identify student learning needs and the degree to which they are or are not being met by existing services. Gifted education has long been interested in student needs, often measuring them with ability or intelligence tests. But having an advanced level of need (or ability) is not sufficient to determine if a student requires additional, supplementary services, and if so, what type of service. This is why we try to be careful and use the term *unmet academic needs*. For example, in roughly 5% of American schools, the average student achievement is around the 95th percentile on a national norm. This means that for 5% of American schools, half of the students are above 95% of their peers from around the country (Lohman, 2006). The traditional model of gifted education would see many, if not all, of these students as gifted. But the more important question, and the one most relevant for schools, is whether or not these students are being sufficiently challenged in their learning so that they can continue to grow and develop.

Simply knowing a person's level of ability, need, or intelligence is necessary but not sufficient to answer this question. For this reason, much of the next chapter will talk about how to determine what needs are currently going unmet by the curriculum and services that are already offered in your school or district. This perspective of gifted education being in place in order to better challenge students who are otherwise underchallenged, is nothing revolutionary. The following is the federal definition of giftedness:

> Children and youth with outstanding talent perform or show the potential for performing at remarkably high levels of accomplishment when compared with others of their age, experience, or environment. These children and youth exhibit high performance capability in intellectual, creative, and/or artistic areas, possess an unusual leadership capacity, or excel in specific academic fields. *They require services or activities not ordinarily provided by the schools.* Outstanding talents are present in children and youth from all cultural groups, across all economic strata, and in all areas of human endeavor. (U.S. Department of Education, 1993, p. 3, emphasis added)

The italicized sentence in this definition is often overlooked but it makes an important point. In addition to exhibiting high-performance capability, gifted learners are those who require services or activities not ordinarily provided. To us, this is critically important, as it states that part of the goal of gifted education is to seek out those who require services or supports that are not provided by a given school as part of their regular curriculum. This is why any good gifted education program must start by understanding who is and is not likely to be appropriately challenged by existing services (in Chapter 4, we discuss the need to modify services when the existing model[s] do not address gifted students' unmet academic needs). In the ideal world where every child is perfectly challenged by a universally flexible range of services, schools would have no need for gifted or special education.

One of the implications of what we've presented so far is that gifted education, with its identification procedures and services, is inherently local. The needs of one particular building could be different from a building across town, which means the services will need to look different as well. "Gifted" is not a static, permanent trait of people, but rather represents a dynamic and ever-changing need for services beyond what is currently being provided. Although the services offered and level of interventions might look different across different schools, what should be universal is that every building has a plan in place for how it will search out and select or create services to make sure all students are challenged in their learning. It doesn't matter if what is needed is teaching a 16-year-old to read or a 9-year-old how to do calculus. The goal for every student is the same—to alleviate unmet academic needs so that every student is appropriately challenged. How this happens and what the process looks like is the meat of a gifted education plan.

A further implication of our second point from above is that programs or interventions are provided to those who have a need for or would benefit from them. This also means that students are not kept out of programs or services unless there is evidence that students will not benefit from them. There is a somewhat-famous statement in gifted education that if an intervention or curriculum is something all students would want to do, could do, or should do, then it's not really gifted education. For example, learning math with manipulatives is something that many students would probably prefer to lengthy worksheets. It's also something that is probably good for all students to practice so that they can think more broadly about math and not just apply math with pencil and paper. Because of these facts, the chance to learn math with manipulatives should not be restricted to identified "gifted" kids, as many more kids would likely want to work with them, should work with them, and could learn better with them. The same can be said for curriculum on critical or creative thinking, project-based learning, or real-world applications. All of these topics are important for all students to learn and be exposed to and as such, they should not be reserved solely for identified gifted students.

Every district must function within the broader context of the state in which it exists. There are also national laws and regulations to consider as well as best practices and standards. For all of these reasons, the following section outlines the current state of the nation with regard to gifted education requirements followed by an overview of what some states do. After reading this section, we recommend the reader review his or her state's page on the National Association for Gifted Children's State of the States report as well as the Davidson Institute's state policy page for his or her particular state. Although we think it's important to know what is happening across the country with regard to gifted education, state-level requirements are the most relevant to crafting gifted education plans.

STATE OF THE NATION

Often, the "why" of gifted education is a state law or regulation requiring identification, services, or both. Throughout the country, there are laws at the state and federal level that districts need to comply with. Of course, these laws are enforced to a wide degree—some, we would argue, are not being enforced at all. Still, what we present in the following section are the main laws at the federal level that relate to gifted education followed by an overview of state rules and regulations with a few in-depth examples. As we said earlier, any gifted education plan should address how the district will be in compliance with any state laws or regulations. For some, this will be easy (because there aren't any state regulations), whereas for others, this will be an exhaustive process.

HIGHER EDUCATION OPPORTUNITY ACT

Before we outline what individual states require in terms of gifted and talented education, it's worth addressing what is actually required by the federal government. Most veteran gifted education practitioners would say there isn't any federal mandate for gifted education (which is true), but in the last 10 years, a number of changes have been made to federal law that relate to advanced learners. First, in summer 2008, President Bush signed the Higher Education Opportunity Act (HEOA) reauthorization into law. This reauthorization made three important changes. First, it redefined "teaching skills" to include the ability to identify the needs of and tailor instruction toward gifted students (among others). This was a consequential change because much of HEOA's emphasis on teaching skills dealt with how colleges and universities prepared teachers. In a less-than-direct way, HEOA mandated that all teachers be trained in how to identify and serve gifted and talented learners. Given the near-nonexistent training that most preservice teachers receive in gifted education, this seemed like a monumental change.

The HEOA also required states to issue report cards on the quality of teacher preparation programs, including information on how they were assuring their preservice teachers' mastery of "teaching skills" as defined in HEOA. In other words, there was some accountability built in to say that each state had to report on how it was assuring all preservice teacher candidates were proficient in the federally defined teaching skills, which, as discussed in the previous paragraph, now included gifted education teaching skills. The final change to HEOA required that any teacher preparation program that received Title II funds must include the "teaching skills" of preservice education students as an outcome. If taken as intended, this would mean any university receiving Title II money would have to at least consider how its programs would support preservice teachers' knowledge development with regard to gifted and talented education. If truly implemented with fidelity, HEOA would have injected gifted education into every teacher education program in the country.

Unfortunately, there's little reason to believe that states implemented the HEOA requirements as intended. Most states simply needed to assure the U.S. Department of Education (USDOE) that their preservice teachers were being trained in such a way that they could meet the needs of advanced learners. Often, this took the form of the state reporting that diversity of student need was addressed in teacher education. No greater level of specificity was required in report cards, and based on our own experience, colleges and universities have changed little in order to better prepare teachers to challenge advanced learners. That said, we bring up HEOA here because it's worth pointing out that there is federal law that requires all teachers to be trained in how to identify and meet the needs of gifted and talented students. Whether or not this is actually happening is an open question.

THE EVERY STUDENT SUCCEEDS ACT

The Every Student Succeeds Act (ESSA) was the 2015 reauthorization of the Elementary and Secondary Education Act (ESEA). ESEA, now represented by ESSA, is by far the most influential federal law for K–12 public schools. Whereas in the past, under No Child Left Behind, the law paid almost no attention to advanced learners, ESSA makes several substantive changes to benefit these students. First, ESSA mandates that state school report cards include achievement data disaggregated by proficiency level as well as by student subgroup. This means that schools and states can no longer just focus on those students who are or are not at grade-level proficiency. Now, they must also report on rates of advanced achievement, broken down by subgroup. Although not mandating any services to influence these rates of achievement, at least now the rates of advanced achievement will be widely reported, including the gaps in advanced achievement among various student subgroups.

Second, when or if a state applies for Title II professional development funds, it must include how the funds will be utilized to improve the skills of educators and schools to identify gifted and talented students and provide instruction based on their identified needs. Although not a blanket requirement for all schools (because it depends on their acceptance of Title II funds), this mandate would require that any professional development funded by Title II funds includes how the capacity of a school to meet the needs of advanced learners will be increased. As of this writing, states are developing their Title II applications, so it remains to be seen how or if states are faithful to these requirements or the degree to which the USDOE enforces them. Still, this change, taken alongside the HEOA definition that includes gifted education as part of strong "teaching skills," suggests there is a movement to consider those students who need additional challenge as part of good teaching and quality teacher education.

The same requirement for states to disaggregate achievement data by level and student subgroup also applies to individual school districts. Whereas some states have already been doing this for years (e.g., online databases reporting the rates of achievement across three, four, or five categories for every school), all schools will now be required to do this. This is significant for the purposes of this book because it means that all schools will soon have access to the rates of above-level achievement for individual student subgroups. This will make identifying unmet needs easier and will allow for individual districts to investigate, measure, and plan interventions to address excellence gaps.

Finally, any individual district that receives Title II professional development funds must use that money to increase the capacity of teachers to meet the needs of "all students"—ESSA specifically states that "all students" includes gifted and talented students. In other words, if a school accepts Title II money, it must include some professional development addressed at advanced levels of student need. Given the ubiquity of Title II funds in schools, this could result in an explosion of professional development related to advanced learners. We stress "could" because the effect depends on the level of proactive enforcement by the state as well as the U.S. Department of Education, in addition to the priorities of the school districts.

One final change that is not a mandate but is significant nonetheless, is that schools may now use Title I funds to identify and serve gifted and talented students. In the past, these funds were restricted to low-income learners, but a change in ESSA allows them to also be used to address advanced learning needs. Schools will have the ability to choose how they wish to use Title I funds, under the priorities of their individual state, but at least increasing the capacity of schools to identify and meet the needs of low-income students who are above grade level has some support. We are especially hopeful that this change will give schools some resources to focus on and create interventions to address income-related excellence gaps.

IMPLICATIONS FOR GIFTED EDUCATION PLANS

A downside to so much new federal legislation related to gifted education is that it isn't yet clear what components will be enforced or what degree of oversight the USDOE and individual states will enforce. However, although there might not be hard, fixed mandates going forward at the federal level, there are opportunities. If not necessarily requiring districts to do more for advanced learners, new legislation has at least given them permission to do so, as well as provided access to a pot of funds. For example, districts could use the ESSA requirements in order to "get a foot in the door" with regard to district-wide professional development for teachers via Title II funds. Similarly, the broader availability of above-level data could be useful in identifying student needs and aligning them with services (something we will address in Chapters 2 and 3).

In the end, there is a renewed federal focus on both the requirement to identify and meet above-level needs as well as funding to support such efforts. Districts that are considering making significant moves or changes in this area might consider the Javits Gifted and Talented Students Education Program grants. This program, which has been funded on and off for almost two decades now, supports programs that meet the needs of gifted and talented students with an emphasis on those populations that are traditionally underrepresented (limited English proficient, economically disadvantaged, and disabled). Districts have received funds to implement 3- to 5-year projects related to better meeting the needs of advanced learners from underrepresented populations. Again, although there is no sweeping federal mandate to support gifted education, there are far more opportunities than there have ever been.

STATE-LEVEL RULES AND REGULATIONS

Although our discussion so far might make it seem as if the federal government is actively involved in assuring that the needs of advanced learners are met in school, the reality is that most of the heavy lifting takes place at the state level and/or school district level. As we said in our introduction to this book, a number of states have legal requirements related to gifted education in K–12 schools, many of which are far more detailed and prescriptive than the federal regulations we just described. At the same time, some have next to nothing (or actually nothing), while even those that have adopted legal requirements have widely variable policies.

In this section, we outline the state of the nation as far as state mandates, funding, and regulations related to advanced learners. Of course, as we write this, much of the information is likely out of date, especially as states across the country work to implement the Every Student Succeeds Act. The National Association for Gifted Children (NAGC) maintains a website clearinghouse of state-specific gifted education information related to laws and policies (https://www.nagc.org/resources-publications/gifted-state) that is a good place to look for the most up-to-date information. Individual state gifted associations also tend to be good places to go to understand what is actually required in your state and how any regulations are enforced. Much of the information we present below comes from the 2014–2015 State of the States (NAGC, 2015). The report itself includes far more information than we will summarize here, but our purpose in the following section is to give readers an idea of what some states require.

FUNDING

Of the states that responded to the State of the States report in 2015, 27 reported that funding was available to school districts to support gifted education. However, these dollar amounts varied widely, as did the mechanism through which the funds are dispersed. For example, for 2014–2015, the State of Iowa allocated $37,675,133 for gifted education with each district receiving funds based on its number of students in the district. In a similar fashion, neighboring Minnesota allocated $11,389,325 (less than a third as much money with roughly twice as many K–12 students as Iowa), and provided these funds via a direct $13 per pupil allocation to all districts in the state. This is not based on the number of identified students, but rather on total enrollment. In other words, every district received $13 for every K–12 student it served in order to addresses the needs of advanced learners. Alternatively, states such as Arizona, Michigan, Illinois, and Connecticut provided no funding for gifted education. There are also states that fall somewhere in the middle. For example, states such as Wisconsin, Colorado, and Montana maintained a set amount of money to be used to fund grants to districts based on proposed services. For the purposes of gifted education plans, funding isn't as influential as the legally mandated services, except to the degree that the funding might actually help support those services. Unfortunately, it's been our experience that, more often than not, states require more things of schools than they are willing to support with funding.

In our experience and based on the State of the States report, the two most common funding mechanisms are the per-pupil allocation (either based on the number of gifted students or the total number of students enrolled in the district) or the grant-based system. An important consideration for a new gifted coordinator is what accountability there is for the use of any existing funds, how they are allowed to be used, and what services can be provided within the limitations of those funds. States do not tend to provide funding with zero strings attached. It's important to understand any accountability that comes with accepting state funds and how this might influence a district's gifted education plans or policies.

MANDATED SERVICES

As with funding, the degree of legal mandate for identification and services varies widely both in what is written as well as what is enforced. Of the 40 states that responded to this particular question in the State of the States survey, 32 reported having some kind of legal mandate for gifted education. In most cases, this mandate comes in the form of state law (32), while for others it comes via department of education policy (11), administrative rules (11), or guidelines (8). Of these states, most require students to be identified as well as served in K–12 schools (28). However, four states reported that identification was required, but not any particular services (e.g., Kansas, Nebraska). We point this out because of what we mentioned earlier—

that the entire point of identification is to more appropriately meet students' needs. Identification is a means to an end, and the needs being met are always more important than the label.

Of those 32 states with legal mandates, four fully fund these mandates (e.g., Oklahoma, Iowa), while 20 partially fund (e.g., North Carolina, Texas), and eight do not fund at all (e.g., Rhode Island, New Jersey). What is required of states (when anything is required) can range from individualized education plans for all identified students to vague and unenforced "appropriate services." In at least 18 states, districts must submit their gifted education plans to the state, and in at least 12 of them, the state must approve of the plan (see Table 1). Note that two of the states where such plans and approvals are required are represented in the chapter commentaries in Part II of this book (Arizona and Florida). However, although on paper Arizona districts are required to submit their gifted education plans to the state, since cutbacks in funding in 2010, this doesn't really happen. Although we believe that all states and districts should have a plan for how they will challenge students whose needs fall outside the scope of the standard, grade-level curriculum, in these states such a practice is mandated by law.

Most often, these state-level approvals involve the review of district identification methods, services offered, teacher training and personnel, the particular definition of giftedness used, and how parents will be involved. For example, in Arkansas, every school district must log in to a department of education website to enter information, such as how many students were served, what types of programs they were provided with, how staff was trained to deliver those services, and the process through which students were identified for those services. Once these plans are submitted, they are reviewed before the state schedules a technical assistance visit. All of this assures a high level of fidelity to the state requirements for gifted education.

Alternatively, in the state of Idaho, districts must submit updated gifted education plans every 3 years, but there is no procedure for approval by the state. These plans are required to include: (1) philosophy statement, (2) definition of giftedness, (3) program goals, (4) program options, (5) identification procedures, and (6) program evaluation (Idaho Department of Education, n.d.).

Although not included in the table above, the state of Iowa also requires districts to have and submit district gifted and talented program plans annually as part of their larger comprehensive school improvement plans. Each district is required to report on the following areas in its plan:

1. Valid and systematic identification procedures, including multiple selection criteria for identifying gifted and talented students from the total student population (grades K–12);
2. Goals and performance measures;
3. Qualitatively differentiated gifted and talented program to meet the students' cognitive and affective needs;

Table 1

State Mandates for Gifted Education Plans

State	District Plan Required	Plan Approved by State
Alabama	Yes	Yes
Arizona	Yes	Yes
Arkansas	Yes	Yes
Colorado	Yes	Yes
Delaware	Yes	No
Florida	Yes	Yes
Georgia	Yes	No
Idaho	Yes	No
Maine	Yes	Yes
Maryland	Yes	Yes
Mississippi	Yes	Yes
Nebraska	Yes	Yes
North Carolina	Yes	No
Oklahoma	Yes	Yes
South Carolina	Yes	Yes
Tennessee	Yes	No
Virginia	Yes	No
Washington	Yes	Yes

    4. Staffing provisions;
    5. In-service design (professional development); and
    6. Program evaluation process (Iowa Department of Education, 2016).

Each district must also report a budget for its programs and services as well as the qualifications of the personnel administering the program.

In a similar fashion, Tennessee requires written gifted education plans for each district. However, unlike in Iowa and Idaho, these plans, once approved, need not be resubmitted unless changes are being made. Otherwise, it is assumed that the district is still implementing its most recently approved plan. According to the Tennessee State Plan for the Education of Intellectually Gifted Students (Tennessee Department of Education, 2010), these plans must address the following areas:

    1. Philosophy
    2. Program goals
    3. Referrals
    4. Evaluation
    5. Eligibility
    6. Service delivery options

7. Grievance procedures
8. Data tracking system
9. Forms
10. Alternative/enrichment programs (p. 23)

As should be clear by now, we believe gifted education and gifted education district plans are necessary in order to assure all students are properly challenged. This same emphasis is reflected in the fact that the most common factors that are required in state plans are identification policies and plans for programming. Many states also require specific program goals, plans for staffing and staff training, and procedures for appeals or communication with parents or other stakeholders. Even when not required in your particular state, these examples show the most common components of gifted education plans. For specific examples, see Part II for the webpage where we have uploaded links to a variety of district plans and materials.

What we've presented so far represents what other states and districts across the country do in terms of formal policy. Any district needs to take into account federal laws (such as the Title II requirements from ESSA) as well as the state-specific rules and regulations related to services and whether or not a formalized plan needs to be provided to the state education agency. However, even when law doesn't require such a plan, it's still a good thing to have. As we noted in the introduction, too often outstanding programs disappear with the retirement of a single staff member or the hiring of a new administrator. This leaves a new person to reinvent the system from the ground up. That doesn't need to happen. Formalized plans and policies, covering some of the topics we've presented in this chapter, can assure that all staff members and schools are on the same page with what is supposed to happen and when, and can also help assure compliance with any relevant regulations. In each of the commentaries included in Part II, the authors reference the state requirements and how their districts responded to them and addressed them in their plans.

In synthesizing what we have seen in state requirements as well as in our experience in the field, there are a few essential components we believe should be included in any gifted education plan. All of these will be discussed in the remaining chapters in Part I:

1. Include details regarding the process that will be undertaken each year to determine who is likely to be underchallenged by existing services—who is likely to have his or her needs met by existing services and who is likely to need something more?

2. Identify where, how, and when different levels of need will be addressed. What are the typical service options? What will happen if none of these service options will alleviate a student's particular need?

3. Identify what will happen when needs are identified that are outside the level or scope of traditional interventions. For example, what will the gifted

services look like for profoundly gifted students who are radically accelerated in specific subject areas?

4. Identify scopes and sequences for students who participate in various interventions such that they will always have something to do next year. See an excellent example of this about Paradise Valley in Part II.

5. Make it clear where and how staff will be trained in the logistics of services as well as in how to deliver the services.

6. Explain timelines for identification, service provisions, program evaluation, and options for family involvement in the process.

7. Explain what will be done to proactively seek out students from traditionally underrepresented populations (e.g., low-income, racial/ethnic minority).

CHAPTER 2

UNDERSTANDING AND IDENTIFYING LEARNING NEEDS

- What are the local learning needs of gifted students?
- How can we ensure that all students are academically challenged at school?
- Why do we need to provide gifted services?

Rhea is fascinated with butterflies. She archives thousands of pictures of butterflies on a website she created for this purpose. She creates theme-based digital scrapbooks that she enjoys sharing with her friends. Rhea researches and archives data about the different species in a very detailed inventory. She also keeps a database on the different butterflies found in various countries and continents. Rhea enjoys interacting with other butterfly aficionados through various online clubs. Her parents have taken her to several butterfly museums in several states while on family vacations.

Jairo grew up in a family of amateur and professional musicians. His father, uncles, and grandfather played in a Mariachi band when he was a child living in Mexico. Jairo loved hanging around them while they practiced, performed, and talked about their music. He was especially enthralled with the words from the songs. He spent countless hours thinking about and talking about the stories and the history told through the songs. From an early age, he began writing his own lyrics for songs and eventually turned his lyrics into insightful and dramatic poems. He was in his element reciting his poems to large gatherings of family and friends during special events. Jairo's new teachers are unaware of these skills. Most of Jairo's friends will only listen for a few minutes, and because his written and spoken English is not yet developed, his teachers are unaware of his talented linguistic abilities.

Cory is enthralled with black holes. He reads everything he can find on the topic; watches over and over every story, show, or documentary he can find on black holes; and continually scours the Internet for new information. Cory's parents take him to planetariums, space centers, and science museums to help him pursue his interest. Cory seeks out scientists through online forums so that he can ask questions from experts. He can easily speak with adults about how black holes occur and in what conditions, their range of sizes, how they are detected, how many have been identified and where, etc. Few of Cory's classmates care much about black holes. They usually think it's pretty neat for a few minutes and then move on to other things.

Rhea, Jairo, and Cody are not typical learners. Each possesses characteristics of gifted children who need more than the regular school curriculum can offer. They need to be able to pursue their areas of interest, and their teachers need to allow that to occur. These three children are not the "best" students in their classes:

- Rhea's class is learning how to collect and document information and cite sources for a research project. Rhea loses interest quickly when her teacher is instructing the class. She has far surpassed the basic method for researching and archiving data other students are learning, but her teacher is insisting that she follow the same steps. She chooses not to.

- Jairo's teachers feel it very important that he learn basic words so that he can develop his vocabulary because he is an English language learner. He has no opportunity to write or tell stories that interest him. He is saddened by the rote learning, and is turning away from the instruction, his teacher, his school, and his poetry writing.

- Cody prefers to read nonfiction books whenever he can. When forced to read fiction, he seeks out stories about phenomena in space. Lately, his teacher has not allowed him to read anything related to space because she wants him to broaden his interests. Cody has decided not to read the stories his teacher selects for him, and he is currently failing in three subjects: reading, writing, and science—the very subjects he relies on to research and maintain his website and communication with his black hole club.

Rhea, Jairo, and Cody fit profiles of gifted children in different ways, but clearly, their classroom instruction does not factor in their unique learning abilities. These students are at risk for becoming alienated from school. Their cases all highlight just how diverse advanced learning needs can be. Yes, there are lists of common "gifted" characteristics. But as we outlined in Chapter 1, the main characteristic is that they have an unmet need on the advanced end of the spectrum. Because of this, one of the first steps that must be taken when thinking about a gifted education plan for a school district is how to determine what unmet needs exist. This is one of the primary reasons that gifted education is and must be seen as intensely local. Students vary across districts, as do the standard, general education services that are made available to them. Because of this, what level of need requires additional, supplementary services will vary across districts (and even schools). For this reason, a critical first step is planning for how unmet needs will be measured and understood so that they can be addressed by appropriate services.

ENSURING ALL STUDENTS ARE CHALLENGED

Regardless of the school, district, or state, there seems to be a systemic problem related to addressing the needs of all students. This problem can be exacerbated when classes contain a large variation in student ability. Peters, Rambo-Hernandez, Makel, Matthews, and Plucker (2017) conducted a study using national data as well as data from California, Texas, and Wisconsin in order to understand the variability of student need that exists within "grade-level" classrooms. They found that anywhere from 20%–49% of students in English language arts and 14%–37% of students in math scored a year or more advanced compared to their grade-level expectation. Further, 15% of students in reading and 6% of students in math scored 3 or more years advanced. Given this wide range of student needs that exist in a single "grade level," we are concerned about the large percentage of students who are going underchallenged. The unfortunate reality is that, more often than not, the high-ability students and high achievers are left to their own devices so that more care can be given to the struggling students. It's unquestionable that students vary widely in what they need. The question now is in what fashion these students can best be challenged and at what point they require something beyond what the general education classroom can provide.

CONNECTING INSTRUCTION TO LEARNING NEEDS

Effective teaching strategies and learning activities often utilized for gifted learners are not novel. In fact, the majority have been practiced in classrooms around the country and beyond for years. It is the way in which teachers use the strategies that makes them effective with gifted students. Relate your teaching strategies to your understanding of *how* gifted students learn and *what* motivates them to learn. By doing so, you will help them make the critical connections they need to relate to the content they are expected to learn. Table 2 demonstrates how several common

Table 2

Gifted Students' Characteristics and Related Learning Needs

Characteristic	Learning Needs
Curious about many topics	Extended learning opportunities
Process information quickly	Acceleration
Possess great memory	Testing out
Grasp underlying principles	Curriculum compacting
Make generalizations	Holistic approach
Are highly sensitive	Community building
Prefer to work alone	Independent projects
Relate well to older students	Apprenticeships and mentors
Have advanced sense of humor	Leadership opportunities
Require little direction	Student-directed learning
Maintain deep concentration	Metacognitive opportunities

characteristics correlate with specific learning needs that can be addressed in any classroom or program.

In an ideal world, every student's education would be personalized. Students would develop their individual interests at their own pace and level of complexity using lessons and resources made available by teachers who facilitated student-directed learning. As with the students depicted in the examples, there are those who learn and achieve more when they can make choices in what and how they learn. In this chapter, we attempt to demonstrate the importance of modifying instructional practices to address gifted students' diverse learning needs.

All students need opportunities to learn new material every day they are in school. For continuous learning to occur for gifted children, they may need a modified approach, a faster pace, or permission to study new material at a greater depth, as seen in the cases of Rhea, Jairo, and Cody. Understanding how to teach to the learning behaviors common among gifted students is essential. A modified approach will help your students connect to the content you want them to learn while engaging them in more meaningful learning.

All students require and deserve academic challenge. Although this simple statement seems a given, the reality of knowing just where the students' challenge levels fall can seem daunting to teachers. Whether in a mixed-ability classroom or a gifted classroom, gifted students' entry levels into curriculum vary dramatically. Ensuring challenging instruction then requires consistent use of diagnostic and formative assessments to determine student groupings and students' entry levels into the curriculum. This process allows teachers to form informed flexible learning groups and tier learning activities accordingly.

Determine the degree and the area of challenge students need by assessing readiness levels and identifying entry points related to the content being addressed. Routine use of preassessments in the various content areas provides the information needed to determine your students' entry points. Ongoing formative assessment helps you monitor student progress so that you can eliminate unnecessary practice on material your students have already learned. Students feel challenged and become engaged in learning when their teachers give credit for previous learning and provide opportunities for self-directed learning.

TEACHER SCENARIO

Mrs. Garcia is a gifted cluster teacher at Esperanza Elementary School. As such, she is accustomed to having a range of ability and achievement levels in her classroom. Mrs. Garcia looks over her class list for the upcoming school year. She sees that she will have eight gifted identified students in her class and 18 regular education students.

Mrs. Garcia sees that three students have been identified as gifted on a nonverbal test, three students identified on verbal and quantitative batteries; one identified in verbal, quantitative, and nonverbal batteries of an ability test; and one identified on an IQ test. Of the eight gifted students, three are English language learners, one is learning disabled (dyslexic), one is profoundly gifted (PG), two have ADD/ADHD, and one is identified with no other diagnosis. Although all of these gifted students have drastically different learning needs, they are all identified as gifted. This means that they each have a higher than average ability to learn so they are grouped together with a teacher who has had training in how to teach gifted students. Mrs. Garcia will need to identify the strengths and challenges each student has and then modify her instructional approach accordingly.

Mrs. Garcia has been teaching for several years. She knows that her ELL gifted students may have highly advanced verbal strengths (in their native language) and aptitude for acquiring language. She is also fully aware that her profoundly gifted student may have more complex learning needs than the others, and that her twice-exceptional gifted students will likely need some accommodations in order to work to their ability and intellectual level. Mrs. Garcia sees this as a typical group of gifted students clustered into her heterogeneous class. She is excited about the upcoming year, and is looking forward to working with her wonderfully creative and idiosyncratic gifted students.

ADDRESSING UNDERREPRESENTED POPULATIONS

A few states' criteria for gifted identification rely only on qualifying ability test scores or IQ test results. On the other hand, many states' gifted identification criteria require a cut score from an academic achievement test in addition to qualifying ability score(s). When the gifted identification also requires evidence of accelerated learning in academic areas in addition to high ability, some students of underrepresented populations (that have high ability but have not yet developed skills or are unable to demonstrate mastery) may not have their abilities noticed.

Through no fault of their own, the vast majority of teachers in the United States become teachers with minimal or no exposure to or training in gifted identification or any aspect of gifted education. With this lack of exposure, teachers are naturally better able to recognize potential in students of their own ethnicity or culture, which adds to the underrepresentation of giftedness in culturally diverse populations. With a preponderance of White teachers in American schools, most of whom had teacher preparation coursework lacking in gifted education training, the reasons for underrepresentation of students from certain racial, ethnic, income, and language backgrounds are understandable. How educators can overcome these disparities becomes the critical question.

States whose gifted mandate requires an academic achievement element—in addition to an ability or IQ test score—can create alternative methods for identifying and serving students with high ability and then work on developing the students' potential so as to increase academic achievement. Experience shows that, when these students with high ability—who are not yet experiencing high achievement—are grouped with others of similar abilities for at least some of their daily core content, they are likely to experience more rapid academic growth than they would if not learning alongside others of similar intellect.

Given past trends, the absence of alternative measures and methods for identifying and serving giftedness in underrepresented populations will naturally contribute to the underrepresentation of minority populations in gifted education. In addition to using multiple measures to identify giftedness, a school needs to provide multiple pathways toward curriculum and instruction. Schools commonly struggle with this latter aspect.

TEACHER SCENARIO

Ms. Ybarra teaches fourth grade at Arrowhead Elementary School, a Title I school. This year she was also assigned the role of gifted cluster teacher for her grade level, which means the gifted students would be grouped into her class. Unfortunately, there were only two gifted identified students in fourth grade.

Looking over the gifted testing records, she noticed there are six students who fell short of qualifying by just a few percentage points. As is the practice at Arrowhead Elementary School, Ms. Ybarra was able to "flex" these six students into her gifted cluster class so they could work along with the two gifted identified students. This gave Ms. Ybarra a significant group of students with higher than average ability for which she would plan lesson extensions. Although not officially identified as gifted, these students will be retested next year to see if they qualify.

Many schools use similar approaches to help identify and serve students from underserved populations. Some call their programs talent searches, talent pools, or watch lists. The important part is accepting that they would benefit from learning with other gifted students and having a method for grouping these students together with a teacher who has understanding of how to effectively modify his or her instruction accordingly.

Let's return to Rhea, Jairo, and Cody. As seen in her research on butterflies, Rhea is a keen observer, can sustain longer periods of attention and concentration than others her age, and is more independent and less concerned with peer approval. Jairo has an advanced vocabulary in his native language and enjoys writing and reciting poetry. He makes valid generalizations about events and people, has vast knowledge of the geography and culture of Mexico, and recognizes complicated relationships and intricate patterns that others do not see. And Cody intuitively understands complex concepts involved in the study of space. He has an incredible memory and readily grasps underlying principles related to space. Clearly, their abilities differ dramatically. Their teachers will need to facilitate their instruction and allow them to self-direct their learning in certain areas.

DIFFERENT APPROACHES TO LEARNING

The vast majority of students use a linear-sequential method of thinking to process information in a "pieces-to-whole" manner. In contrast are those students who look at problems in a "whole-to-pieces" fashion. This allows them to see the overall whole, or gestalt, and is estimated to be the method of choice for processing information for about 30% of the general population, many of whom are gifted identified.

You most likely notice differences in the way gifted students learn as compared to how other students learn. Some of your gifted students may not follow the same steps as others when working out problems, yet they usually arrive at a correct solution. These students may simply "see," or visualize, the solution to the problem. Yet, when asked to explain how they arrived at the solutions, they cannot always do so to the teachers' satisfaction. When forced to describe the steps they took, they typically begin with the solution, then attempt to *create* steps that would explain their solution. If the steps they explain do not lead to the solution they arrived at, the teacher may think that the student did not truly understand the problem. In truth, the students may not know *how* they arrived at the solution . . . in many cases, it just came to them!

HOLISTIC THINKERS

Students who favor a holistic approach to learning tend not to rely on rote memorization but on seeing relationships among concepts.[1] These students can create vast webs of interconnected ideas that build upon each other. You can see this with students who enjoy learning experiences that integrate various subjects, topics, or concepts, such as in project-based learning (PBL) and problem-based learning and when working in thematic-based instructional units. For example, a student may become immersed in a science experiment in which he draws a hypothesis based on historical information, relates it to current events in the news, then uses the information when writing a story or article. When forced to learn in a sequential fashion like his classmates, he may not reach the same depth of understanding that he would otherwise. His learning activities did not encourage him to make the connections he needed in order to become immersed, or interested, in the lesson.

Take the example of Robert, a seventh-grade student, who explained beautifully and intricately his thoughts comparing two scenes in a play. When asked to write out what he described, he paused for an extended period of time, before saying, "I am trying to think of a way to say the same thing using the fewest possible words." This approach is not uncommon with gifted learners. Oftentimes they simply do not feel the need to spend time articulating what they already know; they would rather move on to new learning experiences—even those that may not be in line with the teacher's plans.

STUDENT-DIRECTED LEARNING

For anyone who has parented or taught gifted children, it comes as no surprise to learn that not all gifted students are model students who eagerly follow school rules all of the time. Their passionate desire to learn topics of their own choosing makes some gifted students less willing to acquiesce to classroom expectations and more likely to thrive when given opportunities to pursue areas of interest. Their heightened sense of justice, their intense sensitivities, and their creativity makes them ques-

---

1   The term *holistic thinking* refers to a big picture mentality in which a person recognizes the interconnectedness of various elements that form larger systems, patterns, and objects.

tion, feel, and produce differently than others. These wonderful traits actually help the students become productive learners when their teachers appreciate this part of their learning process.

Understanding *why* gifted students need different educational services is the first step in planning programming for your school or district. Behaviors and characteristics common to gifted students describe why these students' learning needs are difficult to address in a mixed-ability classroom. Becoming familiar with methods of instruction that are effective with these students is the next part.

Learning with intellectual peers. There are numerous benefits for gifted students when they have time to learn together on a daily basis. Gifted students tend to be very competitive with one another. They thrive on challenge and complexity when there are others working at a similar level. The students feel more comfortable taking academic risks when working with like-minded peers. In-depth discussions that extend and guide learning are more likely to occur, especially when led by teachers who have experience and training in educating gifted students.

The benefits of learning together also relate to the social and emotional needs of gifted students. These students can feel very isolated in heterogeneous classrooms without gifted peers. They may feel as if no one understands them, and they may have difficulty making friends. In some cases, gifted students' feelings of isolation turn to alienation, and sometimes the students become nonproductive and tune out of school and learning. The social, emotional, and academic needs of gifted students are critical factors to consider when planning for gifted education programs. Another critically important factor not always considered is the ways these needs are represented in different populations.

A common misconception many educators hold is that gifted students are ideal students who are easy to teach. The truth is that higher intellect is oftentimes associated with behaviors at school that challenge some teachers and may even disrupt students' learning and teachers' instruction. Table 3 depicts some of the strengths many gifted students share and relates those strengths to possible challenges in the classroom.

CONCLUSION

Many gifted students think and learn differently from their chronological peers. They need consistent and appropriate academic challenge in order to learn. Gifted students feel accepted, and typically raise their own challenge levels when learning along with others of similar ability. This helps students understand that it is okay to not always succeed at everything they attempt, which can help them find value in the learning process. Regardless of students' areas of identification, you can encour-

Table 3

Gifted Children's Strengths and Related Challenges (Clark, 2012; Seagoe, 1974)

Strengths of a Gifted Child	Possible Related Challenges
Acquires and retains information quickly	Impatient with others; dislikes routine
Inquisitive; searches for significance	Asks embarrassing questions
Intrinsically motivated	Strong-willed; resists direction
Enjoys problem solving; able to use abstract reasoning	Resists routine practice; questions; uses abstract reasoning procedures
Seeks cause-effect relations	Dislikes unclear and illogical areas
Emphasizes truth, equity, and fair play	Worries about humanitarian concerns
Seeks to organize things and people	Constructs complicated rules; often seen as bossy
Large, advanced vocabulary; broad knowledge base	May use words to manipulate; bored with school and age-peers
High expectations of self and others	Intolerant, perfectionist; may become depressed
Creative and inventive; likes new ways of doing things	May be seen as disruptive and "out of step"
Intense concentration; long attention span; persistence in areas of interest	Intolerant, perfectionist
Sensitive, empathetic; desire to be accepted	Sensitivity to criticism or peer rejection
High energy, alertness, eagerness	Frustration with inactivity, may be seen as hyperactive
Independent; prefers working alone; self-reliant	May reject parent or peer input; nonconforming
Diverse interests and abilities; versatility	May appear disorganized or scattered; frustrated over lack of time
Strong sense of humor	Peers may misunderstand humor; may become "class clown" for attention

age their growth by promoting challenging activities to all gifted students. Providing gifted students with the opportunity to not succeed (with ease) provides the opportunity to learn.

If the goal in learning is to acquire knowledge, then we must find ways to access and build on prior knowledge. Helping your students make connections to existing knowledge integrates the learning process and makes learning meaningful. Accept that your gifted students have different learning needs and provide for these differences by:

- using a variety of materials and approaches,
- narrowing the learning gaps through the integration of studies,
- providing student choices, and
- allowing gifted students to spend time learning together.

CHAPTER 3

IDENTIFICATION—WHAT MAKES IT GOOD?

GUIDING QUESTIONS

- What are we trying to accomplish when we "identify" gifted students?
- What are the costs and benefits of particular identification policies? Why devote additional funds and services to kids who are already privileged?
- What does it mean to "use" multiple measures in student identification?
- What instruments or tools should be used for identification?

There are few topics that are more complicated within gifted education than how to identify students for or place students in gifted education services. And yet, this is often one of the first tasks a new coordinator is asked to take on. As we noted in Chapter 1, it's also one of the actions most often required in state rules and regulations for gifted education and one that is most often subject to state approval. All too frequently, policies or assessment tools are (at best) inherited from long-ago retired staff and little rationale is available regarding why they exist; at worst, they are based on personal anecdote or outright myths. Note that we said *identifying students for services* as opposed to *identifying students as gifted*.

The first thing we need to make clear is that the purpose of identification in K–12 schools should be to identify students who have needs for or would benefit from additional programs or services beyond what they are already receiving. The idea of universal, permanent placement in a specific gifted program whereby a student is identified at a point and then placed in a service that does not benefit him should be discarded in favor of needs-based instruction. Giftedness is not a trait of some fixed number or percentage of people. Instead, we should place emphasis on identifying needs, which we, as an educational system, meet by identifying students for specific services. Before we dive into the details of how to create a gifted education or advanced academic identification protocol, there are a few essential criteria for any "good" identification system.

1. Identification criteria must align with the services offered and the needs met by those services.
2. When implementing any kind of identification process, schools must plan to serve the needs that the process will identify. In other words, identification is a means to an end, and the end must justify the means, even when this means providing service within the regular classroom.
3. All identification systems (also true of all educational assessment) must pay for themselves in terms of greater educational benefit to the students.

Before we talk about each of these in turn and then get into specifics about measures, processes, and criteria, we want to give a real-world example of an identification system that violates all three of these criteria.

> Jefferson Elementary uses group-administered cognitive ability tests as its sole identification criterion. Students who receive a verbal *or* quantitative score at or above the 98th percentile (national norm) are pulled out of class for 30 minutes per week to engage in a creative problem solving/creative thinking curriculum.

Let's unpack this. First, there is little evidence of alignment between the assessment process and the intervention provided (violation of point #1). Students who score very high on a quantitative or verbal ability test *might* have a need for a creative thinking program, but they also might not. Further, there are probably many students who don't score high on verbal or quantitative reasoning who would benefit from a creative thinking curriculum. Put simply, the need identified and services provided do not align. This will result in missed students as well as the "wrong students" (those who won't benefit) being identified.

Second, by identifying high-ability students in verbal and quantitative domains, we have (in theory) identified particular needs—those in quantitative and verbal domains. Jefferson Elementary did this because it believed that students who scored this high are likely to require specialized services in order to continue to grow in their learning. But did the students receive a service to ameliorate those unmet needs? Not really. It's likely that even after receiving the creative thinking curriculum, these students will still be underchallenged in their areas of strength. The same rule would apply if there were no service at all. What's the point of identifying a student need if there are no additional services and the classroom teacher isn't able to meet the need on his or her own? Because of this, the process violates point #2.

Third, and related to the second point, is that if a school administers a 3-hour assessment (or a 12-hour battery of assessments, portfolios, and interviews) but then, at best, provides 30 minutes per week of intervention, was the identification process worth it? Was the time and money put into identification worth it given the intervention provided? We believe as a general rule that if the service or intervention provided as a result of being identified doesn't provide a value greater than the cost of the identification process, then it's not appropriate. Cost can include actual money spent to administer the test(s), but it should also consider the time spent by the student and teacher in taking and interpreting the test. Every assessment takes time, but hopefully the benefits outweigh the costs. In the following section, we highlight how to make sure your identification plans meet these criteria. Now that we've given a commonly practiced example of what not to do, we will try and outline the best practices for how to implement our three identification criteria.

Alignment, Alignment, Alignment!

We hope by repeating our first criterion enough times (alignment!) we make it clear just how important it is that the identification process be aligned in domain and content with the program or intervention to be provided. The needs that are identified need to be the same needs that are served by an intervention. Let's consider another hypothetical example. Which of the following "interventions" is likely to be the easiest to identify students for? In other words, for which program will it be easiest to craft an assessment that will locate students who are ready for and will benefit from the program?

A. K–12 gifted education
B. Undergraduate education
C. Graduate school
D. Medical school

The answer is D—medical school. Why? First, because the "program" in this case is well defined. There's a clear set of curricula and set of topics and skills to be taught. This makes it easier to craft or choose assessments to align to that program. Further, the test used to identify students for the program—in this case, the Medical

College Admission Test— is closely aligned to the program to be provided to those who pass through the identification process.

Can we say the same for typical K–12 gifted education? Are all students identified likely to do well in the program, and can we say that not one of the students who weren't identified would have done well? Even undergraduate education is a bit of a stretch because the "program" that a particular college student receives varies widely by institution and by major. There's such a wide variety of what "college" means that making one test (or process) that can find all of the kids who need or would benefit from college is nearly impossible.

K–12 gifted education has long suffered from alignment problems. Students are often identified using a range of measures or via multiple pathways, but then all of those students identified are placed in the same generic "gifted" program. Such examples cannot be strongly aligned. If you take something away from this chapter on identification, it should be that identification processes and tools need to measure similar skills as those that will be fostered in the service to be provided to the identified students. Violating this rule will cause talent to go overlooked, will result in students being placed in services they have no need for, and will likely result in many parents knocking on your door asking legitimate questions about the lack of coherent agreement between identification and services.

How does one make sure an identification process and interventions are aligned? There are two ways to go about evaluating alignment—one can be done only after an identification process and program have been in place for some time, and the other can be done at any point, even before a program or identification process have been implemented. The first and most ideal way to check alignment is to evaluate the degree to which students who have been placed in an intervention have benefitted, have had their needs met, and have generally succeeded in the intervention. In this case, an identification process has been in place and has been used to place students in some intervention, and we now have some evidence of student success in the program. We refer to this as an *empirical test of alignment* because you would have actual data to test the degree of alignment. Those same data could also have an opposite effect, where they disconfirm the progress by showing that the students being identified do not actually have the prerequisite skills and, because of this, are not doing well in the program.

For example, if you select students for participation in AP Physics based on teacher recommendations, but then all of the students who were recommended do terribly in the class, then there is clearly an alignment issue. Some skills necessary to succeed in the intervention are not being assessed in the identification process. *If* you have data available on how students have performed on the identification system and on how they have performed in a particular program or intervention, then you can compare those two as an empirical measure of alignment. If a school identifies a need using an ID process, then one of the ways the quality of that process can be evaluated is by the degree to which the students identified benefit from and are successful in the program with which they were provided. Of course, knowing if someone has benefited from or was successful in an intervention assumes that the intervention had an explicit goal to begin with.

The empirical test of alignment is something the ACT test, a college entrance exam, has done for years. One way to evaluate the quality of the ACT as an identification system is to measure the relationship between the ACT score and how well students do in the intervention with which they are provided—first semester undergraduate coursework. One of the reasons this relationship is only moderate is because there are so many skills that go into being successful in college that are not measured by the ACT—what Kuncel and Hezlett (2010) refer to as *motivationally determined outcomes*.

To improve this identification process, the process and program need to be brought into closer alignment. If there is a specific program in place to develop a specific set of needs or skills, then, all else being equal, a strongly aligned assessment of those particular skills will yield better predictive power than will a more general measure of ability or intelligence (Kuncel & Hezlett, 2010).

Before we go on to the second method that can be used to check alignment, there is one caution for the first method. The first method only works if the curriculum of the program was challenging enough that not *everybody* would have benefitted. For example, a "gifted education" program that was simply the regular curriculum but with all of the identified "gifted" students clustered together is likely to result in everyone doing well. Why wouldn't they? It's the regular school curriculum! This on its own does not mean there is strong alignment between the identification process and the intervention.

When evaluating alignment you must also make sure that the intervention is sufficiently rigorous that only those students who have a need for it would be likely to benefit. Absent this requirement, any identification system will look good because every student will be as likely to do as well as any other student. If all students would like to do it, all students should do it, or all students could do it successfully, then it's not really a "gifted" intervention or program.

Unfortunately, evaluating empirical alignment only works if you have one or more years of data on a past identification process—program implementation combination. If you are starting from scratch, you won't have this. Instead, what you'll have to do (based on earlier chapters) is identify some observed need or program goal that you hope to meet with some service or intervention (see Chapter 4). For example, you could have observed that not enough low-income students were earning high scores on AP tests, or you could have observed that too many Hmong students weren't performing as well as other students in first-grade math. Or, like the country as a whole, you could just be concerned that there are too few students from all groups scoring at advanced levels. Regardless, you have some need that you hope to meet with some program or intervention for those students who have the observed need.

The second way to check for alignment in the absence of any data is to engage in a construct comparison. We refer to this as the evaluation of *conceptual alignment*. This entails a structured comparison of the constructs, skills, and dispositions measured by the identification process that you're developing and the constructs, skills, and dispositions covered in the intervention.

Evaluating conceptual alignment isn't as simple as saying you have an unmet need in the area of creative thinking so you're going to provide students with a Creative Problem Solving (CPS) program. Just because both the need/identification tool and the program have the word "creativity" in them doesn't mean they both cover the same constructs. Two of the most common ways to assess creative ability in gifted education are with the Torrance Test for Creative Thinking (TTCT) or one of several teacher rating scales that include measures of student creativity. But before you can assume that these measures would result in strong alignment with your proposed CPS curriculum, you need to evaluate what each of the two actually means by "creativity." Perhaps the teacher rating scale you're considering is really about visual and performing arts creativity, whereas the CPS intervention is really focused on creativity more broadly. In a very simple way, these are not at all aligned, just as we wouldn't have alignment if we identified using a language arts test but then provided an advanced math program. Standardized instrument manuals can be reviewed for a better understanding of what they mean by "creativity," which can then be compared to the content addressed in the program.

Likewise, in the academic areas, the skills measured on a particular math test can be compared with the math objectives and concepts addressed in a particular advanced class or intervention. One math test might focus heavily on numeracy, whereas the program you're considering is all about measurement and geometry. Even though they are both about "math," there would be only weak alignment. Conceptual alignment isn't as ideal as having an empirical measure of the alignment between the identification process and the intervention, but it's a lot better than going by name alone.

Although not a third way to check alignment per se, there are also identification systems and programs that are aligned by design. For example, full-grade acceleration as an intervention already has a researched identification process. It's called the Iowa Acceleration Scale, and it includes measures of all of the skills and abilities that are likely necessary for successful performance in an above-age classroom. Similarly, success in the Advanced Placement SpringBoard program is likely indicative of future success in regular Advanced Placement courses. Put simply, for some interventions, someone else has already done the work of alignment, leaving you with one less thing to do.

IDENTIFICATION AS PROGRAM PLACEMENT

Imagine a world in which no high school graduates go to traditional colleges or universities. Formal educational simply ends at 12th grade or students all go on to nonacademic pursuits. Despite this imaginary world, all K–12 schools continue to administer the ACT college readiness test. Would this make any sense? There's no program for which the educational system is seeking to identify students, the data are not used by the teachers or schools for planning, and yet there's a national assessment movement anyway. As strange and illogical as this might seem, this happens in K–12 gifted education every day. Every day students are screened for gifted education eligibility even though there is no potential for any differentiated instruction or targeted intervention to be provided to those students who are identified (at least, not a program that will alleviate the unmet need). The golden rule here is to not engage in identification unless there is a service in place that will be provided to those identified.

Even if both identification and services are required by state rule, there is no point in identification unless there are also services that the school is able to provide. We concede that this seems a rather negative outlook, but we present it in this way to drive home the point that assessment and identification are means through which to provide more appropriate services to students. If these services don't exist, then something is wrong. These services could be "simple interventions," such as compacted units or extension activities in the general education classroom, or as extensive as full-grade acceleration. It all depends on the level of need and where it can best be met.

IDENTIFICATION: THE COST-BENEFIT ANALYSIS

All assessment in schools, including gifted identification, should follow a simple rule. An assessment is only worth giving if the resulting differentiated instruction pays for itself in terms of educational benefits to students. Applied to gifted education, this means that no identification process should take more time, effort, or money than the educational response. For example, if the process to decide on whether or not to identify a student takes a total of four tests and rating scales requiring 18 hours over the course a semester and the best potential outcome is that a student receives the intervention of "differentiation in the regular classroom," then the identification system isn't appropriate. Similarly, if a particular assessment is administered to all third-grade students (universal screening—see below) at a cost of 2 hours and roughly $45 per student and the best-case scenario of benefit to those students is that they will be labeled as "gifted" in the school's data management software and potentially provided with in-class differentiation (at the discretion of the individual classroom teacher), then once again the ends do not justify the means.

Both of these example indentification systems are costly and time consuming and, in the end, would not result in better educational experiences to students. An informed teacher would see that a student has been identified and could, on her own initiative, implement an extensive process of curriculum compacting and differentiation in order to challenge her appropriately, but this kind of ad hoc programming is not ideal and cannot be relied upon. Conversely, a plan for service supported by school administration and policy is recommended, as will be discussed in Chapter 4.

How to "Do" Gifted Identification

As we have said several times, we want to encourage the identification of advanced learning needs and potential for learning as opposed to the permanent trait of giftedness. In the book *Beyond Gifted Education* (Peters, Matthews, McBee, & McCoach, 2014), one of us (Scott) shared a general outline for coming up with a gifted identification process. One of the first steps in this process is the observation that something extra is needed—that some students are being underchallenged or are likely to require something beyond what they are currently receiving in order to continue to grow. That need should have led to the creation or selection of some kind of intervention that, if provided, would alleviate the unmet need. With regard to identification, the question becomes how to create or select a process to tell the school which students have an unmet need and would therefore benefit from the intervention that the school has chosen to provide.

How to Choose Measures

Often the discussion about identification comes down to which test a district can use or purchase for the purpose of gifted identification. Many districts adhere to the philosophy that identification doesn't have to rely solely on published standardized tests and that it can also involve portfolios, observations, teacher ratings, or even student performance in past classes or programs. In practice, we see that these informal measures can present many challenges to implement. As noted previously, it all comes down to alignment and where the best data on student need can be found. If you are at the point where you are trying to develop an identification process, then you should at least have some idea of the differentiated services in mind. If not, go back to Chapter 2 and think about what needs might be going unmet.

Once you have a general outline in mind of the service that is needed, the question becomes which measures or processes best indicate readiness for and probability of benefitting from that intervention. Because most often there won't be years of past data to use to check for alignment (as discussed) we will proceed as if alignment evaluation option two (conceptual alignment checking) is the best way to decide which measures best align to a particular program. Because there is no way to do this in the absence of particular programs, we will use several examples in this chapter and will also make reference to several examples from the district chapters later on in this book.

How to Set Criteria

Selecting measures or tools to be used for identification goes hand in hand with selecting criteria themselves, thereby answering the question of what level on a particular measure indicates a need for a particular service. Whether using a standardized intelligence test or a portfolio evaluation system, a decision has to be made regarding at which point the data suggest a student will benefit from a service versus when he or she will not. Who will be placed in the program as opposed to who can have her needs met through existing services is the primary question. There are three considerations when choosing cut scores/thresholds for identification regardless of the tool.

1. The criteria should be at the point where the general education curriculum or existing programs and services can no longer meet the child's needs in the area of talent; and/or

2. The criteria should be at the point where a student above would benefit from and be successful in the program whereas students who score below would not.

3. The criteria should be set based on the local, general education classroom curriculum; hence this will vary from district to district or even building to building.

There is some greater nuance to these points. First, meeting one of the first two criteria really should involve meeting the other. If a child has a need for advanced math that cannot be met by the general curriculum and if the advanced program option was appropriately designed, then the student should do well in the advanced intervention. However, because of the alignment issues discussed above, this is not always the case. This brings us back to how to set thresholds for participation in a program. Figure 1 represents the Response to Intervention model.

In this model, the standard curricular offerings of a school are represented by the Tier I box in the middle. Most often, Tier I makes up the general educational classroom setting plus any teacher differentiation. It can include more than that if such services are provided as standard. For example, if students are able to self-select into Algebra I as an eighth grader without any special identification process, then that too can be seen as part of Tier I—the grade-level math option plus the Algebra

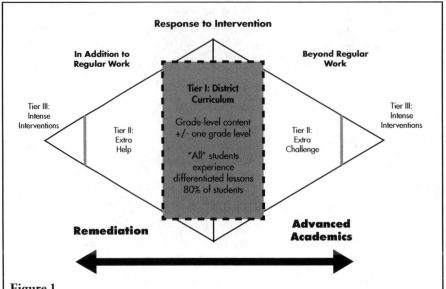

Figure 1
Response to Intervention continuum. Created by James Kueht and Ruth Robinson and used with their permission.

I option. This makes for a larger overall box for eighth graders in the area of math for this particular school.

We bring this up because point #1 from above relates to the lines between Tier I and Tier II on both sides of the box. That's where the criteria for inclusion in gifted identification should be. On the advanced side of the RtI diamond, this line represents the point in a content area scope and sequence where a teacher can no longer challenge a child on his or her own, even with access to resources, proper differentiation, etc. At some point, a child's needs are just too advanced for the content being taught in a grade-level classroom. That's where the identification criteria should be set such that when a child reaches that level, he receives a Tier II intervention. The same is true for Tier III. At some point, a child is so advanced that he is still underchallenged even with the Tier I core instruction and the supplemental interventions provided in Tier II. Conceptually, this is where gifted education criteria should be set.

Let's consider an example related to point #1 from earlier. Pretend that Mr. Jacobs is teaching fifth grade at Washington Elementary School. Mr. Jacobs has been teaching for some time and has a deep understanding of his curriculum. He has designed his language arts instruction with differentiation in mind. In fact, he builds three grade levels of remediation (covering as low as second-grade standards) as well as one level up (covering sixth-grade language arts standards) into every lesson. However, despite this impressive level of preparation, he sees that 15% of his incoming students scored three or more grade levels above where they are in school. Because his curriculum, including strong differentiation, is only designed to reach up a single grade level, he cannot reach those 15% of his students. Including those who are two or more years advanced would make up 24% of his students. Although he feels like he can stretch and meet those who are ready for the seventh-grade material, he also feels that other interventions beyond that level are necessary. In a metaphorical sense, this represents his own Tier I box. It's worth noting that these numbers are fairly conservative regarding the percentages of K–12 students who are above level in American schools (Peters et al., 2017). This mental exercise helps him and his school get an idea of at which point students need additional intervention beyond what he can provide in his classroom.

The reason this is so similar to identification consideration #2 from earlier is that if a school decides that this particular level of need cannot be met in the general education classroom and has designed, created, or selected some intervention for those students who are above that line, then the students who are selected should be the same as those who will benefit from the interventions. In other words, if the program was created for the students above that line, and the curriculum of the program is based on that level of need, then those students selected should also turn out to be the ones who are most likely to benefit.

An important point needs to be made about the third identification consideration. Determining the level of mastery or need at which a student can no longer be challenged in the general education classroom is no easy task. For one, this level can be different for every district or even every school or classroom, because the students and teachers will all be different. Likewise, all students are different and they change from year to year. Class size also changes from year to year. Some teachers are also more adept at differentiating up than down, while still others don't differentiate at all. For these reasons, coming up with criteria and revising them continuously based on these factors is critical, even though it can be a challenge.

We maintain this is an appropriate way to set cut scores or admission criteria to interventions, even if it's inherently imperfect. That said, there is another way that is much easier but also a less-precise estimate. Instead of setting criteria based on actual knowledge base and mismatch with the grade-level curriculum, a school can set a general policy of what range of learners a single grade-level teacher is expected to challenge on his or her own. Again, an example might be illustrative.

Given the large range of student readiness that exists within grade levels, Washington Elementary School has a policy that all teachers are expected to differentiate up and down three grade levels in math and reading without additional staffing support, and prior to any additional interventions being considered. Beyond this level, there are instructional resources teachers that push-in or pull-out students for additional challenge or support, and there are also special full-day programs for students with even more extreme needs. General education teachers also receive ongoing professional development to help them reach this up and down three-level goal. Applying such a policy to the nearest national estimates of the percentage of students who are above grade level (Peters et al., 2017), on the advanced end in math translates to 10% of students needing Tier II or Tier III in English language arts and 2% in math (because they are more than 3 years advanced). Note that we are not suggesting that a single fifth-grade teacher be expected to teach students who need eighth-grade content, but this is just an example of one alternative way that criteria could be set. A school could set a policy of what range of expectations are the responsibility of the general classroom teacher as opposed to when other options are available.

There is one final consideration when setting the level of criteria necessary for program placement. The greater the risk of a negative outcome that could stem from the wrong decision being made, the more conservative the criteria should be. This means that if the student could be harmed in some way if he or she is placed in an intervention and isn't actually ready for it, then the criteria should be more restrictive.

The opposite is also true. If the risk of harm is nonexistent, then the criteria should be lower (assuming the program can handle and benefit the additional students). This same philosophy should apply when students could be "harmed" by being denied services. If the risk to the child not being served is great and could result in that student falling behind or underachieving, then the criteria should be more inclusive. This should be seen as a "when in doubt" rule—with a potentially risky program, when in doubt, don't place the student. However, if not serving the student with a program is potentially risky, when in doubt, place the student in the program.

This issue of relative harm is discussed at greater length in Chapter 3 of *Beyond Gifted Education*. In our experience in gifted education, the default is too often not to serve, regardless of the potential harm that could result from such a decision. We think this is a mistake. "Risk" in an educational program is complicated. In most education circumstances, risk isn't of bodily harm or even mental anguish. Instead, it's more likely to take the form of a student who was placed in a program who needs to go back to the general classroom setting because it isn't going well. There could be behavioral, social, or emotional challenges that go along with such a move. There are also logistical complications. Risk can also come in the form of lost learning. When a student is incorrectly left out of an intervention that she would have benefited from, then the risk looks more like lost potential.

WHO TO SCREEN

If so far this has all seemed a bit daunting or confusing, you're in luck, because this next section has clear recommendations.

Golden rule: Screening a larger percentage of kids will result in fewer kids being missed.

Figure 2 helps illustrate this point. All identification results in some gifted student being missed (false negatives) and some students being identified even though they won't really benefit from the program (incorrect identification rate; McBee, Peters, & Waterman, 2014). This is due purely to imperfections in psychoeducational measurement. Screening fewer students will increase false negatives. This is depicted by the far right end of the figure. In the extreme, if we screen no students for gifted services, we'll miss 100% of the kids who would benefit. Alternatively, if we use universal screening and assess everyone, we'll miss the fewest students (but still some), but we also might identify some by mistake, simply due to imperfections in testing and identification procedures. How many to screen is a question of balance and the competing priorities of efficiency and effectiveness.

A simpler discussion of this golden rule is that once you've selected your identification measures and criteria (from the earlier discussion), you should screen the largest percentage of your student population as you can get away with. In an ideal world, this would mean everyone. If you decide that the American Awesome Achievement Test (AAAT; not a real test) is aligned in content to the intervention you're hoping to provide, then it should be given to all students. Of course, for financial, logistical, or political reasons, this isn't always possible. It's possible that the AAAT takes 10 hours to complete at a cost of $1,000,000 per student. In such cases, there is a middle road to be taken between universal screening and a false negative rate of 100%. We'll discuss how to design optimal, nonuniversal screening methods in the next section.

We mentioned that even with universal screening, even the highest quality identification system will miss some students. This is because no assessment system has perfect reliability and validity. There is some level of error present in any assessment system—some kids who do have a need for a program will always be missed by any identification system. Table 4 (from McBee, Peters, & Waterman, 2014) shows just how many students would be missed (false negatives) under varying reliability levels and cut scores. For example, an identification process with extremely high reliability (.95) and a generous cut score (top 10%) would still miss 16% of the students it was supposed to find. Remember that this assumes universal screening and that whatever assessment process is being used is aligned to the program to be provided (is a valid measure of "giftedness"). It can only get worse from here.

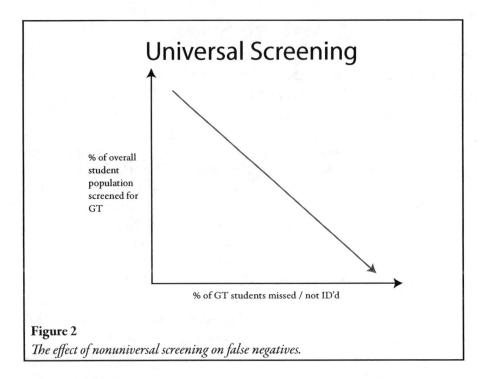

Figure 2
The effect of nonuniversal screening on false negatives.

Table 4
Performance Analysis of Single-Assessment Identification Scheme Under Varying Test Reliabilities and Cutoffs

Cutoff	Reliability	Sensitivity	*p* False negative	*p* Incorrect identification
90th percentile	1.00	1.000	.000	.000
(z =1.28)	.95	.843	.157	.157
	.90	.776	.224	.224
	.85	.725	.275	.275
	.80	.68	.32	.32
	.75	.641	.359	.359
	.70	.604	.396	.396
95th percentile	1.00	1.000	.000	.000
(z = 1.645)	.95	.815	.185	.185
	.90	.738	.262	.262
	.85	.679	.321	.321
	.80	.628	.372	.372
	.75	.582	.418	.418
	.70	.541	.459	.459
99th percentile	1.00	1.000	.000	.000
(z = 2.33)	.95	.763	.237	.237
	.90	.665	.335	.335
	.85	.592	.408	.408
	.80	.53	.47	.47
	.75	.476	.524	.524
	.70	.428	.572	.572

There are only two ways to make this 16% shrink: (1) increase the reliability level of the assessment process, or (2) lower the cut score. There are challenges with both of these options. First, it's very difficult to obtain reliability levels above .95. In portfolio or observation methods, these levels are all but impossible. The truth is that in education we are trying to measure human traits, not something as manifest and cut and dried as ball bearings. Assessment is not an exact science. With regard to the cut score, it's true that a lower cut score will miss fewer kids, but it will also increase the number of students identified overall. By definition, the lower the cut score, the more students identified. This might mean you miss fewer of the students you want to find, but you would also drastically increase the size of your service population by increasing the incorrect identification rate. These are students who would be served by a program or intervention even though they aren't ready for it and aren't likely to benefit. As we mentioned earlier, if the program involves a low level of risk, then maybe this isn't much of an issue.

SHOULD WE SCREEN?

When we refer to screening we do so in a specific way. Screening phases or assessments are typically given to an entire population—all of those eligible. Those who score "positive" or above a certain level then pass through the screener to a more invasive, complicated, or costly assessment phase. For the purposes of gifted education, it's this second phase (also called the *confirmation phase*) where a student is actually identified. The screening phase is typically a faster, shorter, less expensive way to determine for whom it is worth administering the confirmation assessments.

All of this brings us back to the opening question of this section: Should we screen or should we just give everyone the confirmation assessment? The answer is: It depends. If your intervention can tolerate larger numbers of students, then a lower cut score and screening all kids might make sense—meaning having no screening phase and instead just implementing universal testing for giftedness. Fewer students would be missed, but the program would have a lot more kids enrolled. At the same time, if the intervention is fragile or potentially risky for any student who is incorrectly placed in it, then perhaps missing some students is okay in order to protect the integrity of the program as well as avoid negative effects on students. This takes us back to the earlier rule. If an intervention is potentially risky to those who are inappropriately placed in it, then perhaps missing some kids is okay.

Before we move on to two-phase screening systems, we should address the question of when in a K–12 career to screen or assess for giftedness. This is a common question. The most honest answer is that you should screen or administer identification methods whenever there is an opportunity to deliver services. For example, if you have an accelerated and compacted math program that will cover grades 6 and 7 of math in sixth grade, then you should identify toward the end of fifth grade. Similarly, if you want to see which students can have their needs met in the general education classroom and which need some additional intervention, you should identify every year. A simple rule is that you should identify as temporally close to the delivery of the differentiated service as possible. Note that what is absent from this recommendation is any discussion of ideal grade levels. That's because we are no longer "identifying giftedness" in children. Instead, we are identifying student needs that might be addressed through a particular intervention at a particular point in time. Because students' needs change over time, we want to assess those needs as close to the program delivery period as possible.

All of that said, there are a few important considerations that we will only touch on here. First, younger children are harder to assess with just about any process or test. This is for a variety of reasons, including attention span and limited reading ability, both of which can limit the validity of data. If a student can't read the test on her own, then it must be administered orally, which takes much more time and resources. There is some consensus that these additional challenges taper off around grades 2 or 3, although this is by no means a hard and fast rule. This doesn't mean you should never identify before then, but early identification often requires assessments beyond what the district is already using or more time-consuming procedures.

Although we recommend identification to occur as close to when programming is offered as possible, this doesn't mean a new round of testing or identification is needed every time. Sometimes successful completion of an intervention is the best indicator of need to continue with that intervention. We discussed this with regard to alignment earlier on in this chapter. Consider sixth-grade students who were identified for a section of prealgebra. If there is an intervention offering algebra the following year, then there's no reason to conduct what we often think of as formal gifted identification for the algebra class. Instead, those students who are successful in prealgebra and master the necessary prerequisite skills are likely to benefit from moving on to algebra. Simply passing the prerequisite class (or receiving whatever grade is sufficient with "mastery") is all the identification you need.

Nonuniversal Screening

Much of the preceding section argued that universal screening for an intervention is the best way to go. And it is. It will always result in the fewest students being overlooked, but universal screening is not always feasible. Perhaps the criteria that you believe are most strongly aligned to an intervention include lengthy observations by highly trained raters/observers. Alternatively, they might include individual intelligence tests that are very costly and time consuming. Either way, it's not realistic to give such lengthy and costly assessments to an entire grade of students. You should do so if you can. Your other option involves a look back at the golden rule: Screen as many students in the population as you can get away with. In other words, screening 70% of your population will result in missing fewer students than if you screen 25%. More is always better in terms of missing the fewest students who need additional challenge. But as soon as you decide you cannot get away with universal screening, you have to decide who is going to get screened and who is not. This is where things get complicated.

The Broward County School District (Florida) had a gifted education program with an individual intelligence test score of 130+ (two standard deviations above average) as the criteria. Ignore the alignment issues for a minute. Given that this is one of the largest school districts in the nation, it was not about to screen tens of thousands of students with individual IQ tests. Instead, it administered an IQ test to any child who was nominated by his or her teacher as potentially gifted. Roughly 16% of the district's second graders were nominated for IQ testing (see Card & Giuliano, 2015) and then given an IQ test. Compared to universal screening where 100% of students are assessed for program eligibility, in this case, only 16% of students were assessed. This can be viewed as if the screening phase criteria were the most "gifted" top 16%. What makes things even worse is that we don't even know if they were the right 16%. But we leave that for later. If, in an ideal world, the false negative rate is around 16% (same by coincidence), the false negative rate in this case would have easily exceeded 50%, simply because such a high cut score was required to pass through the screening phase and on to the actual identification/confirmation phase.

Figure 3 (from McBee, Peters, & Miller, 2016) shows the accuracy of an identification system by overall reliability, cut score, and the correlation between the two phases (how strongly related they are on a scale of zero to one)—the screening phase and the confirmation phase. The top left figure presents a scenario in which the nomination and confirmation phases are only weakly correlated, such as in a case where the two phases are really measuring different things. Moving left to right and top to bottom, the relationship between the two phases improves. The different lines within each graph represent different nomination cut scores. These cut scores determine who gets to move through the first phase to the second. The bottom line represents the 90th percentile, meaning that only 10% of those screened will move through to the second phase. As we said earlier, this always results in the most students missed. That's why it's always on the bottom. The confirmation phase is what

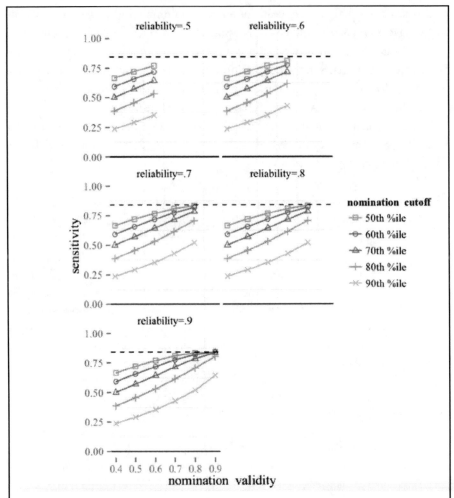

Figure 3

Sensitivity of a two-stage, single-assessment system by nomination reliability, validity, and cutoff.

Note. From "The Impact of the Nomination Stage on Gifted Program Identification: A Comprehensive Psychometric Analysis" (p. 266), by M. T. McBee, S. J. Peters, and E. M. Miller, 2016, *Gifted Child Quarterly, 60,* 258–278. Copyright 2016 by National Association for Gifted Children. Reprinted with permission of the authors.

determines who is identified as gifted. The nomination phase just decides who gets access to the confirmation phase.

In the Broward County example, the general teacher nomination was the screening phase and the IQ test was the confirmation phase. It's impossible to know exactly how strongly correlated a generic teacher nomination is with an IQ score. But based on data from other aptitude tests and other teacher rating scales, we'd estimate it's no higher than .70 (scale of zero to one with 1.0 being perfectly correlated) and likely much lower. Assuming the teacher nomination was highly reliable (which it likely was not because we are again talking about humans here) and that the reliability of an IQ test is very high (which it is), then the "+" line on the third graph will tell us how many students we missed. At best, assuming very reliable screening and confirmation assessments, the system used by Broward County missed approximately 30% of the students it was supposed to find. This is where the + line is the highest on the far right of the figure. Under a more realistic scenario, where the weaker reliability of teacher nominations is factored in, plus the fact that parents could bypass this step and seek out their own IQ test at their own cost, it's more likely that the accuracy was closer to .50—translating to 50% of students being missed. This is due to three factors: the reliability of the underlying measures (in this case, two), the correlation between the two measures, and the cut score. In the case of Broward, the reliability was likely rather low (because of the natural inconsistency across human raters), the relationship between the two phases was likely moderate at best, and the cut scores on both phases were very high ("gifted" as individually defined by each teacher on the nomination phase and the top ~2% on the confirmation phase). These three things combine to make for poor system accuracy.

What does this all mean if you're trying to create an identification system that does not rely on universal screening? There are three key things you want in a quality two-phase/nonuniversal identification system:

1. highly reliable assessments,
2. phases that are strongly related/correlated, and
3. a much more inclusive cut score on the nomination phase than on the confirmation phase.

First, you need as reliable of measures as you can find for any and all assessment tools or procedures. This means you want very high-quality standardized tests as well as very reliable nominations or observation protocols. Some published tests and protocols come with reliability information, but many, including those homemade by a district, do not. Any subjective rating scales (e.g., rubrics, observation tools) are notoriously unreliable because they involve subjective human judgment and often many, many different raters. Think about the inherent inconsistency in grading student essay writing assignments. Even with a detailed rubric, many factors will be left to the subjective judgment of the individual grader. This translates to weak reliability. Humans are naturally unstandardized, which is a challenge for reliability. Any subjectively scored or rated instruments will suffer from weaker reliability for this same reason. This doesn't mean they should never be used, just that they are harder to use to gather highly reliable data.

Let's return to Figure 3 for a moment to consider what happens when less-reliable measures are used for identification. Examples of these would be teacher ratings, student portfolios, teacher recommendations, or even classroom grades. Another less obvious example is no screening phase at all. If students are only given the confirmation phase after a parent requests this testing, then the system is inherently unreliable. After all, the considerations that motivate a parent to request testing aren't likely very strongly related to a child's score on a standardized ability or achievement test. In any of these cases, one of the top two charts in Figure 3 is likely the best representation of a system with poor reliability. The first implication is that the lower the reliability, the lower the cut score an identification system can tolerate without devastating consequences to system accuracy. In the top left chart of Figure 3, the system has a reliability of .50. If a screening cut score at the 90th+ percentile were used, this system would miss more than 60% of the students it was supposed to find. To combat this and try to maintain system accuracy ($\sim$75% correctly identified), the screening phase cut score would have to be closer to the 50th percentile. Overall, as the reliability of an identification system decreases, so must the cut scores used for identification, or else the overall system accuracy will be very poor. As reliability increases, higher cut scores can be utilized.

Regarding the second point from above, if you're going to have a two-phase system, one where you evaluate <100% of students using your confirmation assessment for eligibility, then you want the content measured by the screening phase to be as closely related to the content measured by the confirmation phase as possible. If this sounds similar to the alignment discussion from earlier, that's because it is. In the Broward County example, teacher nominations were only moderately related to IQ scores. Requiring a teacher nomination in order to "be gifted" will always harm the quality of the identification system. When Broward changed its practice and replaced the required nomination with a shorter, standardized screener, one with higher reliability that was also more strongly related to performance on an IQ test, the overall system improved. The ending message is that you want the screening and nomination phases to be measuring similar things such that high scores on one are likely to mean high scores on the other.

It's important to again emphasize that just because your screening phase uses a creativity rating scale and your confirmation assessment is a creativity test does not mean those two are strongly correlated. In the McBee et al. (2016) article we reference an example of the Gifted Rating Scales—School Form. Its Creativity subscale is only correlated .14 with the Torrance Test of Creative Thinking. This might as well be a zero relationship and would result in very poor system validity with a high degree of overlooked talent. Those students who pass through the screening phase will not do well on the confirmation phase and vice versa. These two phases must be strongly related not in what they purport to measure, but rather in that students who do well on one also do well on the other. Whether or not they measure the same thing is less important except to the extent that none of the students who would do well in the confirmation phase are stopped by the screening phase.

With regard to the third key component from above, the score necessary to move through the screening phase and on to the confirmation phase must be lower than that of the confirmation phase. Much lower. In the Broward example where the system missed approximately 30% of students, this was with a nomination cut score of the 80th percentile. If that were to be raised to the 90th percentile, the system would miss 50% to 65%. There is an actual empirical process to determine the ideal cut score on the screening phase—one that balances false negatives with those passed through on accident. However, it's easier just to aim for the top 20%–50% to move through the screening phase (cut scores of 50th to 80th percentiles) and on to the confirmation phase. If, instead of being nominated as "gifted" in order to pass through to the confirmation phase a student need only be "above average" (top 50%) or in the top third (top 33%), the percentage of students missed will be much lower. It's even possible to get an accuracy rate via a two-stage screening system that is very close to that of a universal screening system, but with closer to 30%–50% of the cost. We think that is a bargain and is something every school district should include as part of its identification process if utilizing universal screening isn't feasible.

This recommendation for a two-stage system assumes your assessments are already highly reliable and strongly related (see #1 and #2). This all relates back to the golden rule of assessing as many people as possible for eligibility. If you have a high cut score on the nomination phase, you won't assess many people. A lower cut score means assessing more with whatever your confirmation phase is, but it also means missing fewer students who really need the service.

So far in this section we have been less than kind to teacher ratings or nominations, and we think this deserves a little more explanation. As we mentioned earlier, any time a student is required to get a teacher nomination in order to be identified as gifted, this will always cause students to go overlooked, and these students are more likely to be from low-income or minority families (Card & Giuliano, 2015; Grissom & Redding, 2016). In most cases, we do not believe this is due to outright racism or animus on the part of teachers. Instead, it's due to the natural variability in teachers. Teachers vary in their prior life experiences just as students do. When a teacher is asked to nominate a child as gifted or to rate a child on the frequency of her behaviors, that teacher has to rely on his or her expertise, education, and subjective judgment. Just as there are high-quality raters, there are also low-quality raters. This natural variability is a barrier to quality identification because it introduces natural and inevitable unreliability. However, teacher ratings can be used in other ways, such as one of several pathways to identification (called an "or" rule). In this case, instead of requiring a teacher nomination, it is simply one way in which a student can be put through to the confirmation phase (e.g., he or she can pass through the screening test or be nominated by a teacher). In this fashion, a student who has a teacher who is not as familiar with gifted education does not get held back. He has other pathways to potential identification. These challenges are not unique to teacher ratings or nominations; it's just that they tend to be one of the most common, less-than-reliable measures used for gifted identification.

COMBINING MULTIPLE MEASURES

A topic referenced many times in the online district materials as well as in the Part II commentaries is using multiple measures for identification. For years, the use of multiple measures has been gifted education orthodoxy. Position papers and best practice articles have been written about how the use of multiple measures is the best way to go about student identification. Despite this wide agreement, far less has been written on *how* to use multiple measures. After all, as soon as more than one assessment or process is utilized for gifted identification, some decision must be made regarding how the process will work together or combined. In this section, we try to provide some guidance for any time more than one instrument, step, or process will be used to identify students for gifted and talented services.

TWO PATHS

"And" rules. Put simply, any time more than a single instrument or process is used for identification, there are two ways those instruments can be combined as multiple measures. The first is called the "and" rule because it requires students to meet all of two or more criteria in order to be identified. In this fashion, it can also be considered the "multiple hurdles" method because a student must be able to clear all of several hurdles in order to be identified. For example, the famous Enrichment Triad model by Joe Renzulli proposed that giftedness was the combination of above average ability, task commitment, and creativity. Based on this, some schools have created identification systems that require students to score above a certain level on a measure of academic ability AND a measure of motivation/task commitment AND a measure of creativity. The name of the "and" rule should be obvious. In order for a student to be identified, she must score high on all of the multiple measures.

The "and" rule has two major characteristics or implications. First, it will result in the smallest identified population. Every time a hurdle is added, more students will be weeded out (both correctly and due to assessment error). Add enough hurdles, and nobody will be identified purely due to measurement error. We view this as a negative/drawback to this method for combining multiple measures. The more hurdles you add, the more opportunities there are for someone to trip and not get identified, even though she should have been. However, the upside to the "and" rule is that the identified students will be very homogenous; they will have very similar needs. In the Renzulli example, identified students will all have high ability, high creativity, and high motivation. This will make providing services and interventions much easier for a school because the students will have more consistent needs than if other, more inclusive identification procedures were used.

As we mentioned throughout Chapter 3, the accuracy or correctness of an identification process depends on what students are being provided once they are identified. However, one thing that can be said about "and" combination rules is that they make more sense for more drastic, more intensive, higher risk, Tier III-type gifted services or interventions. Two examples of this might be drastic grade acceleration (e.g., a 14-year-old graduating high school) or a dedicated profoundly gifted program. In such cases, a school might rightly want to be very careful in making these decisions. The negative side effect of missing some students at the expense of nobody getting drastically accelerated on accident might be acceptable. All of that said, we do not see the "and" rule as the best method of combining multiple measures for identifying students for most gifted education services.

"Or" rules. The second method for using multiple measures is called the "or" rule, because it allows students to be identified if they meet any one of several possible criteria. Instead of having to jump over several hurdles, a student need only jump over one of several potential hurdles. Because being identified only requires one jump instead of several, one of the key characteristics of the "or" combination rule is that it will identify larger numbers of students. Whereas with the "and" rule every time a new step or instrument is added fewer students are identified, the opposite is true with the "or" rule. Every time an additional pathway is added, more students will be identified. For example, if students can be identified with high math scores OR high reading scores OR a teacher recommendation, more students will be identified than if the teacher recommendation pathway was not an option.

When "or" combination rules, also known as multiple pathways, are used, larger numbers of students will be identified (compared to a single ID process or an "and" rule) and these students will be more diverse in every sense of the word. For example, whereas under the "and" rule students had to score high in ability, creativity, and motivation in order to be identified, under an "or" rule, a student would only need to score high in any one of these. This would result in some students being identified with high creativity, but very low motivation and ability. This is not inherently good or bad, but it does carry implications for programs and services. Identifying "more" students might seem appealing, but then those larger numbers of more diverse students will need to be served by appropriate interventions.

In general, "or" combination rules are preferable to "and" combination rules because they are less likely to miss students who would benefit from gifted services. This means that for most typical gifted services (e.g., enrichment, gifted clusters) "or" rules make more sense because they allow students to be identified if they meet any of several criteria. In this fashion, "or" rules are inherently more inclusive.

Hybrid. It's also possible to use a combination of the two rules. For example, perhaps a school requires two of five criteria to be met in order to be identified. This represents a kind of middle ground between the two combination rules. The resulting students identified will be more homogenous and smaller in number than if an "or" rule were used, but less homogenous and larger in number than if an "and" rule were to be used. Although this might seem appealing because of the hybrid method's balance between the other two rules, it also adds a lot of extra logistical steps and complication to the process. This is another place to consider the cost-benefit analysis of the identification system. Every time an identification process becomes more cumbersome or complicated, it becomes even harder to rationalize with appropriate services.

Multiphase Identification

Everything we have discussed so far assumes that all of the various instruments for identification were given to all eligible students. As we mentioned earlier in this chapter, any time nonuniversal screening or testing is done, more students will be missed. This includes places where students are not tested for identification until they first meet an earlier screening criteria. Multiphase identification systems are a special application of the "and" combination rule. If a student is not tested for gifted services until she is first nominated by a teacher, then that student must be nominated AND score high on the gifted identification process. However, there is one additional complication. The quality of such systems is completely dependent on the quality of the first phase. After all, the first phase doesn't decide who is gifted; it just decides who gets evaluated for gifted education services. This means that if the first phase is low quality or that the criteria were set too high, a two-phase system can miss very large percentages of gifted students. Again, we refer the reader back to our earlier discussion of screening and nonuniversal screening as well as to two articles by McBee, Peters, and Waterman (2014) and McBee, Peters, and Miller (2016) for more details on how to best combine multiple data points in gifted identification.

Lingering Issues

Is It Okay to De-Gift a Child?

We are asked this frequently. Before we answer, we want to change the questions to "Is it okay for a child previously served by a gifted education intervention one year to no longer be served by a similar intervention the next?" The answer is, absolutely. It's completely reasonable for some students who need and end up doing well in a particular intervention one year to no longer need a similarly advanced intervention the following year. Does that mean they are no longer gifted? To us, this question is irrelevant. What matters is that students should be able to move in and out of different types of services as their needs dictate—not based on whether or not the student *is* gifted. Ability, achievement, motivation, and need are all developmental. They are not fixed attributes of a person. Instead, they change over time as a result of a number of factors. For this reason, it is inappropriate to identify once early in school and then leave any identified students in services for all of the time without assuring the services are addressing an unmet need. Conversely, if a student does not—or no longer—demonstrate a need for that type of services, then it is inappropriate to say that because he didn't have a need in second grade that he will never benefit from any advanced academic services. If a system is going to allow for multiple on-ramps—multiple opportunities to enter an advanced service or intervention—then it must also provide off-ramps.

Some of the schools used in the later chapters are in states that require students to be identified as "gifted." This could seem to conflict with much of what we have said throughout this chapter. But we believe it's possible to have it both ways. The simplest way to do this is to label any students in need of a Tier III intervention at any particular time as "gifted," whereas the others are considered "talent development" or "challenge" students. Again, the label is irrelevant. This way a district is still identifying students as gifted while also identifying based more on student need. Another option is to have a wider range of labels than just gifted or not gifted. For example, in addition to these categories, a school could add categories of "gifted and being served by an intervention this year" or "gifted but being served in the Tier I general education classroom this year." In such a fashion, a student might carry the gifted label for several years, but for some of those years she has her needs met in the general education classroom. Much of this is semantic, but the challenges are certainly real.

COMMUNICATING WITH PARENTS

The most important thing when communicating with parents about a gifted identification process is that the school is able to communicate the logic behind the criteria used for identification. As we've stated throughout this chapter, the identification process should locate those who have a need for and would benefit from additional challenge in a particular domain. That means that when approached by a parent, a GT coordinator needs to be able to articulate how the existing process does this. Further, he or she needs to be able to say that even if a child wasn't identified as gifted, that there is reason to believe this is because he or she will be appropriately challenged by other interventions (e.g., the general education classroom) this year. *Not being identified should never mean a student goes underchallenged*. Instead, it should simply signal that Tier I interventions are sufficient to challenge a child in this content area and at this point in time. Much of the conflict between schools and parents over gifted identification is due to unclear or illogical policies—the latter being a common alignment problem. Hopefully, many of the steps laid out in this chapter can help make the process better overall such that the main lingering task is a matter of good communication.

It's important to acknowledge another group of families who may take issue with some of the practices described in this chapter. This chapter describes methods to identify students who are in need of more challenge than the current Tier I classroom can provide. However, not all families seek out the gifted label because their child needs more challenge. Some seek greater social-emotional support; some seek a wider, like-minded peer group for their children; and yes, some simply want the label as a status symbol (although we believe this is not a large group).

Concerns over social-emotional needs are certainly fair, but based on the existing research base, are also often overstated because there is little research to suggest "gifted" or advanced learners suffer from any higher incidences of social or emotional challenges. Concerns about being able to access like-minded peers who have similar interests are also valid. But a student should not have to be identified as gifted in order to receive these things. All students should be able to access mental health support when needed, and schools should be on the look out for student needs in this area. Although gifted students show no higher rate of mental health challenges, they also show no lower rate, meaning they still have these challenges just like anybody else. Similarly, schools should create opportunities for students to work with diverse groups of peers as well as similar-ability peers. This should not solely be a benefit afforded to identified gifted students. In the model presented in this chapter and much of this book, "gifted" is an educational designation used to better align instruction with an advanced level of need. That doesn't preclude other services or domains, but this focus is narrower than many others presented in the field of gifted education. In closing, remember that identification of giftedness is not enough. Although it is important to identify, it is even more important to appropriately serve students in ways that meet their unmet academic needs.

CHAPTER 4

CREATING GIFTED PROGRAMMING

GUIDING QUESTIONS

- What is the difference between "provisions" and "programs" for gifted students?
- What models or gifted programs should I consider implementing based on my school/district needs?
- What do equitable gifted services look like?

A comprehensive K–12 program plan should include policies and procedures for identification, curriculum and instruction, service delivery, teacher preparation, formative and summative evaluation, support services and parent involvement.

—NAGC Exemplary Standard

In this chapter, we will be discussing a variety of gifted program models and services. To help clarify the differences, we have loosely defined several broadly used terms in Table 5. Note that they are closely related and may seem to overlap in some cases.

Table 5
Gifted Program Terminology Defined

Term	Definition
Gifted services	A general term used to identify the services a school or district employs to place and educate gifted students. Gifted services may entail only one specific model or a range of programs provided in one educational setting (district, school, or classroom).
Gifted program	A plan or set of plans designed to educate gifted students. Some districts may use "gifted program" as an umbrella term for a variety of services.
Gifted program model	A specific plan for delivering gifted services. Models typically refer to an established plan for grouping and teaching gifted students.
Pilots	An initial attempt to try out a specific gifted program model with a certain group of students.
Instructional interventions	Program elements or strategies used to teach new skills or apply skills in new situations.
Provisions	Instructional methods or strategies to broaden students' understandings.

INTRODUCTORY SCENARIOS

Angelica is a third-grade English language learner (ELL) from Mexico. Testers from the Language Acquisition Department first tested Angelica to determine her level of English language development when she enrolled in the district at the beginning of second grade. Angelica's parents only spoke Spanish, so she was a monolingual Spanish speaker when she began school. Angelica was placed in an English language development class with others who were learning the language. Unlike the others, Angelica learned English very quickly and within a short time period surpassed her peers. The language acquisition tester and teacher both noticed the rapidity with which she was learning English.

Having received training in recognizing giftedness, the testers referred Angelica for gifted testing. She scored in the 99th percentile on the Naglieri Nonverbal Ability Test (NNAT2), a language-free ability test. Upon identification, Angelica was placed into a gifted cluster classroom in third grade along with a group of other gifted identified students. This was done because the high measured nonverbal ability suggested there might be some hidden potential and because of the low potential for risk of cluster grouping as an intervention. After spending one year in the gifted cluster classroom, in fourth grade Angelica took the Cognitive Abilities Test (CogAt) and scored a 98% in the quantitative battery. She then received content replacement with other gifted students in math and continued in gifted cluster classrooms throughout her elementary school years. Angelica excelled in this environment learning along with the other gifted students.

Tristan is a twice-exceptional student who was identified as gifted through the process of special education testing in fourth grade. Although his teachers knew he was bright, his learning challenges masked his higher than average abilities. Through special education testing on the Stanford Binet V (SB-5), the school learned of his high IQ. Tristan had an incredible memory, perceptive insights, and a craving for learning. He also had extreme challenges organizing *everything* . . . his papers, his desk, himself. Tristan had ADD, dysgraphic, and dyslexic. He struggled emotionally with the expectations in class and with his inability to complete work.

Tristan was added to the school's gifted roster and participated in gifted enrichment class on Tuesdays along with several other gifted students. Tristan also received services through special education to support his learning challenges. With the combination of enrichment to spark his creatively imaginative thoughts and his resource support, Tristan felt motivated to learn and made outstanding progress.

Anvi is a highly gifted and radically accelerated student from India. Her parents claim that she was reading sight words when she was 2 1/2 and picture books before turning 4 years old. By her kindergarten year she was reading and comprehending chapter books. Anvi was also accelerated in mathematics and was interested in the brain and how the brain works. When tested on the CogAT in the spring of her kindergarten year, Anvi scored in the 99th percentile on all batteries. Upon application and acceptance, she entered the district's self-contained gifted program for highly gifted students where she learned at a radically accelerated pace along with intellectual peers.

Stephen was identified as gifted on a test of general ability. Stephen was an interesting student. He did not stand out to his teacher in the ways she expected of gifted students. However, his great imagination set him apart from others. Stephen was able to think very quickly and solve problems impressively. He displayed characteristics of a creative and insightful thinker. Stephen thrived in telling animated stories, using rich vocabulary that drew in his audience. This exceptional child naturally fell into role-playing within the context of what he was learning, and was known to ad-lib brilliantly during class plays and presentations.

Stephen's artistic talents were exceptional, as well. He loved to draw and would typically create diagrams, storyboards, and messages in code instead of writing steps and outlining content. Stephen demonstrated this talent in his homework (although some assignments were never completed or turned in). Stephen's teacher recognized his talent and encouraged him to build upon his ideas. She was pleased that he could spend some time with other gifted peers during pull-out enrichment classes for gifted students because she knew that he thrived when he was allowed to explore ideas and be creative with the other gifted students.

Angelica, Tristan, Anvi and Stephen represent four gifted students who require quite different approaches toward learning at school. If they were placed in the same gifted program with the same instruction, then it is highly unlikely all of their learning needs would be met without significant accommodations. As alluded to in the examples, the gifted programming and/or instruction that would benefit these students must be tailored to address their strengths and areas of challenge. Each of these students requires a teacher who has understanding of how gifted children learn in general; she can then provide specific interventions based on their individual needs, much like we see with special education services. These scenarios clearly demonstrate that differentiated characteristics and learning needs of gifted and talented students require a differentiated instructional approach.

Despite their learning differences, these gifted students should also have opportunities to work together, with other gifted students, and to learn from one another. Although these students certainly need to interact with intellectual peers, clearly each of them might not be a perfect peer for each other. However, there will most likely be other gifted students grouped with them, allowing for various other gifted students to interact with on a daily basis. Intellectual peer interaction can motivate gifted students to take academic risks, explore new content, and delve more deeply into material. One of the main benefits gifted programs provide is the setting and opportunity for peer collaboration. This benefit holds true in any formal gifted service model wherein students are grouped together.

These students are all considered gifted by their schools' identification criteria, but each might not demonstrate success in a way that is acknowledged and appreciated in standardized instruction. Even though some may consider each of these students to have special needs, some students such as these are often left out of gifted programs because of a focus on their deficits. For example, they may be denied gifted education services if they do not meet the academic achievement criteria used to qualify for gifted services in their school. If their schools did not group gifted students together or provide comprehensive gifted programs, it is likely that:

- Angelica would remain with English language learners with no attention to her areas of extraordinary strength.
- Anvi may have been grade skipped with no additional interventions or enrichment.
- Tristan would receive only special education services to help him compensate for his disabilities.
- Stephen's needs may have been overlooked altogether because he was a nonconforming student.

Keep in mind that simply grouping gifted students together does not guarantee a successful education for these students. Grouping on its own isn't a magic bullet. It is what occurs in those groupings that determines how effectively learning needs are met. This will be discussed in more depth later in the chapter.

PROVISIONS AND INTERVENTIONS

In this section, we discussed the importance of developing gifted programs that reflect the needs of the school or district's gifted students, which varies dramatically in different schools, districts, regions, and/or states. Just as a "one-size-fits-all" curriculum will not meet the needs of all of our diverse learners, neither will one standard gifted program. Create the structure of your gifted services so that it matches your students' needs. Clearly, this requires that teachers and administrators recognize and understand the spectrum of learning needs of the gifted students in their school and district, and purposefully plan ways to motivate, challenge, and expand the abilities of the students.

In *Aiming for Excellence: Gifted Program Standards*, Landrum, Callahan, and Shaklee (2001) wrote,

> Developing program models for gifted students rests with the states or school districts within a state. [There is] no single best way to develop programs for these students, who are so varied in their interests, talents, abilities, and learning styles. Thus, programs should be flexible and dynamic, multi-leveled, and designed to meet the individual needs of each child who receives services. The goal is to expand students' abilities, not just to establish a program.

In this next section, we describe some of the provisions and interventions schools and classroom teachers can make to address instruction for advanced learners. Note that these provisions and interventions are simply tools to consider for different students and different circumstances. No one provision or intervention is perfect, works only on its own, or works for every student. Rather, each can be seen as part of a repertoire of tools that should be considered to address the varying needs of gifted students. Also note the difference between interventions, provisions, and programs. Provisions and programs are described and discussed in detail throughout the chapter. Interventions can be seen as both large and small scale, such as steps a classroom teacher can implement daily to ensure all students are engaged and learning. Interventions typically include content enrichment and/or acceleration, both of which can be accomplished in many ways, in any classroom setting, and by any teacher. They simply require that the teacher (and sometimes the school administration) understands the need and importance for interventions.

PROVISIONS VERSUS PROGRAMS

When contemplating gifted services, it is important to differentiate between "provisions" and "programming" when it comes to gifted education. Schools commonly rely on provisions, or interventions, in lieu of formal gifted programs. Although provisions can address many learning needs of gifted students, they should only be considered part of the comprehensive programming of formal gifted programming unless the school or district is unable to create a formal program.

Program provisions are not usually established procedures and therefore are not typically recognized as formal gifted programs. These provisions include instructional modifications and accommodations that teachers routinely make. Due to the individual nature of provisions that schools make, provisions cannot always guarantee informed interventions. In most cases, there are few resources allocated toward provisions primarily because they do not constitute district-level and/or administrative support.

Gifted programs generally describe a specific process for providing educational options for students in ways that differ from regular classroom curricula and/or instructional practices (Callahan, Moon, & Oh, 2014). A good program includes appropriately challenging curriculum, a supportive environment for divergent learning, and time learning with other gifted students. Specific programming that addresses gifted students' learning needs should be provided, but when this is not the case then provisions can help meet those needs.

In an *ERIC Digest* article titled, "Developing Programs for Students of High Ability," Sandra Berger (1991) wrote, "[A gifted program] is a comprehensive, sequential system for educating students with identifiable needs" (p. 2). Berger made the distinction between programs for students who are gifted students and provisions for these students. Provisions made for gifted students in the school or classroom can help you meet some of the needs of your gifted students. However, provisions made for gifted students cannot be considered comprehensive programs.

Provisions put in place for gifted students range from a stop-gap measure to well-designed systems that schools can make when formal gifted programs do not exist and cannot be created. As noted previously, this alternative approach is often teacher dependent, meaning that the degree of efficacy and willingness to implement with fidelity varies drastically. Provisions typically do not involve a high degree of administrative support, resources, or accountability and require minimal articulation between departments. They are generally built into existing systems, as they represent modifications to general curriculum and instruction.

Provisions can be highly effective when implemented by teachers with training in gifted education and differentiation instruction. Program provisions do not typically represent a cost to the school or district, but rather the modification of existing resources to better serve students. Popular program provisions and interventions described in this chapter include:

- flexible grouping strategies,
- differentiated instructional strategies,
- content enrichment, and
- acceleration.

Provisions should:

- cater to individual needs of students through a differentiated curriculum;
- provide further extension in those topics or areas in which the students are demonstrating exceptional ability;
- enable opportunities for students to undertake studies in related topics or learning areas;
- allow students to undertake studies in different and additional areas of interest;
- make more time for students to study important areas in which less satisfactory progress is being made;
- include opportunities for accelerated progress in specific subject areas or across the curriculum; and
- enable access to a range of additional programs.

Although these provisions describe what benefits all students at all levels, gifted students need them at higher levels to engage in appropriately challenging curriculum and instruction.

FLEXIBLE GROUPING STRATEGIES

Flexible grouping within classes, along with strong differentiation of curriculum and instruction, are requirements in any effective gifted service, program, or model. We flexibly group students in order to differentiate instruction according to the group members' learning needs. This process can, and should, occur in any classroom where gifted students learn.

Flexible grouping generally relies on pretesting (or diagnostic or formative assessments) provided before and/or during instruction in order to form flexible learning groups. With regard to flexible grouping, pretesting represents a simple process teachers can use in any setting to identify students who can show mastery of a concept, standard, or objective so they can study and learn new material and pursue their thoughts and ideas in a more complex manner.

Flexible grouping can occur within a grade level and/or within a classroom. Within-class groupings typically consist of placing students of similar ability into small groups for specific instruction. Flexible learning groups continually change as they are formed by ability, achievement, interest, learning preferences, and/or teaching objective based on specific units of study or assignments.

The benefits of flexible grouping depend upon the instruction occurring within the groups. One of the most important benefits is that the teachers are continually assessing students in order to form and reform flexible learning groups. This continual assessment process allows for instruction targeted at students' needs, which sets the stage for differentiated instruction for various student groups and leads to more personalized learning.

Flexible ability grouping allows schools to match a student's readiness with instruction, delivering the right content to the right student at the right pace and at the right time (Rogers, 2002).

DIFFERENTIATED INSTRUCTIONAL STRATEGIES

Undoubtedly, the most common provision used for gifted students' instruction in most classrooms is seen with differentiated instructional strategies. Differentiated instruction for gifted learners provides them an equal opportunity to learn when they are appropriately grouped. This sometimes can mean grouping students across grade levels or providing a self-contained gifted program for radically accelerated learning needs (as typically seen with mathematics instruction). Teachers can tap into students' background knowledge, readiness, preferred learning style, and interests. Differentiated instructional strategies may involve pretesting, compacting curriculum, tiering assignments, content enrichment, and acceleration in different content areas.

Whether in a self-contained gifted class, a pull-out class, a cluster-grouped class, or the regular classroom, differentiated instruction includes extended learning opportunities that typically take the form of independent or small-group projects, tiered assignments, or extension menus. Although considered a provision, differentiated instruction, like flexible grouping, can occur in any—and should occur in every—classroom setting and gifted program. When differentiating instruction for gifted learners, allowing for student-directed learning will increase engagement and can enhance rigor in authentic learning experiences.

One of the most commonly used differentiation strategies involves variations of tiering lesson activities, assignments, and projects to meet the diverse needs of the students within the class. To tier lessons, teachers implement varied levels of activities to ensure students work at challenge levels. With gifted students, this usually means exploring ideas at levels that build on prior knowledge and prompt continued growth. Teachers can tier lessons by challenge level, product, process, depth and complexity, etc. Once again, tiered lessons exemplify best practice in education and should occur as part of all teachers' instruction whenever possible, and with all students, whether gifted, high achieving, average, low average, or remedial. Tiered lessons exemplify teachers' efforts to address all students' learning at the levels they need.

CONTENT ENRICHMENT

Content enrichment represents an expansive approach for differentiating instruction that can take many forms. Content enrichment commonly involves open-ended questioning and problem solving that can lead to creative and divergent thinking. Enrichment typically emphasizes critical thinking skills, creativity, and project-based learning. Enrichment allows gifted students to explore the content at a much deeper level and application to real-world scenarios while linking the learning to multiple disciplines.

Sometimes content enrichment is offered through itinerant (traveling) teachers on an intermittent basis, such as one class period a week. Although sometimes overlooked, it is extremely beneficial for enrichment teachers to consider aligning instruction in gifted enrichment classes to the content and/or topics being learned in the regular classroom (Naglieri, Brulles, & Landsdowne, 2008).

Content enrichment can benefit all learners and can become an integral component of instruction. Examples of content enrichment include infusing depth and complexity, individual explorations such as "passion projects," and independent study. Enrichment can engage, stimulate, and challenge gifted students, especially when learning in a mixed-ability classroom. Due to gifted students' abilities to make connections quickly and think holistically, content enrichment can extend curriculum content being learned in any classroom. Students are encouraged to investigate a topic in greater depth, integrate various subject areas to build on background knowledge, and research and explore universal concepts.

ACCELERATION

The National Association for Gifted Children (n.d.) stated that,

> Education acceleration is one of the cornerstones of exemplary gifted education practices, with more research supporting this intervention than any other in the literature on gifted individuals. The practice of education acceleration has long been used to match high level student general ability and specific talent with optimal learning opportunities. (para. 3)

As with the other interventions noted, acceleration can occur in any educational setting and can take many forms, such as whole-grade acceleration, early entrance, subject area acceleration, and curriculum compacting to name just a few. Acceleration can be appropriate for students who are radically accelerated academically and who learn at a faster pace given they are motivated learners. Research has shown that the benefits of acceleration for gifted students are strongest when students are grouped together for their accelerated learning experiences (Steenbergen-Hu, Makel, & Olszewski-Kubilius, 2016). Ability grouping combined with acceleration allows children to learn with peers, which can motivate and challenge students in any program or classroom setting. Table 6 illustrates the various provisions described previously in the chapter and provides a brief description of who can benefit from each method.

GIFTED PROGRAMMING

Gifted programming requires a formal commitment from the school or school district to effectively embed gifted services into formal school practices. This commitment factors in class schedules, identification procedures, placement criteria, curriculum and instruction, and staffing, to name a few critical pieces. These procedures and practices rely on administrative support and guidance and need to be purposefully considered into all school or district plans.

Once designed and established, gifted programs should ideally become part of school policy, such as part of a larger RtI process with the goal of everyone being challenged as often as possible—not just an add-on for gifted kids. Having the district's gifted program services adopted by the school's governing board establishes legitimacy and is often required by state law or regulation. Doing so shows a commitment from the district and provides support in program implementation and necessary teacher preparation. A board-adopted plan also helps ensure that gifted program needs are factored into regular school operations. This high-level administrative support demonstrates the district's obligation to ensure an appropriate education to all students, including our high-ability learners.

Table 6

Gifted Programming Provisions

Method	Who Benefits?
Flexible grouping strategies	All students can benefit from flexible grouping, as it allows them to learn with peers according to readiness, pace, learning style, interest, and other factors.
Differentiated instructional strategies	All students benefit from instruction differentiated according to their learning needs. These strategies should be available to all students, regardless of their learning levels. Students with advanced learning needs and those with learning challenges can benefit the most.
Content enrichment	All students can benefit from content enrichment, and it should be made available to students learning at all levels. Instruction for gifted students is sometimes provided through an itinerate gifted teacher during pull-out periods.
Acceleration	Students who are advanced academically in one or more areas benefit from content acceleration. This acceleration can occur in specific subject areas within a regular classroom, in any gifted classroom, or across grade levels. Some highly advanced students may benefit from full-grade-level acceleration, especially when the other forms of acceleration are not available or are not sufficiently challenging.

It is much more difficult to cut gifted education programs than provisions because of the attention and support that effective well-planned gifted programs entail.

CRITICAL ELEMENTS OF EFFECTIVE GIFTED PROGRAMS

In her classic book, *Growing Up Gifted,* Dr. Barbara Clark (2012) described the essential elements of a comprehensive gifted education program: flexible grouping, curriculum differentiation, continuous progress, intellectual peer interaction, continuity, and teachers with specialized training in gifted education. Flexibly grouping students within a classroom or grade level according to learning needs in order to differentiate curriculum accordingly helps ensure students are continually making academic progress while learning with intellectual peers. Grouping gifted students together with teachers who have ongoing training can also ensure continuity of differentiated instruction daily, monthly, and yearly.

Administrative advice: Gifted programs will be stronger and more sustainable when they are well established within all schools in the district. Districtwide programs require data collection, professional development, and curriculum and instruction, all of which strengthen a program.

IDENTIFYING A PROGRAM MODEL

Identifying a program model or models should be determined by the needs of your gifted student population. Building a gifted program based on the needs of your school's gifted population usually requires some degree of mind shift for teachers and administrators. Although unusual in practice, offering a continuum of services is ideal to address the vast range of gifted students' learning needs. As seen in Chapter 2, some gifted students need acceleration in some or all content areas, some need enrichment, and some need a combination of both.

It is not uncommon for some schools' gifted program models to address specific needs. For this reason, teachers in most gifted programs find it necessary to implement interventions such as those described earlier in this chapter. In Part II of this book, you will see a range of examples of how the services and interventions outlined in this chapter have been successfully implemented in different school districts. In the following sections, we provide a brief overview of the types of program models depicted later in the book.

SELF-CONTAINED GIFTED PROGRAMS

Self-contained gifted programs are those in which gifted (or gifted and talented) students are grouped together on a daily basis for instruction. Schools vary in how self-contained gifted programs are designed and structured. Some, such as the program described in Chapter 6, reserve self-contained gifted programs for highly and profoundly gifted students. Self-contained gifted programs with this level of entrance criterion can coexist in conjunction with other gifted programs with alternative entrance criteria, as there should be levels of interventions available to address the range of observed need. Other schools/districts offer self-contained gifted programs for any gifted identified student.

School districts that provide a self-contained gifted program typically select a site(s) to house the program and have gifted students transported to the program from other district schools. This requires that schools provide transportation to the site, which can cause challenges. Other school districts offering self-contained programs require that parents transport the students daily when coming from other district schools.

Anvi, from our earlier scenario, would thrive in a self-contained program for highly gifted students who are radically accelerated in their learning. In this case, however, the teacher would need to include interventions that would cater to Anvi's radically accelerated learning level.

Written by a third-grade student in Polson (district discussed in Chapter 8):

The purpose of a self-contained gifted program is to improve learning for students who learn or think differently. I also think that this type of program creates more opportunities for students to challenge themselves than a regular classroom may. I want to be in this program to be in a class with other students who learn like I learn.

At my current school I feel like everyone is wearing a yellow shirt, but I'm wearing a bright red shirt. I want to be in a class that might have more kids wearing red shirts. I also want to be with kids who think like me, learn like me, and have the same thirst for knowledge I have.

CLUSTER GROUPING

In cluster grouping models, gifted identified students are grouped together into one classroom at each grade level with a teacher who receives specialized training and support. In this model, when classrooms are composed appropriately, all classrooms at a grade level have a narrowed range of abilities so that teachers can better address students' challenge levels in every classroom. Gifted students have opportunities to learn daily in all content areas with intellectual peers.

In this model, we group gifted identified students together into one classroom in each grade and then use achievement assessments to determine students' academic strengths and needs. Teachers then provide appropriately challenging instruction through acceleration, enrichment, and lesson extensions for those students who demonstrate the need for them.

SAMPLE CLUSTER GROUPING CONFIGURATION

Gifted clusters generally contain 4–10 gifted identified students. When there are more than 10 gifted students identified at a grade level, principals can create a second gifted cluster classroom. See Figure 4 for placement suggestions when fewer or more than the recommended numbers of gifted students exist.

Prior to placing students into classrooms, assign all students to one of the following categories at a grade level. Assignments to the groups are determined by both formal and informal methods that combine standardized test scores with teacher observations and other anecdotal data. Achievement data from the local school population determines student placement into the designated groups (with the exception of the gifted identified students). "Group 1—Gifted" includes all formally identified students regardless of their achievement levels, including twice-exceptional, ELL, culturally and linguistically diverse, and underachieving gifted students. Assign all other students to groups using the descriptors that follow.

Grouping categories consist of:

- **Group 1—Gifted:** Gifted identified students.
- **Group 2 —High Average:** Highly competent and productive students.
- **Group 3—Average:** Students achieving in the average range when compared to others.
- **Group 4—Low Average:** Students struggling in math or reading and scoring slightly below grade level but able to achieve at grade level with some support.
- **Group 5—Far Below Average**: Students who struggle in most subject areas and who score significantly below proficiency levels on standardized tests.

Creating classroom compositions occurs by working with teachers from the sending grade levels, with the building principal, and ideally with assistance from gifted education specialists and special education teachers when possible. One visual method incorporates the use of colored cards. Using this method, each group is represented by a designated card color (or card with colored sticky dots) to identify the groups, as determined by the student's ability or achievement level. Each classroom teacher assigns her students to the appropriate card color. Colored cards in the grade level are then combined to create the class combination as described in Figure 4 (Brulles & Winebrenner, 2011).

Stephen, Tristan, and Angelica could all be served well in a gifted cluster grouping model. However, their cluster teachers will need to learn differentiated instructional strategies that work well with each of these students after gaining an understanding that they all have high ability, yet very distinctive learning needs. Grouping the students together is just the first step. The instructional methods the gifted cluster teacher incorporates for the students determines the efficacy of the model.

30 Students in 3 Classes	Gifted	High Average	Average	Low Average	Far Below Average
A	6	0	12	12	0
B	0	6	12	6	6
C	0	6	12	6	6

Figure 4
Placement suggestions for cluster grouping.

CONTENT REPLACEMENT OR HONORS CLASSES

Content replacement classes, sometimes also known as honors classes, allow gifted students to learn core content, most commonly language arts and mathematics, at an accelerated and/or enriched level on a daily basis. These classes are typically provided to gifted and talented students in lieu of the standard grade-level curriculum. Offering content replacement classes requires that grade levels schedule core content area classes at the same time period each day. Although this pull-out model requires additional staffing, it can also reduce the class sizes in the general education classes in these content areas, as the gifted students leave their regular classroom for instruction in these core classes.

Teachers using this model usually find that they also need to modify their instructional methods to accommodate the diverse needs of the gifted students in their classes. As with instruction in other models, content replacement classes require that teachers incorporate rigor, acceleration, and depth and complexity according to the students' learning needs.

ITINERANT MODELS

Itinerant models, also known as pull-out or push-in models, can serve as alternatives when full-time services are not available. In these models, a gifted teacher typically meets with gifted students at a particular grade level on a regularly scheduled basis, commonly for one period a week, but sometimes more often. Instruction in these models usually consists of enrichment activities designed to develop creativity and critical thinking. Students like Tristan, from our earlier example, enjoy spending time in a pull-out gifted class working on projects that require higher level thinking activities with his gifted peers.

One major concern with pull-out programs is that the regular classroom teacher commonly feels less responsibility to plan for gifted students' instruction on a daily basis because of the regularly scheduled pull-out time with the gifted specialist. Another is that during times of school budget cuts, the gifted itinerant teacher's position is oftentimes identified as an area in which to reduce staffing because it represents an added position that is not critical to students' daily instruction.

Philosophical, Cultural, and Practical Considerations

At this point in the chapter you may be wondering how to get started and who to address first. Take comfort in knowing that no two schools or districts function exactly the same and with good reason! As noted earlier, for programs and services to be effective, they need to address the needs of the school population. This includes the students, the staff, administrative support, and the community, all of whom provide valuable information and different perspectives to consider in building programs and services. School and district initiatives and state mandates also factor in heavily.

In Chapter 5, we will share logistical information that will help put effective structures in place that can assist with program development and evaluation. In this next section, we examine some of the philosophical, cultural, and practical considerations that can impact the decisions we make when developing services.

Who Makes These Decisions and What Impacts the Decision Making?

First and foremost, all schools need strong administrative support to build and support gifted services. And like most things in schools, principals and other administrators change roles. For this reason, we emphasize the need to develop services that can be built upon, modified, and sustained (even when there is a change in school leadership). Indeed, the continually shifting school initiatives, standards implementation, school policies, curriculum, etc., we experience in schools encourages constant examination of school services of all kinds. School leaders must continually provide oversight in managing systems and integrating new initiatives.

Embedding gifted services into general education discussions can strongly impact efficacy of the efforts. (For example, interventions for gifted students would ideally be inherent within the RtI framework as opposed to an "add-on" to existing instruction.) In schools that incorporate RtI, the principal at the school level and directors at the district level typically lead these discussions. However, these individuals may not be completely aware of the urgency often felt by parents or teachers who advocate for change in their gifted services. Those drawing attention to the need to create change must:

- provide information to those in the position to lead the change,

- rely on the voices and stories of students, and
- document and share student achievement data.

Clearly, administrative buy-in is needed to propose changes and staff support is required for successful implementation. The obvious challenge is that the vast majority of educators receive no training in gifted education prior to teaching. This situation reinforces the need to invest time in sharing ample amounts of information about gifted students and their learning needs prior to suggesting new services.

Other important constituents who can impact gifted program development may include human resource departments as pertaining to staffing, teachers unions and associations, or bargaining agreements, especially pertaining to class sizes, staffing, stipends, and state mandate requirements. The assessment department is oftentimes involved in the testing and identification process and in providing gifted student achievement data to document progress and help determine curricular needs. Language acquisition departments can provide information about which ELL and former ELL students need to be tested, and collaboration with the special education department can help identify and serve twice-exceptional gifted students. A detailed description of how one school district collaborates with various school district departments is seen in Chapter 6.

How Are Programs Developed and Who Decides What Interventions Are Made?

Just as there is no single best model for serving gifted students, there is no singular method for developing gifted programs. There are, however, processes that are important to take into account throughout the process. Consider the tips suggested in Figure 5.

Whereas it takes a village to develop sustainable gifted programs, interventions, like provisions, can be made more easily and readily. Interventions are typically made in response to students' current needs, such as the provisions noted earlier in the chapter. Differentiated instruction, such as curriculum compacting, extension lessons, tiered lessons, as well as subject or content acceleration, are all interventions that classroom teachers can make in any gifted program model.

Teachers can determine the appropriate instructional interventions gifted students need using diagnostic and formative assessment. Diagnostic assessments can include informal pretests that the teacher provides prior to instruction. Informal pretests provide teachers real-time information that can guide daily instruction. They allow the teacher to assess student readiness to assist with forming flexible learning groups within a classroom for focused lesson planning purposes. Pretesting students provides data that informs student readiness and challenge levels within a specific concept, topic, or standard. Pretests should be considered fundamental

1. Remember that building strong and sustainable gifted services takes time. Spend your first year learning the systems and needs of the school and the district. Study the educators' and parents' philosophies on gifted education and gifted programming.
2. Start by sharing information and resources with stakeholder groups. Ask questions and seek input. Present basic information on the characteristics and learning needs of gifted students by:
   A. speaking at staff meetings,
   B. offering book studies,
   C. holding parent meetings, and
   D. meeting with district and school administrators.

3. Study methods for providing professional development to teachers, both informally and fomally. Identify and prioritize staff professional development needs.
4. Examine your school/district data to analyze gifted students' achievement. This information will help you determine programming needs.
5. Network and find others in similar situations to share ideas when planning.

Figure 5
Top tips to start building programs.

procedures for gifted students, as all teachers have the ability to preassess students regardless of the educational setting or gifted program.

Similar to diagnostic assessments, teachers in any setting can use formative assessments with gifted students to determine what interventions are needed *during* the instructional process. Formative assessments are typically informal methods used to gauge students' readiness to move on, go deeper into content being studied, or accelerate learning within a particular unit of study. Skilled teachers use both formative and diagnostic assessments routinely to inform and guide all students' learning, but they are critical for advanced learners.

What Happens When a Program Model Is Not Serving a Gifted Student?

Not all gifted program models can adequately serve all gifted students. As discussed in Chapter 2, gifted identification indicates that a student has high potential and may be capable of achieving at higher than average levels. Although there are common characteristics gifted students share, there is host of differences in their learning needs. These differences in needs cannot all be addressed within one gifted program model unless interventions are included for some students.

Even with the best intentions and interventions, at times a gifted identified student will need something very different from what the gifted program can provide. With this unfortunate occurrence there will be times when a gifted student needs to discontinue participation in the existing gifted program and have different interventions provided in a regular classroom or in an alternative placement. The important piece here is that all students receive attention to their learning needs and that these needs vary and deserve flexibility in how they are addressed regardless of the students' designation or identification.

Some larger school districts are able to offer a continuum of services or at least different options. In Part II, you will see explicit examples of alternate methods that both large and small districts utilize. The descriptions will provide ideas to take into account when modifying services in any school district. To be able to serve a range of gifted students, we recommend establishing a continuum of services whenever possible. See Chapter 6 for an example of a school district that relies on such a combination: cluster grouping K–6, content replacement in grades 4–6, and a self-contained program for highly and profoundly gifted students who are radically accelerated in their academics. In this district's case, these three services combine to provide a comprehensive continuum that, when implemented appropriately, can effectively service a range of gifted students' learning needs.

EQUALITY VERSUS EQUITY

Public perception of the need for gifted education has been impacted by many factors throughout recent history. Given the lack of federal attention in the form of mandates or funding, gifted education is simply not a priority in most states, which then carries over to the districts and schools.

With increased attention to equity in our schools, we can advocate for the learning needs of all students, including our most advanced learners and those with exceptional potential. Giving all students equal opportunities to learn requires that we respond to their learning needs. If schools provided equitable attention to all students' learning needs, then we would not need to advocate for gifted education or gifted programs. Teachers would have received training in how gifted students learn and in how to teach them prior to entering the classroom.

An important question to ask is, "What happens when schools do not plan for and provide equitable approaches to learning?" Nationally, about two in five advanced learners fall behind (out of the ranks of advanced achievers) as they progress through school (Xiang, Dahlin, Cronin, Theaker, & Durant, 2011). Similarly, a 2009 report from the Jack Kent Cooke Foundation (Wyner, Bridgeland, & DiIulio) found that only 56% of high achievers from low-income families retained their status as high achievers in reading by fifth grade. These students' skills are not being fostered, resulting in an incredible loss of talent both for the individuals and for a society that badly needs more innovators and creative thinkers. Return to your school district's mission and vision statements, as discussed in Chapter 2, and answer the question, "Are all our students provided equitable opportunities to achieve their goals within our school structure?" If not, how can you help them learn?

In this chapter, we have stressed the importance of developing gifted services that reflect the needs of the student population. We recommend forming a committee that represents all stakeholders: teachers, principals, and parents. This will help ensure you have the voice of all of those who will support the services and will increase buy-in from all parties. When designing your services, begin with a needs assessment by referencing the NAGC Pre-K–12 Gifted Programming Standards. Then identify the various components your committee will need to define and describe. Figure 6 is a sample list of the components of a district gifted education plan.

CONCLUSION

In this chapter, we have provided you with an overview of various programming options available. If you don't have anything in place yet or recognize the need to change your services but are not sure what to implement, begin by searching for unmet needs to see if you need additional services. Even when there are no existing programs or services in place, this is part of why we identify—to get an idea of what is needed.

Importantly, the program models and the interventions described need not occur in isolation. In Part II, you will glean several examples as to how these program models can work in conjunction with each other to meet the broad range of our gifted students' instruction. School districts that can develop services that combine multiple program models and/or include various interventions can meet a broader and more diverse population of gifted students, thus avoiding the question, "What happens when a program model is not serving a gifted student?"

Our intention in this chapter was to demonstrate that different gifted students may need different options; likewise, different districts will need different programming options. Despite the variations, some type of gifted services should be an integral part of the school day for all gifted students. As noted, in Part II, we demonstrate similarities and differences in what programs use in a rural setting, a suburban setting, a large diverse school district, and a countywide school district.

- Statement of commitment
- Philosophy and purpose
- Mission statements
- Definitions and descriptions
- Gifted identification process
- Programming
- Staffing
- Professional development and preparation
- Curriculum and instruction
- Addressing social and emotional needs
- Program evaluation
- Parent collaboration and community involvement
- Budget

Figure 6
Components of a district gifted education plan.

CHAPTER 5

LOGISTICAL CONSIDERATIONS

GUIDING QUESTIONS

- How can parents help advocate for and support gifted services at their schools?
- Who should we approach at the school or district level when advocating for change?
- What are some ways to monitor progress when implementing and supporting gifted services?

In this final chapter of Part I, we want to leave you with practical advice, based on our experiences and those of our colleagues, on how to help build sustainable gifted services. With this emphasis, we focus on the importance of communication, collaboration, and accountability reflected in some of the processes employed when creating effective gifted services. Many of the topics addressed here are geared toward program administrators and coordinators and deal with common challenges related to getting new gifted and talented services off the ground. We encourage you to consider how these methods might play out in your own school district, as every community is different. When reading this chapter, consider the type of structures that need to be put into place, the families you will need to communicate with, and the existing structures already in place. Who do you need to connect with to make this happen? What level of support do you already have? What resources do you have available? What kinds of challenges are you likely to encounter?

COMMUNICATION

Something you will see referenced often in the Part II commentary chapters is the importance of communication—communication with general education teachers, administrators, school board members, and parents. Every one of the chapter authors in Part II has experienced successes as well as significant setbacks at the hands of parents or administrators. Much of this comes down to effective communication. In some states, effective communication is actually mandated. For example, in Wisconsin, state law requires that provisions be made to involve parents in the identification and programming process. But even if communication isn't required, an important logistical lesson is just how important it is that the gifted education coordinator make sure everyone is on the same page regarding what is happening, for whom, and why. We see communication as an investment that pays large dividends. If you invest an hour in planning effective communication, you might save 2 hours in answering e-mails and phone calls. As noted in Chapter 1, if everyone isn't clear on why some students are being served and not others, on why there is gifted education in the first place, and why particular identification criteria are used, then the program will not last long.

The three most common pathways for communication mentioned in Part II relate to websites, newsletters, and parent groups. But before we talk about any of these, it's important to emphasize that just "having" a parent advisory group for gifted education isn't going to help with communication if parents have to seek out its existence on their own. Similarly, if parents need to know about a listserv in order to receive the newsletter, then only those who are in the know are going to be informed. Regardless of how communication is approached in your district, it needs to be proactive. The goal needs to be keeping everyone informed, not just those who seek out information, have the time and energy to do so, or speak the dominant language in which information is communicated.

THE IMPORTANCE OF PARENT COMMUNICATION

Like it or not, parents are often the catalyst to making things happen in a district. They can advocate for change with the school board in ways that district employees cannot, and they can also scuttle plans that haven't been effectively communicated.

For this reason, we are big fans of parent advisory boards. These can take a range of forms. We've seen parent advisory boards as simple as once-a-semester meetings where district employees share updates and answer questions, but we've also seen them take a much more active role. Some host their own professional development for parents and teachers, some (see the Paradise Valley example in Part II) have liaisons with the school district in order to assure open lines of dialogue, and some serve as informal parent support groups. We've also seen parent groups that span districts and include entire geographic regions. In most cases, the district takes a hands-off approach to these groups—often helping to facilitate their creation but then letting parents take the lead as they see fit.

Sometimes these parent groups are difficult to navigate for a GT coordinator who is representing the district while also trying to expand services for students. Again, this points to the importance to clearly communicate roles and purposes. If nothing else, parent advisory boards can help communicate with other parents, can communicate information to parent groups at individual buildings, can serve as guides to new parents who might have children on the radar of the GT coordinator, and can help with strategic planning. We know of parent groups that were actually the primary drafters of district GT plans. We really do mean what we said at the start of this section: Parents can be the impetus for strengthening gifted education in a district. It makes great sense to work together to demonstrate flexibility and transparency in efforts. It all comes down to communication.

Administrative advice: Be transparent with your parents and parent advisory group. They can be a tremendous advocate for you or can strongly hinder your efforts. Your combined efforts will be more effective when you treat parents as partners and plan together.

STAKEHOLDER COMMUNICATION

In a similar vein to parent advisory groups is the importance to liaise with other stakeholder groups. Larger districts often have parent communication liaisons or chief diversity officers whose jobs involve engaging with different communities in a district. We know of specific examples where Spanish-speaking parents were never involved in the GT advisory board because: (a) the parents didn't know it existed, and (b) it wasn't seen as an inclusive place for them. District personnel need to resist the urge to simply let those who want to be involved be the only ones who know what's going on. Communication needs to be proactive in the sense that the goal is reaching 100% of stakeholders, not simply those who are willing and able to come to parent meetings.

Websites, newsletters, and listservs are effective ways to communicate with both teachers and parents. All of these can be utilized for free through Google Sites, Google Groups, and Google Docs. It doesn't take an advanced level of technology savvy to keep a running Q&A on Google Docs or to send out notifications about upcoming identification testing through a Google group e-mail list. Some information can be sent to all district parents and teachers, posted in building newsletters, and shared at back-to-school nights or parent-teacher conferences. Similarly, once a student gets on the radar for potential GT services, the student's family can be added to another Google group in order to receive updates regarding programs, services, and ways to contact the district. All of this becomes more important with larger programs or larger school districts. (See Chapter 6 for specific examples of these communication tools in action with parents, teachers, and administrators.)

If the entire district is in a single building with only a handful of teachers, then face-to-face communication on an individual basis is possible. However, in such situations, the person who is facilitating gifted education for the district is probably also in charge of several other areas, thus necessitating technology to help facilitate communication. There is no single best way to stay in touch with stakeholders, but we do want to emphasize just how important this communication is to the long-term success of gifted education in a district. The best-planned gifted education plan in the world won't go anywhere if it isn't rolled out and communicated effectively.

School board members and district and building administrators are often the first line of communication for many families. When there is a concern or when a parent needs to reach out regarding a need for additional services for his or her child, it's likely to be to a teacher, administrator, or school board member. This is why it's so important that all of these people know what is going on, are able to talk about it, and (if needed) are able to defend it. It's never good when a principal is approached with an issue she didn't know was going on in her building or if a school board member finds out about a program for the first time from an upset parent.

Gifted and talented coordinators should schedule periodic visits with every district administrator as well as formal presentations to the school board. He or she should make a schedule rotation for when each administrator gets a visit. These visits can be a time to share updates to policies, but also as a way to gauge any potential unmet needs. As we discussed in earlier chapters, much of gifted education begins with observing an unmet need and building-level staff are often the best ears to the ground when looking for such needs.

Like parents, individual administrators or school board members can also be the catalyst to furthering advanced education in a district. In the Wisconsin example in Part II, the author discusses how a new director of curriculum and instruction came to the district and was successful at instilling a sense of urgency regarding the needs of advanced learners. This person was then able to recruit advocates on the school board, who, in turn, provided funding for additional training as well as instructional coach stipends for each building. Similarly, the fact that the Paradise Valley school board receives frequent updates regarding enrollment (and their associated finances) helps assure their continued support. All of this relates back to effective communication. We've seen too many cases where school personnel want to hide their gifted education programs or policies out of worries too many parents might want these services for their kids or out of fear of elitism claims. But these issues are better dealt with head on via engagement with all stakeholders and proactive, ongoing communication.

FUNDING

As we presented in Chapter 1, in most states there simply isn't a lot of funding for gifted or advanced education. Most states do not fully fund their mandates, which leaves individual districts to find resources to support learning needs that cannot be met through regular education offerings (Tier I). First, we want to emphasize that because we are no longer talking about a singular "gifted education program" but instead are talking about domain-specific interventions or services, the cost should not be as high. Yes, some districts will have the need for a stand-alone profoundly gifted program (see Large and Mega district examples in Part II). But many more students simply need a little more challenge and not to be several grades accelerated.

It's worth pointing out that both the Large and Medium-sized district examples used the increasing numbers of students leaving the district because of a lack of advanced educational opportunities as a catalyst for change. In both of these districts, this decreased enrollment meant decreased district revenue. Although not a carrot to provide services, the potential loss of funds when families leave the district is often a powerful stick. Although providing a particular service might cost the district $10,000, that amount is more than made up for if only two students (on average) stay in the district (in Wisconsin). Of course, education shouldn't be about money, but at the end of the day money helps allow services to happen. Sometimes the "student need" or educational argument might not win the day and what it takes is dollars and cents.

With scarce funding for education in general, a common concern is that schools must address issues that pertain to the general population prior to funding programs or services for gifted students. This situation requires that school districts rely on local levels of support for high-ability students, which then falls into the hands of school boards, superintendents, principals, teachers, and parent advocates.

Program Administration

School boards have the ability to create policy, which can solidify services and make it so that schools cannot opt out of providing services. This can help embed gifted services into district initiatives. Superintendents can make gifted education a priority in the district and ensure that district leaders and principals carry out its implementation and provide ongoing support. Principals hold the position of school leadership and, as such, can structure classes with gifted education in mind. Most commonly, this appears as ensuring that differentiated curriculum, special classes, and acceleration are included at the site. Nothing, however, is as meaningful as the teachers' efforts to understand and respond to the learning needs of her gifted students in a purposeful manner. Parent advocates oftentimes lead the movement to make needed changes in how their children are served. It truly does take a village!

When considering change, begin by analyzing your current situation. Identify what is working and what needs modification in your model of gifted services by answering the following questions:

- Does your school program meet state gifted mandate requirements?
- Are curriculum and instructional strategies used by the teachers designed to meet the needs of *all* of your gifted identified students?
- Is there professional development in place that supports and ensures a quality program that serves diversity?
- Does the school and district administration support a systematic approach to maintaining the model (i.e., budget, communication, district-level collaboration, professional development, scheduling, and staffing)?
- What measures are in place to evaluate the service model? Does program evaluation include parents, teachers, students, and administrators?

Making changes to the gifted program in your school or district takes time. As an administrator, you will most likely begin implementing change using existing staff. Bear in mind that it is possible for change to take place with existing resources and limited financial implications when needed. We recommend beginning by providing staff development to all of your teachers on the learning needs of gifted students as well as any information you have on existing student learning needs. Often information on these needs can come directly from teachers. Then look at ways to form instructional groups so that your gifted students spend time learning core content together from a teacher who has participated in the training.

GIFTED COORDINATOR DUTIES

The strength and success of a gifted program relies heavily on the departments' administrative assistance. The office staff represents the "face" of gifted in the district. The staff sets the tone for the department and provides the public's perception of the district's gifted services. Gifted student enrollment into the district can continue to grow when parents feel supported. Critical administrative functions that provide for a systemic structure supports all programs, services, and staff. Possible job duties for a gifted coordinator and office administrative support can include: design, develop, and support a continuum of gifted programs and services;

- analyze and utilize district data for program and curriculum development;
- establish and maintain database for gifted student information;
- recommend policy and procedures for department development;
- supervise and evaluate gifted specialists;
- create and manage department budget;
- create and provide staff development based on needs assessments;
- coordinate gifted testing and reporting procedures;
- recruit and staff for gifted education department needs;
- ensure compliance with state mandates and alignment with district initiatives;
- build and maintain stakeholder communication and relationships; and
- represent the school district in community forums and to the media.

USING A (GIFTED) DATABASE

We strongly recommend that schools and districts create and maintain a comprehensive gifted database. The database will allow schools to monitor the number of students being tested and served and can help ensure that all gifted identified students are receiving services. The gifted database should include the names of the students identified as gifted, the dates the students were tested, the name(s) of the test(s) used, and the area(s) of identification, along with any other information you wish to document. Include all available test scores used in the identification process, including both qualifying and nonqualifying gifted cluster placement scores. Information included in the database can be used over several years to recognize patterns, such as which schools have more accurate identification methods, and to make sure that any student who has been identified as gifted will continue to be served as a gifted student (Winebrenner & Brulles, 2008).

You may find that your school district prefers to follow a longer term plan to implement changes in its gifted programming. If so, consider the following plan:

1. The planning year would include providing professional development

opportunities, scheduling informational meetings for all stakeholders, and planning out a timeline for implementation with benchmarks.

2. The pilot year would involve implementing the program in at least one school, but preferably a few depending on the size of the district.

3. The following year the school district would then expand to other schools after making necessary program modifications that emerged during the pilot year.

You would continue holding ongoing informational meetings and supporting teachers with professional development during the planning, pilot, and implementation years.

CREATING SUSTAINABLE SERVICES

Throughout Part I of the book, we have attempted to demonstrate the need to embed gifted services into all major aspects of the school functions. Doing so will provide the framework for creating sustainable services that outlive district personnel. We want all district staff and leadership to constantly be reminded to consider the learning needs of gifted and talented students in all school-related functions. Hence, the need for gifted coordinators to collaborate with school departments and other administrators.

COLLABORATION AMONG ADMINISTRATORS

We build understanding and support through relationships and collaboration. Collaboration between the gifted coordinator and principals is imperative for designing building-level support. If gifted services involve students changing classrooms, such as with grade-level flexible grouping, ability grouping, push-in or pull-out, etc., then scheduling of special area classes (i.e., art, music band) needs to occur opposite the academic service the gifted students are experiencing.

Collaboration between the gifted coordinator and district-level administrators allows for systems to develop. Gifted students' learning needs are much more likely to become embedded into school/district culture through collaboration at this level. This collaboration and support produces shared expectations and helps build sustainable systems.

Administrative advice: It is critical that any "general education" or district/ schoolwide committee include representation by the gifted education department or committee (a district RtI committee is a perfect example). Too often gifted education is seen as unrelated to these other initiatives, and nothing could be further from the truth.

RELYING ON THE DISTRICT'S MISSION STATEMENT

A quick review of your school district mission statement will usually provide a strong direction on how to approach school district administration when advocating for gifted services. Most mission statements include language that announces the district's intention to help all students develop their potential, challenge all students, individualize instruction according to students' needs, or such similar language. Using the language of the district's mission statement in the context of our gifted learners suggests that opportunities to learn require some intervention for these students.

Examples of mission statements:

- "Our mission is to *cultivate the potential in every student* to thrive as a global citizen by inspiring a love of learning and civic engagement, by challenging and supporting every student to achieve academic excellence, and by embracing the full richness and diversity of our community."
- "We are committed to *providing each student with optimal learning opportunities so that they can reach their full academic* and social potential."
- "In our schools students should be accepted, appreciated, nurtured, and *challenged according to their individual needs.*"
- "We provide a nurturing environment committed to achieving excellence. *All students are challenged to reach their maximum potential* by learning at their functional level to provide a solid foundation of skills, knowledge and values . . ."

Because gifted students are typically advanced learners that need instruction beyond what is offered at the grade level, the language in the mission statement should rightfully encompass those learning needs.

PROACTIVELY FINDING GIFTED STUDENTS WE ARE LIKELY TO MISS

As discussed in Chapter 3 on gifted identification, we remind you to pay close attention to monitoring effectiveness in identifying and serving gifted students from diverse populations. Check to see if your policies and procedures for gifted identification and programs include tests that identify diverse populations. If not, focus some staff development on gifted student identification procedures for the underrepresented populations. Over time, watch for growth in the number of your currently underrepresented groups. If underrepresentation remains a problem, this is a perfect example of an unmet need that requires additional services and interventions.

Determine from your school or district's enrollment records the percentage of students in each group. Compare that data to the percentage of identified gifted students from each group. If the percentages are discrepant, seek alternative identification methods, criteria, or procedures that will increase identification and service to the underrepresented populations. You will find some practical methods for doing so in the district chapters that follow.

Administrative advice: Compare your student demographics to your gifted identified student population and use this comparison data to determine if specific populations are underrepresented. Then explore alternative tools and methods for gifted testing that may provide for a more equitable identification procedure. Proactively work to increase the numbers of underrepresented students identified as gifted.

To find other students we are likely to miss, consider including special area teachers in your teacher training on recognizing giftedness or when nominating students for gifted testing. Those teaching art, music, drama, band, orchestra, choir, etc., will notice strengths and talent in students in ways not observed in the classroom. These talents oftentimes transfer into academic areas with encouragement and attention from classroom teachers. Including special area teachers will also provide data needed to group these talented students with gifted identified children working in the content areas. Exposure to others with exceptional abilities can inspire and motivate students in various areas of learning.

Enrollment

Maintaining awareness of the gifted student enrollment provides a number of benefits to the district, the schools, the strength of the gifted program, and gifted students. The increased number of gifted students enrolled in the district draws school staff awareness to these students' learning needs and contributes to the support of their instruction. This becomes particularly true when you begin to diversify the gifted population, showing that you are working at developing potential of all students, regardless of other special needs, achievement levels, gender, or age. This awareness can build acceptance between teachers, staff, and other students due to the broader range of gifted students identified and served. It creates an inclusive mentality that encourages equitable identification methods and services.

Administrative advice: Attention to gifted education also informs the public that your school is reaching out to and teaching students at the highest level possible.

Professional Development

Determine the areas where professional development is needed and then develop the schedule accordingly. We recommend designing professional development based on gifted student achievement data, input from teachers and principals, and school/district initiatives. This is another place where gifted education needs to be a consideration at the table.

A few additional suggestions to consider when designing professional development opportunities:

- Invite all district teachers to workshops you create with gifted students in mind to build understanding and strengthen support.
- Tap into in-house resources to utilize district teachers to provide training on areas of expertise.
- Utilize a variety of training formats: afterschool workshops, before school meetings, face-to-face and online trainings, local conferences, webinars, PLC's, etc.
- Access free and low-cost training through gifted education Twitter chats and webinars offered through national gifted associations, such as the National Association for Gifted Children (NAGC).
- Provide training for teachers of the gifted when adopting new curriculum.

When making professional development opportunities available to all staff members, the teachers become aware of the characteristics of gifted students and learn to identify gifted students in all populations because of the ongoing training they receive. With continual attention to this type of training, the school develops a culture that is accepting of the presence of giftedness in all subpopulations. Importantly, this type of professional development trains teachers to offer compacting and differentiation opportunities to all students, which can lead to increasing achievement for all students.

Most effective gifted programs provide teachers with collaboration time. Teachers, in general, typically have insufficient time to plan with colleagues. Common planning time is even more rare with teachers of the gifted because oftentimes they are the only ones at their school or in the district.

Administrative advice: Use free Google tools to create a digital resource site where teachers can participate in workshops, collaborate with one another, study archived presentations, and learn from others' contributions.

When planning for any type of professional development, administrators must consider the varying needs of their faculty (notice the ongoing theme of needs-based interventions for kids and adults alike?). Some topics, especially those rooted in whole-school programming, are necessary for the entire staff. Other topics should be offered to new staff in order to align the expectations and procedures used throughout the school. With respect to gifted education techniques, the general consensus is that all teachers should receive training. Inviting all teachers sends the message that the training is important to the school and that all teachers are responsible for having preparation in addressing the learning needs of the school's gifted students. Furthermore, training all teachers ensures that strategies can be modified and used with all learners in the school. As noted earlier, best practices are often effective for all students.

The most powerful training can quickly be pushed aside, however, if teachers do not have sufficient time to learn, practice, and plan for how they will use the training. Allowing educators to process the information provided in the training, and to devise a concrete way in which the training can be applied to their classroom, fosters a greater likelihood that the educators will use what they learn as a regular part of their teaching repertoire (Winebrenner & Brulles, 2008).

Administrative advice: Creating data charts provides information useful for determining training needs and curricular improvements. Use this type of achievement data to design workshops, in-service topics, and curriculum, and to monitor progress in these efforts.

MONITORING AND EVALUATION

Regardless of the program model selected or the services provided, it is essential for schools to monitor the success of the program with respect to student achievement, gifted program enrollment, and parent communication, to name a few. Attention to gifted department record keeping makes it possible to track, reference, and report on these elements. With time, this reporting can correct the discrepancies and be used over several years to recognize patterns and areas that need improvement.

We also recommend that schools maintain an active record of teacher training opportunities, topics, and attendees. The goal is to ensure that teachers are receiving adequate and appropriate training. By analyzing the data recorded, it will become clear which topics have been thoroughly covered and which require additional sessions. This attention to detail will help ensure that the teachers delivering instruction to gifted students are sufficiently prepared to teach these learners.

Administrative advice: Use input from the district's major stakeholder groups, curricular and district initiatives, and educational trends and data from existing services as evidence that current services need revisions or improvement.

USING THE NAGC PRE-K–GRADE 12 GIFTED PROGRAMMING STANDARDS

The NAGC Pre-K–Grade 12 Gifted Programming Standards provide a framework schools can use in a variety of ways to develop, evaluate, and/or improve gifted programs or services. The 2010 standards are categorized as follows:

- Standard 1: Learning and Development
- Standard 2: Assessment

- Standard 3: Curriculum Planning and Instruction
- Standard 4: Learning Environments
- Standard 5: Programming
- Standard 6: Professional Development

In Appendix A, we have provided a complete description of each standard, along with descriptive student outcomes correlated with evidence-based practices. These guidelines can serve as a "blueprint for quality gifted education programs" that schools can use in a variety of ways, such as: (1) developing initial programs and services; (2) informing schools of areas where improvement is needed; (3) ensuring attention to all aspects of gifted programming; (4) guiding professional development; and (5) advocating for administrative support. These program standards plus whatever requirements exist in your state (if any) are the best place to start determining what needs to go into a comprehensive gifted education plan.

These comprehensive standards are recognized throughout the field as an ideal for which to use at any and all stages of program development. Included in Appendix A are two charts: a Gap Analysis Chart that can provide documentation showing where attention and improvement is needed and an Action Plan Chart where specific action steps can be planned.

These tools can help schools help direct attention to specific areas of need and map out concrete steps for moving forward to enhance and strengthen gifted services. Even if some degree of a "plan" already exists, the gap analysis chart can be a great way to reflect on what is happening and how it can be improved.

CONCLUSION

In closing, we would like to emphasize that change takes time. To ensure that gifted programming changes are effective and sustainable involves creating systems that align with district goals and using data to document the purpose of the efforts. Embedding these efforts into existing structures ensures stronger outcomes that can continue to be built upon in response to student and teacher needs. Importantly, sustainable changes also necessitate buy-in from stakeholders, and this support comes from building relationships and the willingness to seek input from all those involved in educating our gifted students.

Remember that strong gifted programs not only take time to develop but also will change over time. Educational trends, district initiatives, state policies, shifting student demographics, and staffing all have significant influence on how programs develop and evolve throughout the years. Identifying what once worked well and recognizing indicators that change is needed help districts improve educational opportunities for students.

In this chapter, we attempted to convince readers to take small steps and consider a wide range of needs and supports. Emphasis on the critical need for clear and consistent communication was woven throughout all topics in the chapter. Communication to support parents, to encourage district-level collaboration, and to support staff will strengthen your services and bode well for enjoying sustainable services.

We close Part I with an invitation to collaborate with us and gifted coordinators around the county. Along with the links to other resources promoted in the book, we invite you to view gifted programming plans of others around the country and upload your own to share with others. We have set up a public Google site where you can upload your own district's GT plan as well as view plans from other districts at http://goo.gl/NcCA9L. We do this in keeping with the main theme of the book—there's no need to reinvent the wheel every time, and even if you can grasp a few ideas from other district plans, then that's time you can spend on plenty of other things.

PART II
DISTRICT PLANS

Introduction and Overview

Part II of this book provides readers a rare opportunity to see how four gifted coordinators approached the process of building comprehensive gifted services in their own districts. Our intent is to show the behind-the-scenes work of the district plans and policies—how they were developed, how they've changed, what the real world looks like compared to what's on paper, and how things have evolved over the history of gifted education in each district. Their stories allow you to reflect upon the obstacles they encountered within this process and learn from their experiences. Although there are similarities across all of the commentaries in Part II (e.g., references to student needs), you'll also note a number of differences. These differences relate to state funding, mandates, as well as overall philosophy for how to best meet the needs of advanced learners in these very different districts.

We selected four districts that represent very different state contexts, geographic locations, and sizes. These include the following:

- an immense countywide district in Florida with more than 220,000 students (County Unified School District);
- a large district in Arizona with 33,000 students served (Paradise Valley Unified School District);
- a small rural district in Montana with 1,600 K–12 students, roughly one third of whom are Native American (Montana); and
- a medium sized suburban district in Wisconsin with 3,000 students (Baraboo School District).

The diversity within these districts reflects the nation's student populations. You will note that the authors each describe their efforts to identify and serve gifted students of underrepresented populations. As representation of diverse populations in gifted programs remains a priority for many school practitioners, in these chapters you will also learn methods the districts employ for serving and instructing their diverse gifted populations once identified.

Among the similarities within the districts profiled here you will notice an emphasis on aligning identification procedures and services to the districts' philosophy, vision, mission, and program goals. Most significantly, you will examine how those are achieved, as Dr. Lauri Kirsch from County in Florida eloquently describes. Throughout all of the chapters you will note that the districts' plans reflect the district's needs. The plans are not intended to serve as a model to emulate, but rather as a demonstration of how these districts' programs were developed based on state requirements and district data (i.e., number of schools, student population, identification processes, administrative support, district allocation of resources, etc.). Importantly, you will also learn how they are supported, modified, and sustained.

You will also see various differences between the inner workings of gifted education in the districts profiled. The districts vary dramatically in their reliance on collaboration within district, accessibility of plans and resources to general education teachers, and levels of training and support provided. Likewise, the scope of services offered varies considerably within the districts. The individual districts may offer their schools choices, may mandate services, or even may fluctuate between offering choices or requiring services based on the needs and numbers of identified gifted students. This is perhaps the one universal of gifted education—it needs to be flexible and based on the needs of the local district (and sometimes even the school) population.

To gain insight into the how the coordinators approached the task of developing gifted services, we asked them to consider how their programs were developed and evolved. We wanted to know their thinking at the time and asked what aspects of the programs they modified, why those modifications were made, and what has been the result of those revisions. With the goal of providing readers examples to draw from, we asked the districts' coordinators to respond to several commonly asked questions new coordinators often consider when developing gifted services. The following questions framed the commentaries included in Part II:

- What was the initial impetus for the creation of the existing plan?
- What is the guiding philosophy for the district's gifted and talented program? What is its purpose or goal?
- What is the history of gifted education in the district? What major changes have happened and when?
- How were stakeholders involved in the drafting of the plan and how do they continue to be involved (parents, administrators, teachers, students)?
- How is gifted education incorporated into general education curriculum and programming decisions as well as other initiatives such as RtI, Common Core, Personalized Learning, etc.?
- What content areas are covered under your district's plan(s)? How is curriculum determined and by whom?
- How does your district seek out, identify, and program for students from traditionally underrepresented groups?
- How are gifted teaching positions staffed, supervised, and evaluated?
- Where do you see the district/the plan heading next? What revisions might be necessary or what corrections are you currently working on?
- What are the state-mandated requirements and components for gifted and talented education plans?

What follows are commentaries written by individuals in each district with deep knowledge of the policies and practices. For the sake of space (and paper!) we did not include all of the district plans or policies in this book. Instead, you can access all of those at the following link: http://www.prufrock.com/DesigningGiftedPrograms. aspx. We believe the plans/documents and commentaries are best read in tandem so that the reader can see what is in the policy and how that policy came to be.

CHAPTER 6

LARGE DISTRICT IN ARIZONA

Dina Brulles, Ph.D.

INTRODUCTION: OUR PURPOSE AND PHILOSOPHY

The guiding philosophy of the gifted programs I developed and support in Paradise Valley reflects that of any other educational program: to engage students in challenging curriculum and instruction on a daily basis and in all relevant content areas so that they can make continuous academic growth. To effectively do so, teachers who have ongoing training and support must facilitate instruction. The school district must also provide support by allocating resources and providing training for administrators and teachers and information to parents.

The purpose of the gifted programs in Paradise Valley Unified School District (PVUSD) is to provide a setting wherein all students can learn and achieve at levels commensurate with their ability and potential. The immediate goal is to help ensure that those students identified and served in our program receive consistent opportunities to thrive academically every year and learn every day. Achieving and sustaining this goal requires a systematic approach and considerable support for the teachers.

One of the district's two major initiatives is to include equitable practices in each department and school, so I work this equity goal into my action plans. We aligned our gifted programming objectives with the district's recently formed equity priorities. Our ongoing efforts to ensure equity in services drew awareness from several national publications and news stations. These include several stories on serving underrepresented populations in gifted with National Public Radio (NPR) featuring Hispanic/Latino gifted students at the elementary and secondary levels:

http://www.npr.org/sections/ed/2016/03/31/472528190/the-rare-district-that-recognizes-gifted-latino-students and http://www.npr.org/sections/ed/2016/04/11/467653193/gifted-but-still-learning-english-overlooked-underserved.

History and Context

A Supportive Governing Board Helps

Within the first 2 weeks in my position with Paradise Valley, I was scheduled to report to the Governing Board on the state of gifted education in the district through a board study session. This study session was scheduled long before my arrival, as concerns had surfaced. The Governing Board wanted to learn more about the current services. My presentation and the ensuing discussions provided the board members with a shared understanding of gifted education and the district's services. I shared data, best practices in gifted education, and state legislation. From this experience I learned that keeping board members up to date can create allies. Now, whenever a board member is questioned about the gifted program, he or she can address those concerns or have confidence in the department's ability to do so. As we noted in Chapter 5, communication of all kind is key.

I continue to share information and data with the administrative leadership team (called the Cabinet). This includes gifted student enrollment data, achievement data, and student and teacher accolades, such as competition results, awards, and media coverage. Our Governing Board formally recognizes the awards and accomplishments of staff and their gifted students at board meetings, as does our communication department, which draws additional attention to our gifted programs.

A Little Background

In 2006, I entered into my current position as Gifted Coordinator (now titled, "Gifted Education Director") with excitement and trepidation. The district held the admirable reputation of having a strong gifted program, which included having a pull-out honors teacher at every one of its 32 elementary schools who taught content replacement in math and reading to students in grades 3–6. It had a district self-contained program and a twice-exceptional program and honors, Advanced Placement (AP), and Baccalaureate Program (IB) at the secondary level. The prospect of leading and supporting this comprehensive program initially felt daunting.

I would soon learn that the district gifted services were more site-based than district mandated. Department records documented how funds were spent, how the district was in compliance with the Arizona State Gifted Mandate, and a long-established staffing structure was in place. However, I found that no programming records, gifted student rosters, professional development plans, or articulated curriculum existed. I was perplexed by the lack of accountability or overall structure.

I was informed that the honors teachers "knew" who the gifted students were in their schools. These teachers did not meet for training or planning; each individual teacher tested, identified, and placed gifted students at his or her school. They each determined their own curriculum and teaching schedules. I discovered that the district had a significant structure in place that provided gifted services in every school and a full-time gifted coordinator. After an initial review I realized there was a tremendous opportunity to build on this existing structure.

TTWWADI (That's the Way We've Always Done It!)

The history of gifted education in the district became immediately evident when I took the position; in fact, the history reflected the current reality at the time. Little had changed since the inception of the program 28 years prior to when I joined the district. This stagnation likely stemmed from an unspoken yet pervasive philosophy that prevailed throughout many of the district's programs: TTWWADI. Fortunately, the district became much more progressive and innovative in successive years.

An impressive structure with an underdeveloped support system existed. Although there was a coordinator with a strong background in gifted education and admirable intentions, there was no obligation that the teachers meet, share, or plan together. Also absent were the procedures necessary for a systemic and systematic approach—everyone knew what was going on, but this wasn't due to a formalized plan. As a teacher-on-assignment (TOA), the gifted coordinator did not possess the authority to schedule in-services, require professional development, or mandate a specific curriculum.

INVOLVING STAKEHOLDERS

A strong gifted parent group was initially in place when I came to the district. Parents had formed a nonprofit group to build awareness of the learning needs of their children and advocate for stronger and more fully supported gifted programs. The parents realized that their children would benefit from a more fully developed gifted program. Parent group leaders met with me monthly to provide input that helped guide the initial changes. Together, we held informational parent nights where I presented on the needs of gifted students and approaches for serving them. We also invited local and national experts to address topics of interest to the parents.

Parents, teachers, and administrators representing elementary, middle, and high school students served on a district committee with me to revise the existing Scope and Sequence of Gifted Education Services. At the time, the state department of education required the submission of this plan as one of the requirements for receiving gifted program grant funding as outlined in the Arizona Gifted Education State Mandate. Once revised, the Governing Board adopted the Scope and Sequence and it became policy. Every 3 years, a committee of stakeholders convenes to update the Scope and Sequence to reflect the change in services.

ARIZONA'S GIFTED MANDATE AND (LACK OF) FUNDING

The Arizona Department of Education has a gifted education mandate that lost its funding in 2010. With no funding attached to the gifted mandate, school districts were no longer required to submit their gifted program Scope and Sequence plans to the Arizona Department of Education. The lack of state support resulted in many districts decreasing attention to their gifted services. In subsequent years, most of the districts in the state also eliminated existing gifted staff positions. Paradise Valley retained its gifted staffing and support, and this choice has paid long-term dividends. Districts that continued to provide gifted education services, such as the case in Paradise Valley, began drawing the attention of parents seeking services for their gifted children. In Arizona, parents may elect to send their children to schools in districts outside of their home school boundaries. Many parents of gifted children ultimately elected to send their children to Paradise Valley.

THE RATIONALE FOR CHANGE

HOW OUR PROGRAM EVOLVED AND EVOLVES

Since I joined the district in 2006, gifted education services evolved into its current comprehensive system over a period of years, and it continues to expand yearly in response to students' needs. We now have strong program oversight, gifted identification, teacher support and training, and curriculum development by obtaining support from district administration. This was accomplished by demonstrating need in several areas, including:
- scheduling of services,
- reorganizing staffing to maximize services,
- reviewing student achievement,
- aligning curriculum and instruction to meet students' needs,
- providing targeted teacher training and support,
- revising budget allocations,

- monitoring gifted student enrollment, and
- examining gifted student demographics.

I provided documentation showing underutilized staffing, underidentified students, and underdeveloped and inconsistent curriculum. With these data, I was granted the opportunity to develop proposals for Cabinet-level consideration in which I addressed the areas noted above.

LOGISTICAL CHALLENGES ENCOUNTERED

Realizing the possibilities for growth, I created a systematic approach that began with sharing information, which district administration supported. I invited schools to voluntarily implement new systems and services. Soon after, I was told by a fellow director, "You don't understand; change happens slowly around here!" With that admonishment, I recognized the importance of treading cautiously while continuing my efforts to strengthen the programs. I also better understood the need to provide colleagues with information that would broaden their awareness of our responsibility to appropriately support and challenge our gifted and talented students.

TESTING AND IDENTIFICATION

Fortuitously, the Arizona state gifted mandate has no requirement of advanced academic achievement for gifted identification. Due to the large number of English language learners (ELLs) and former ELLs in Arizona, the lack of academic achievement criteria for gifted identification allows for students who have high ability that is yet to manifest itself as high achievement. Arizona's system of identifying giftedness based on ability alone encourages schools to identify giftedness based on potential and then work toward developing that potential.

REFINING TESTING PROCEDURES

The gifted testing procedure currently incorporated in the district has been completely revamped from the procedures employed in the past; in fact, we continue to refine our testing procedures every year. After we identify students as gifted, we determine if programming adjustments or curriculum and instructional modifications are needed to best serve those students. This responsive process requires that we continually enhance our existing programs to more inclusively serve the students we identify.

Paradise Valley provides a comprehensive identification process designed to identify all students with high ability and potential with special attention to those from diverse populations. The Arizona state mandate stipulates that schools test three times a year and establishes the gifted identification criteria as 97% or above in any one area (verbal, quantitative, nonverbal) on a state-approved ability or intelligence test. This encourages the schools to continually share information with parents, staff members, and administrators; a precursor to developing strong gifted programs.

QUALIFYING FOR GIFTED SERVICES: OUR TESTING SCHEDULE

The district's testing schedule is made available to parents and teachers at the start of each school year, allowing all stakeholders to plan accordingly. The testing schedule involves the procedures described below and in Brulles (2014).

Fall testing:

- Test any student who may qualify for content replacement or honors classes (grades 4–8) using the CogAT and/or the NNAT2. The test used depends on previous test results and test dates. Students who score between 80%–96% on either test may test again using the alternative test.
- Qualifying students move into content replacement or honors classes upon identification. Some students scoring between 80%–96% may be "flexed" into gifted cluster classes and content replacements depending on school demographics and numbers of gifted students at each school (typically, this occurs in our Title I schools).

Winter testing:

- Blanket test students in certain grades in the Title I elementary schools (NNAT2).
- Blanket test all sixth graders in the feeder system of the middle school that houses the Nonverbal Honors Core, a specialized program for culturally and linguistically diverse GT students (NNAT2).
- Test ELLs and former ELLs at all schools (NNAT2).
- Schedule testing for students who reside outside the district's boundaries or those who attend charter schools, private schools, or are homeschooled (CogAT).

Spring testing:

- Extensive testing, grades K–8, to identify students for fall classroom placements. Teacher and parent nominations are solicited (CogAT and NNAT2).

- Schedule testing for students who reside outside the district's boundaries or those who attend charter schools, private schools, or are homeschooled (CogAT and NNAT2).
- Testing for the G/T Preschool for a nominal fee. School psychologists use the Stanford Binet Early Childhood Intelligence Test.
- Testing for students applying for the Self-Contained G/T Kindergarten Program provided at no cost (NNAT2).

Summer testing:
- Students with IEPs, 504 accommodation plans, or other special needs test individually or in small groups of 2–3 depending on the testing accommodations and modifications stipulated by the plans (CogAT, NNAT2, or IQ tests).
- Testing for the G/T preschool and kindergarten programs continue.
- Students who began testing during the school year's regularly scheduled testing period but who were unable to complete testing due to illness finish testing.

Testing notes:
- Testing for the Uniquely Gifted Program occurs throughout the school year using an IQ test administered by school district's psychologists.
- Outside testing with private psychologists (with experience in identifying giftedness) is encouraged for parents who feel the district administered test does not adequately reflect the child's true abilities and also when the parents would like more detailed information than group-administered ability tests provide.
- The gifted education department works closely with school psychologists using a process wherein students can qualify for gifted programs while undergoing testing for special education services.
- Gifted specialists at every elementary school, and gifted liaisons at the secondary level, provide site-based training to help staff members recognize characteristics and behaviors of gifted students, including those from diverse populations.
- District-level training, including workshops, cluster teacher meetings, gifted teacher in-services, and gifted liaison meetings, offers guidance and direction to the schools' gifted staff to better prepare them to oversee testing nominations at the sites.
- The gifted education department employs a team of retired teachers to schedule and administer the testing.

The district supports multiple pathways gifted students can take as they progress through their school years. The different program models naturally have differing entrance criteria, which require different testing options. This need is most prevalent in the early childhood gifted programs, in the transition from the Self-Contained Preschool Program to either the Self-Contained Kindergarten Program or a kindergarten cluster grouping class and in the transition from the kindergarten programs to first grade in the self-contained program or into the cluster model.

Qualifying criteria for the various self-contained gifted programs become increasingly more stringent between the preschool and elementary programs. This is largely due to the difficulty in accurately assessing young children, necessitating more inclusive criteria—something discussed in Chapter 3. We have found that gifted scores often increase from one year to the next in very young gifted children, which we associate with developmental readiness.

SPECIAL TESTING SITUATIONS

Preschool to kindergarten. Students entering the preschool program need a score of 90% or higher in one area as measured on the Stanford Binet Early Childhood Test. However, students need a 97% or higher to qualify for gifted services in kindergarten, either in the Self-Contained Kindergarten Program or a kindergarten gifted cluster class. Therefore, some students in the gifted preschool will enter into the Self-Contained Kindergarten Program, some will go to a gifted cluster class, and some will not qualify for gifted services in the elementary years.

Kindergarten to first grade. The transition from kindergarten to first grade also requires scheduling a special testing period to determine whether students qualify for placement into the schoolwide cluster grouping model or if they qualify to apply for the self-contained program in the elementary years. Most of the students from the preschool matriculate into the Self-Contained Gifted Kindergarten Program. From here, however, the majority will not qualify for (or need) the self-contained gifted program for grades 1–6. To apply for this elementary years program, students must have gifted test scores of 97% or higher in two of the three areas (verbal, quantitative, or nonverbal) with a score in the third area at 90% or higher. Students with an IQ of 140 or higher may also apply. Therefore, we provide testing using the Cognitive Abilities Test (CogAT) for those who need additional qualifying scores to apply. As an aside, the vast majority of students in the self-contained programs enter with IQ test results administered by private psychologists, and most of these students have IQs well over 140.

Students with IEPs and 504s. We work closely with school psychologists using a process wherein students can qualify for gifted services based on testing for special education services. We also examine previous special education testing records of students nominated for gifted testing who already have an IEP or 504, as we can sometimes use the test results to qualify a student as gifted. When additional testing is needed, we schedule a separate testing period for these students so that we can abide by the requirements noted on the IEP or 504 plan, such as extended testing time, testing in a small group, preferred seating arrangements, etc. This procedure allows us to provide the most opportune testing environment for the students and obtain the most valid data regarding their needs.

Feeder schools into Nonverbal Core. The Nonverbal Honors Core, located at Greenway Middle School, is a Title I school with a nearly entirely Hispanic student body. To qualify for entrance into the program, students need a 90% or higher score on a gifted ability test. We blanket test all sixth graders from schools that feed into Greenway. Those who score in this range on any previous testing automatically qualify for placement in the Nonverbal Honors Core.

TESTING RECORDS

We inform parents that we mail test results within 3 weeks of test administration. We send copies to the schools' gifted teachers to inform the classroom teachers and place the letters in the students' files. The gifted education department inputs scores of both qualifying and nonqualifying students to the student database and adds newly qualifying students to the schools' gifted student rosters. Every time the schools' gifted rosters are changed, we send an updated roster to the schools. This occurs following each school's testing administration, when gifted students enroll into a school, or when they withdraw from a school. We document nonqualifying scores in order to keep track of when the students were tested, which allows us to ensure that one year has passed before we retest the student.

Many parents come to us with testing records from outside the district. Some are from private psychologists, and some are from other schools. We recognize the value of IQ tests administered by psychologists in private settings. We encourage parents to seek outside testing if they feel the district testing does not accurately reflect the child's true abilities or when the parents would like more detailed information than group-administered ability tests provide. I have established a working relationship with the local psychologists whom many of our parents use for gifted testing. Doing so allows me to communicate my preferences in the language the psychologists include in their recommendations to ensure they are providing accurate program placement information to parents.

OUTSIDE TESTING

Students enrolling in Paradise Valley who have previously participated in gifted programs in another school district are automatically placed into the district's gifted programs if their gifted testing records meet the state's identification criteria. Outside testing records are sent to our gifted office for evaluation to determine qualification for services and to recommend programming options to the parents. School districts and states differ in their gifted identification criteria, therefore, some students who were served in their previous schools may need to retest with us if the gifted test used to identify them does not meet the state's identification requirements or if the scores were not equivalent to those accepted by the district. In these cases, the students will test during their school's next scheduled gifted testing period.

INVOLVING PARENTS

Reaching out to and involving parents is critical to the success of gifted programs. The gifted education department provides updates of gifted programming, testing, student placements procedures, parent resources, events, news, and a plethora of information on the district gifted department website. The department also sends out a quarterly gifted parent newsletter with highlights, promotions, and advice for parents of gifted identified students. We have learned that when parents have information they are much more likely to support our efforts.

COLLABORATING WITH UNITED PARENT COUNCIL

The United Parent Council (UPC) is districtwide parent group that actively "looks out for the interest of students." This 501(c)(3) group has several subgroups, one being a gifted committee led by the group's gifted parent liaison, with whom I meet monthly to share information. The gifted parent group also meets monthly, wherein the gifted parent liaison shares information she and I discuss during our monthly meetings. In these meetings, I provide updates on our services, teacher training, parent events, etc. The parent liaison provides input from committee members. This continued sharing of information also helps parents understand the various facets of our programs and efforts.

Outcomes of this collaboration include:

- provide parents and community members ongoing opportunities to learn about issues impacting gifted students,
- collaborate on scheduling guest speakers to present to parents and the community,
- present to parents and community for jointly scheduled informational meetings,
- share programming and instructional information in a timely manner,
- invite parents to serve on committees that support gifted education in the district,
- distribute pertinent information related to news and school district events,
- provide newly identified students' parents with contact information and resources, and
- encourage involvement of parents of gifted students with district initiatives.

PARENT NEWSLETTERS

The gifted department sends out a quarterly gifted parent newsletter to inform parents of our efforts, offerings, and useful resources. This information helps guide parents' conversations and advocacy efforts in an intentional and productive manner. We advertise and highlight events, note student and teacher accomplishments and provide tidbits of information about different programs and services available to our gifted students. In this way, parents recognize that we are proactive, supportive, and responsive to their children's learning needs. See sample newsletters at http://www.pvschools.net/Page/4407.

OUR GIFTED WEBSITE

With the range of gifted services, including gifted testing opportunities and program placements, we have found it critical to provide as much information as possible on the gifted website. Along with the program descriptions, qualification criteria, and application process for each program, on our public gifted website we post short videos of our teachers, students, and administrators sharing information about teaching and learning in each program. When we receive phone calls requesting information about our services, we direct them first to the gifted website. This allows the parents to gain insight into the purpose of the different programs so they can fine-tune their questions when calling us. We post information such as events, parent presentations, tours, and the professional development we provide to our teachers. We also include a brief photo gallery of students learning in the various programs. This transparent display of information demonstrates to the community the district's strong support of gifted education and diligence in our efforts.

OUR PROGRAM REVISIONS: RELYING ON DATA AND COLLABORATION

RATIONALE AND RESULTS

Under my tenure, all aspects of the gifted program are continuously modified based on evolving needs of the district, our students' needs, current initiatives, and constantly changing resources. District administration has supported this program development, in large part due to efforts to continually align to and support the district's goals.

One important example of how the program aligns with district goals is seen in the department's long-range plan. The district creates a 3-year plan articulating its goals, objectives, strategies, and measures of success. Each department and school then writes its plan within this outline. The gifted education department develops highly ambitious, innovative, and rigorous plans that align with the district's plans. These plans have been used as a model for other departments, further entrenching plans into practice, which draws attention to the district's gifted services.

PROGRAM EVALUATION

In efforts to create gifted programs that are responsive to students' needs, we rely on information and feedback from teachers, parents, students, and administrators. We have a rotating schedule of providing surveys to the groups mentioned above and administering a full program evaluation. This schedule is as follows:

- **Year 1:** Surveys to teachers, parents, students, and administrators in each of the programs separately (i.e., cluster model, self-contained program, etc.)
- **Year 2:** Program evaluation for elementary schools
- **Year 3:** Surveys (repeated)
- **Year 4**: Program evaluation for secondary schools

Through this schedule, I learn and document areas of strength and areas that need attention. The results inform my curriculum development and pacing, professional development, communication efforts, staffing, and student enrichment opportunities. I share the results with our district parent group, United Parent Council (UPC), and the Cabinet, who then may share with the Governing Board.

EXAMINING DEMOGRAPHICS

We believe that examining the demographics of the gifted student population presents the first and most critical step in creating testing procedures. We examine data at both the school and district level. Keeping ongoing records in the following categories during each year, and from one year to the next, provides us with accurate information to help administrators plan and carry out professional development, identification procedures, and staffing. We collect and record the following data:

- the percentage of the student population identified and served as gifted, by year;
- the percentage of the student population identified and served as gifted compared to the state average;
- the ethnic representation of gifted students in relation to the school or district's ethnic population; and
- the number and names of teachers obtaining a gifted endorsement or certification or participating in professional development offerings in gifted education.

REVIEWING STUDENT ACHIEVEMENT

I rely on data to draw attention to needs and to build support. Data allow us to advocate and plan for our gifted population's evolving needs. Each year I create presentations for every elementary, middle, and high school, showing graphs of student performance based on the state-administered tests. I use the data to guide curriculum and instruction, professional development, and program modifications. We return to the data during trainings, PLCs, and as needed. Teachers can identify trends and alter their plans accordingly.

The presentations are housed on the district's Gifted Resource Site (GRS) and are not made public. Data are reported by proficiency levels (highly proficient, partially proficient, approaching proficiency, not proficient) for each school in a variety of ways, showing gifted students' achievement:

- in the core content areas tested,
- in the core content areas tested with charts showing data for multiple years,
- by grade level in the core content areas,
- compared to general education students in the core content areas,
- by feeder systems, and
- by gender and by ethnicity.

SAMPLE DATA CHARTS

Figures 7, 8, and 9 contain examples of the data charts we create to show gifted students' performance.

MONITORING GIFTED STUDENT ENROLLMENT

Keeping records of gifted student enrollment takes many forms and serves several purposes in PVUSD. Of great importance to the department, the records draw awareness to the revenue that follows these students from state funding, which builds support for the gifted programs. We will refer to the importance and impact of monitoring gifted student enrollment throughout the chapter.

Arizona's open enrollment policy allows parents to enroll their children in any public school if there is space in the desired grade level. Many parents of advanced learners take advantage of this policy and seek programs that best represent what they want for their gifted children. PVUSD's gifted programs have greatly benefited from this policy and the influx of additional tax dollars has helped expand services for gifted student.

Every year, the gifted department's office manager prepares a spreadsheet documenting the amount of funding brought to the district by gifted students enrolled in PVUSD who come to us from other districts, charter schools, private schools, or

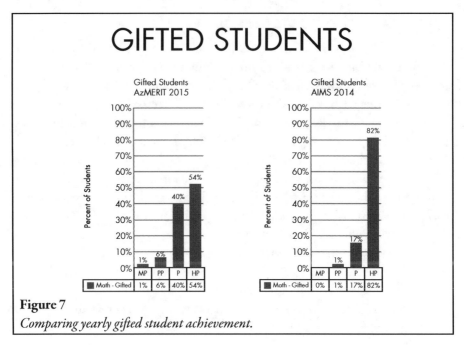

Figure 7
Comparing yearly gifted student achievement.

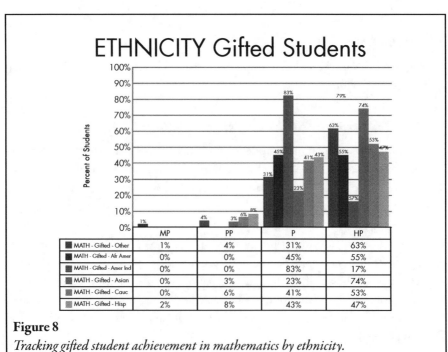

Figure 8
Tracking gifted student achievement in mathematics by ethnicity.

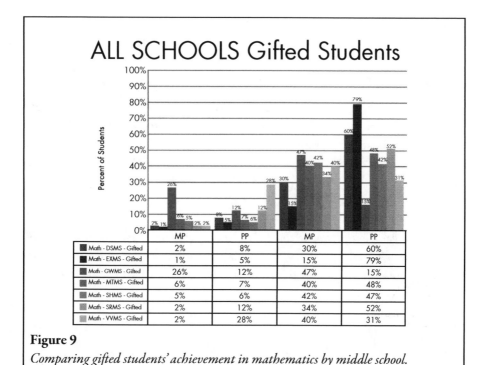

Figure 9
Comparing gifted students' achievement in mathematics by middle school.

those who are homeschooled. We record the following information for each newly enrolled gifted student on this document:

- school most recently attended,
- student's home school/district,
- PV school in which he or she enrolls,
- PV gifted program, and
- gifted identification data.

Maintaining awareness of the gifted student enrollments provides a number of benefits to the district, the gifted program, and the gifted students. The increased number of gifted students enrolled in the district draws awareness to their needs and contributes to the support of their instruction. This awareness builds acceptance between teachers, staff, and other students due to the broader range of gifted students identified and served. It creates an inclusive mentality that encourages equitable identification methods.

Ultimately, monitoring gifted student enrollment in PV expands programming options. The increased number of gifted students also highlights and promotes the need for professional development for all teachers to better understand how gifted students learn and methods and strategies for differentiating their curriculum and instruction. The training and exposure to gifted students also assists in teachers' ability to recognize giftedness in their students, which helps in the nomination and identification processes.

EMBEDDING GIFTED SERVICES INTO DISTRICT INITIATIVES

Gifted education services evolved into its current system of program oversight by obtaining support from district administration and parents and involving other district departments and administrators. We accomplished this by demonstrating need in several areas and through collaboration with other administrators. Efforts included:

- establishing the need for the systemic scheduling of services (Assistant Superintendents);
- reorganizing staffing to maximize services (Human Resources Directors);
- reviewing student achievement (Assessment Director);
- aligning curriculum and instruction to meet students' needs (Curriculum Director);
- providing targeted teacher training and support (Professional Development Director);
- revising budget allocations (Finance Director);
- monitoring gifted student enrollment (Student Services Director); and
- examining gifted student demographics (Title I Coordinator).

I provided documentation showing underutilized staffing, underidentified student populations, and underdeveloped and inconsistent curriculum. With this data, Cabinet members granted me the opportunity to develop proposals for their consideration.

COLLABORATING WITH DISTRICT DEPARTMENTS

Over time, I discovered the benefits of collaboration with the different district departments. Through these collaborative efforts, I built the case that our gifted students need differentiated curricula and resources, trained teachers, alternative assessment methods, gifted testing materials that ensure equitable identification, etc. Working closely with the other departments, we are able to continually address these needs and obtain access to resources that support our goals.

The following scenario describing our math pathways and placements provides an example of how we integrate gifted services into other departments. Figure 10 outlines the varied options for progressing through a math course sequence from grades 6–12. Decisions about placement and movement in these pathways are made on a systematic, yet individual basis and are dependent on a number of criteria, including the results of diagnostic testing, student performance, and teacher recommendations. This process aligns with the goals and objectives of our long-range plan and responds to student needs, thereby creating consistency districtwide for our math curriculum while also meeting the needs of gifted students.

To establish this process, the gifted education department collaborated with the assessment department to formulate a plan for out-of-level testing in mathematics to determine appropriate math placements. The chart shows that the pathways were set to address all PV students' needs. Developing these sequences also required collaboration with the curriculum department, as the alignment of the instructional materials needed to be considered and planned for across the spectrum. Collaboration with the professional development department is needed to train teachers on using the diagnostic and formative assessments that determine placement levels.

District administration supports the process, as it directly aligns with the district's long-range plan. I align curriculum and assessment for gifted students to the district objectives. We build in methods so that school administrators and teachers recognize the critical nature of teaching students at their challenge levels, regardless of the scheduling challenges involved in doing so.[1]

We arrange for the different levels of math instruction in several ways. When students test into a certain level that falls beyond the level of expertise for the classroom teacher, we make arrangements for them to attend the class at another school or provide the course via PVOnline, which includes honors sections of the courses described in the pathway depicted in Figure 10. In this way, all students are able to progress through their math instruction as needed.

In this next section, I provide brief descriptions of the ways in which our gifted department interacts and collaborates with several other district departments. The interactions demonstrate methods for integrating gifted services into existing school structures and building relationships that infuse gifted education considerations into others' thought and planning processes.

Special education and school psychologists. Gifted education falls outside the realm of special education in Arizona, therefore, school psychologists do not specifically test for gifted identification. However, these two departments collaborate in very important ways. I present to school psychologists yearly, sharing information on our gifted identification procedures, placements, and services. The school psychologists find that a good number of students presented to them for special education referrals qualify for gifted identification. The district's lead psychologist and I created procedures for the two departments to follow to assist this interface.

The psychologists send their students' testing records to the gifted education department. We review them to determine if they qualify for gifted services. If so, we record the students' area(s) of gifted identification in the student database and

---

1   Looking at the Math Pathways chart, some may question whether this represents a tracking system. It is important to note that a concern of tracking students for math placement has never been surfaced in the district, as students are not automatically *assigned* to specific tracks. In fact, parents and teachers alike appreciate that students have pathways that fit their individual needs. Students simply have the opportunity to progress naturally at their own levels, and students can move between the pathways when needed.

	Sixth Grade	Seventh Grade	Eighth Grade	Ninth Grade	10th Grade	11th Grade	12th Grade
Alternative Pathway	sixth-grade math	seventh-grade basic math	Prealgebra	Intermediate algebra 1–2	Survey of Geometry	Intermediate algebra 3–4	Algebra 3–4
Conventional Pathway	sixthgrade math	seventh-grade basic math	Prealgebra	Algebra 1–2	Geometry	Algebra 3–4	Precalculus
Honors Pathway	Prealgebra	Prealgebra	Algebra 1–2	Honors geometry	Honors algebra 3–4	Honors precalculus	AP Calculus AB
Accelerated Pathway I	Prealgebra	Prealgebra	Algebra 1–2	Geometry	Algebra 3–4	Precalculus	Personal option
Accelerated Pathway II	PVOnline prealgebra 2	Algebra 1–2	Honors geometry	Honors algebra 3–4	Honors precalculus	AP Calculus AB/BC	AP Calculus AB/BC
Accelerated Pathway III	PVOnline algebra 1–2	Geometry	Honors algebra 3–4	Honors precalculus	AP Calculus AB/BC	AP Calculus AB/BC	Personal option

Figure 10
Math pathways—Sequence of courses chart.

include them on the schools' gifted rosters. Gifted services for these students are then determined at the Multidisciplinary Evaluation Team (MET) meeting. The student study team then determines, with my input, the services and setting that best meets the needs of the students. Unless there is a need for placement into a special class or program, twice-exceptional students are automatically placed into a gifted cluster classroom, and the school psychologist and school's gifted specialist determine which honors class for content replacement would benefit the student.

Title I and language acquisition department. One immediate goal I had when coming to Paradise Valley was to increase representation of the district's Hispanic student population. I enlisted the help of the language acquisition department by providing training in gifted education to the language acquisition testers to help them recognize signs of giftedness in the students they test. With this understanding, they can then advise the classroom teachers on which ELLs to nominate for gifted testing. This is part of our proactive attempt to increase proportional representation throughout gifted education programs. I also provide yearly training to our ELL teachers.

Student services department. School districts typically have a district level administrator assigned to addressing student issues that routinely arise. Interaction with the director of Student Services in Paradise Valley is sporadic but imperative in certain circumstances. This administrator oversees 504 accommodation plans, early entrance procedures, parent concerns, and disciplinary actions such as those involved with behavioral problems. With gifted students, these topics/issues sometimes involve different considerations that require nuanced approaches. The gifted students may have social and emotional concerns that require modifying tactics when dealing with these issues. The Director of Student Services has extensive experience addressing these issues and works closely with me to resolve them.

Curriculum department. Collaboration with the Curriculum Director assists with curriculum alignment within the various gifted program models in the district. This collaboration occurs formally through representation on curriculum committees and book adoptions and informally through meetings. Understanding the vertical alignment of instructional materials for gifted teachers, the curriculum department assists in the communication of the different instructional pathways dictated by the gifted programs.

Instructional technology department. Our gifted teachers take the lead in the vast innovative initiatives of the IT director. This results in a high level of support for our gifted programs that includes ample technology and considerable collaboration between the two departments. The number and type of devices used in the classrooms varies depending on the program and current need. As an example, the self-contained programs have enjoyed a 1:1 ratio of student devices since 2010; that ratio is now several devices to each gifted student.

Ubiquitous technology is critical for the highly gifted students in these programs who are working at highly accelerated levels because the standard curriculum does not suffice. Grade-level textbooks lack the levels of depth and rigor these students need to learn at their challenge and interest levels. Our gifted students rely on technology to access primary sources that are up to date, relevant, and free of prior interpretation. They also need meaningful ways to demonstrate their learning and thrive on the creative possibilities to do so through the use of technology.

A couple of examples of the collaboration between the IT and gifted departments include:

1. This year, the gifted teacher at each school took the lead for the "Hour of Code." The goal of 100% participation was realized throughout the district.
2. Summer Digital Academy—This highly interactive and innovative summer professional development opportunity, taught by IT specialists and gifted teachers, helped workshop participants learn to integrate Google Apps for Education into their existing curriculum. The 3-week long academy ran throughout the summer with six cohorts participating in both face-to-face and virtual collaboration. These types of leadership and collaboration instill attention toward high-level learning activities throughout the district, which benefits all students.

Assessment department. Collaboration with the director of the assessment department occurs in various ways. We use the data collected by the department to create the growth charts shown in Figures 7–9. The director assists us with providing access to out-of-level testing and pulls different groups' achievement data for examination and reports when we request. We also rely on the assessment department for examining achievement levels of students in different programs and in different classes. This allows us to monitor program and teacher efficacy and provide intervention and support where needed.

Professional development department. Professional development workshops are advertised through the professional development department, along with all other district trainings. The gifted workshops emphasize teaching gifted and high-achieving students, but are available to all teachers, early childhood through high school. In fact, the majority of participants who register for the gifted education workshops are not employed as gifted teachers. This open invitation from the two departments spreads the training and interest in gifted education throughout the district, which helps prepare teachers who may move into a gifted teaching position and informs current and future administrators. We know that although robust gifted programs exists in Paradise Valley, some gifted students will either slip through the cracks or wish to remain in the general education setting. This means all teachers should have the ability to teach advanced learners.

Teachers register for the workshops through the PD department's teacher training system that maintains records of the workshops teachers take. Teachers can use these clock hours toward their gifted endorsement offered through the state. Sample workshop titles and professional development details are noted on pages 128–129.

Community education department. Parents and teachers know that gifted students thrive on enrichment activities, not all of which can be explored sufficiently within the school day. To that end, we promote extracurricular enrichment opportunities offered after school through the community education department, as many of these workshops, such as coding, engineering, and architecture, attract our gifted students. The gifted teachers encourage their students to engage in these classes; they suggest specific topics to be offered based on their students' interests.

The gifted education department interacts with community education in several ways, as this is the only department that can take fees for activities. An overview of this interaction include the following:

- **The Gifted Preschool:** This tuition-based program required that we establish a method for registration and enrollment through community education. Additionally, the district's preschools are run through this department so we collaborate for staffing classroom aides and ordering resources.
- **Afterschool enrichment classes:** The fee-based, afterschool enrichment classes are arranged through community education. Working together,

we suggest classes that will entice our gifted students, such as architecture, engineering, coding, and arts-related coursess.

- **Program specific enrichment:** Students in our gifted programs have the option of learning a foreign language using an online foreign language program. This opportunity is arranged between the two departments. We established a system wherein, for a nominal fee, the students can select one of 14 languages and use the program during enrichment period times during the school day or after school hours at their leisure.

- **Gifted Summer School:** Collaboration with community education also allows us to arrange a gifted summer school wherein gifted identified students can immerse themselves in classes of interest to them. Gifted program teachers teach the summer school classes. The tuition and teacher salaries are handled through this department. Sample class titles offered last year include: Adventures in Digital Media, Brain Game Academy, Future Engineers, Geography in Action!, History Mysteries, Linguistic Lovers, Mad Scientists in Training, Mathematician Mania, Native American Crafting, Remotely Operated Vehicle (ROV) Inventors, Speech and Debate, and Super Sleuths.

PROGRAM DESIGN AND SERVICES

SOME UNFORTUNATE HISTORY

When I came to Paradise Valley, students identified on the verbal battery of the Cognitive Abilities Test received content replacement in reading, while those identified on the quantitative battery received content replacement in math. Students identified on the nonverbal battery of the test were included in the last 20 minutes of honors math class on Fridays, where they engaged with other gifted students to play logic games and problem-solving activities. The rationale for these students' limited exposure to gifted instruction was that these "nonverbal" students did not perform at the academic levels of the other gifted students and therefore would not be able to keep up in the honors classes.

Given that the vast majority of our English language learners are identified on the NNAT or on the nonverbal battery of the CogAT, this scenario illustrates a longstanding practice of how these students received inequitable services when compared to gifted students identified on the verbal or quantitative batteries of an ability test. My task was to develop the teachers' understanding that these students' inability to perform at similarly high levels would likely be remedied by including these students in the regular gifted program.

OUR CONTINUUM OF SERVICES

Our mindset holds that all students who are identified as gifted receive services of some type. This mindset propelled us to continue to expand gifted services in response to identified need. The district now provides a continuum of gifted services designed for the specific learning needs of the gifted identified students, preschool through high school. The programs and services included in this continuum offer a number of options for each school level.

Paradise Valley's continuum of gifted services described below developed over time and in response to students' needs. Although all gifted students receive services, we recognize that some gifted students may need something different than their home schools' regular gifted services. This need encouraged us to create supplemental, specialized programs and services that enfranchise students of special populations. These specialized programs are now housed at different school sites throughout the district. Students may apply for any of the district's gifted programs, regardless of their home schools.

The programs and services include:

- **Self-Contained G/T Preschool:** Students may enter the program upon turning 4 years of age. Following this program, students enter either a kindergarten gifted cluster class or the self-contained program (depending on the students' needs).

- **Self-Contained G/T Kindergarten Program:** Following this program, students enter either a first-grade gifted cluster class or the self-contained program.

- **Schoolwide Cluster Grouping Model:** Grades K–4 at all schools; K–6 at most schools. All students identified as gifted on a standardized ability or IQ test[2] are automatically scheduled into a gifted cluster classroom regardless of their achievement levels or areas.

- **Content Replacement and Content Enrichment:** Pull-out services for language arts and/or mathematics provided daily with a gifted specialist, grades 4–6. All students identified as gifted on a standardized ability or IQ test are automatically placed, regardless of their achievement levels.

- **Self-Contained Gifted Program:** Grades 1–6; highly and profoundly gifted students who are radically accelerated apply for acceptance into this program. Modified criteria exist for ELLs and former ELLs.

- **Digital Learning Center Middle School (DLC):** Grades 7–8; highly and profoundly gifted students who are achieving beyond grade level, apply for acceptance into this innovative, technology-infused program. Separate criteria exist for ELLs and former ELLs.

---

2   To identify as gifted in Arizona, students must be tested with a test on the Arizona State Approved Gifted Test List.

- **Uniquely Gifted Program:** Elementary and middle school levels, funded by the special education department. Students in this program have an IEP and gifted identification and are referred to the program by their school's psychologist.
- **Nonverbal Honors Core:** Middle school level, specifically designed for culturally and linguistically diverse gifted students identified on the NNAT2.
- **Honors Academies:** Middle school level; Foreign Language Academy and Pre-Engineering Academy for gifted identified students.
- **International Baccalaureate Program:** Grades K–12; includes a school-wide Primary Years Program (PYP) and application programs for the Middle Years Programme (MYP) and Diploma Program (DP).
- **Honors Classes:** Middle school and high school levels; all students identified as gifted on a standardized ability or IQ test are automatically placed, as well as talented, high-achieving students recommended by their teachers.
- **Advanced Placement Courses:** High school level; gifted identified students, as well as high-achieving talented students who are not gifted identified. A full complement of AP courses offered at each high school, and also online and through telepresence. Middle school gifted students who demonstrate the need may also participate in AP courses.
- **Digital Academy for Advanced Placement Scholars (DAAPS):** High school level; an innovative, technology-infused, project-based program emphasizing AP coursework in an integrated format.
- **The Center for Research in Engineering, Science and Technology (CREST):** High school level; a small, STEM specialty school for biotechnology, sustainability, and engineering.

Notes: All services provide content acceleration to the level needed for each student and also emphasize critical and creative thinking, problem solving, logic, and reasoning. Visit http://www.prufrock.com/Assets/ClientPages/DesigningGiftedPrograms.aspx for a complete description of the programs and services listed above.

With all of the program options, one might wonder how we determine which program is most appropriate for our gifted students. At the elementary level, all gifted identified students are automatically placed into a gifted cluster class. Those students who qualify and demonstrate a need for the self-contained gifted program may apply for the location of their choice. Students at the middle school level who are seeking a specialized program—other than the honors classes offered at each school—may also apply for the program of their choice. The same systems apply to program choices at the high school level.

INSTRUCTIONAL PRACTICES

These specialized programs are housed at different schools throughout the district. Students may apply for, and/or enroll in, any the district's gifted programs, regardless of their home schools or whether they reside in the district. Students attending one of the self-contained specialty programs must provide their own transportation to and from the school if they live outside schools' attendance areas.

Instruction in all of our gifted programs involves acceleration, enrichment, and various extended learning opportunities. Instruction in the gifted programs emphasizes developing the following skills within the content areas: logical thinking, reasoning skills, critical and creative thinking, and problem solving. Depending on the specific program model, instruction in the gifted classes includes:

- accelerated mathematics,
- Latin stems studies as a foundation for interpreting the living languages,
- Socratic seminars,
- Junior Great Books,
- classic and contemporary literature,
- project-based learning,
- core knowledge integrated curriculum,
- advanced problem-solving instruction,
- classic literature,
- 4 level grammar,
- Math Olympiad and Continental Math competitions, and
- grammar and vocabulary instruction using the work of Michael Clay Thompson.

STAFFING AND SUPPORT

THAT WAS THEN

When I joined the gifted education department in 2006, it employed a gifted coordinator, one office clerk, one honors teacher at each elementary school, and four self-contained program teachers. Observing the honors teachers in their schools made it apparent that the district overstaffed this position. In the schools that had many gifted identified students, the gifted specialists had large classes; whereas, in schools with few gifted students, some honors classes had numbers as low as five or six. Small class sizes for gifted students were not justifiable in a time of shrinking school budgets.

During my second year in the position, I recalculated the staffing ratio, significantly reducing the number of honors teachers. The elimination of a dozen gifted teaching positions required collaboration with the president of the teachers association and the Human Resources Department; I provided these groups with data (i.e., number of students being served by each teacher) documenting the rationale for cutting the positions. This staffing move demonstrated fairness and a move toward providing equitable services to all students, which resulted in increased respect for the gifted department by district teachers and administrators. This move ended the perception that gifted students (and their teachers) were treated with privilege by having the luxury of small classes. The staffing recalculation also demanded a higher level of expertise by the teachers, strengthening instruction and ultimately the department, by requiring increased teacher support in curriculum planning and training.

THIS IS NOW

It really does take a village! With gifted students' needs considered by all departments in the district we are able to access support that translates into staffing. Having strong gifted education programs requires a staffing commitment by the district. We are fortunate to currently employ the following personnel to support gifted education services in the district:

- **Director of Gifted Education:** Oversees all aspects of gifted education services offered in the district.
- **Gifted program mentor:** Supports and provides training in curriculum and instruction to honors teachers and self-contained program teachers.
- **Cluster teacher coach:** Supports and provides training in curriculum and instruction to gifted cluster teachers.
- **Office manager:** Oversees administrative functions of the gifted education department, including data collection and reports, testing administration and enrollment, and placement of students into the various programs.
- **Administrative assistant:** Responds to parent and staff inquiries, maintains web content, and orders materials.
- **Testing technicians (approximately five):** The lead testing technician creates the testing schedule for the year, trains and schedules the testers, and oversees the testing administration. The testers administer gifted testing at each school. One additional tester completes the scoring and reporting of all district testing.
- **Gifted education specialists (28, formerly called honors teachers):** Provide daily content replacement in math and language arts to gifted students, coordinate gifted testing with gifted testing technicians, and support gifted cluster teachers at school sites.

- **Self-contained gifted teachers (20):** Provide individualized acceleration and specialized instruction to students in the self-contained gifted program.
- **Gifted education liaison (12):** Provide and facilitate staff development in gifted education to honors, AP, and IB teachers at the high school level; assist honors, AP, and IB teachers in differentiated instruction for gifted students; and serve as a resource to their schools' honors teachers. One honors teacher at each middle and high school fills this role.
- **Gifted cluster teachers:** One at each grade level in the elementary schools, these teachers differentiate curriculum and instruction for gifted identified students cluster grouped in their classrooms. Cluster teachers are staffed by the school principals.
- **Honors, Advanced Placement teachers:** Provide gifted and talented students in the middle and high schools with accelerated and enriched content in the honors and AP courses.
- **International Baccalaureate teachers (PYP, MYP, DP, IB Coordinator):** Provide specialized instruction to students in the IB programs. IB teachers collaborate to provide a content and experience rich experience in accordance with the IB curriculum and philosophy.

Paradise Valley's Gifted Education Director responsibilities include the following:
- design, develop, and support a continuum of gifted programs and services;
- analyze and utilize district data for program and curriculum development;
- establish and maintain database for gifted student information;
- recommend policy and procedures for department development;
- supervise and evaluate gifted specialists and self-contained gifted teachers;
- create and manage department budget;
- develop and provide staff development K–12 based on needs assessments;
- coordinate gifted testing and reporting procedures;
- recruit and staff for gifted education department needs;
- ensure compliance with state mandates;
- align gifted services to district initiatives;
- build and maintain stakeholder communication and relationships; and
- represent the school district in community forums and to the media.

As noted above, the director position I now hold began as a gifted coordinator. Within a couple of years, the district approved my proposal to change the position to a director level. With this change, I was able to promote gifted education as a "stand-alone" department, rather than an area overseen by the curriculum director, as had been the case previously. This change gave me a voice at the table during district-level meetings. As a coordinator, I had to rely on my director—who was not trained in gifted education—to speak on behalf of gifted students. The "director" title allowed me to advocate more efficiently and effectively.

SUPPORTING TEACHERS

TARGETED TEACHER TRAINING

We recognize that teachers need support, ongoing training, and resources. They also need time to work and plan alongside others who are teaching in their roles. Knowing this, we provide a wide range of face-to-face and online workshops; specifically, we offer 30–35 afterschool workshops each fall, spring, and summer. Our gifted teachers teach the workshops and we determine the topics based on teachers' needs and requests.

The range of services provided in the district requires that we differentiate the curriculum, instruction, and assessments procedures. Therefore, we must also differentiate our staffing, professional development, and teacher support. Although many strategies we train on are appropriate for all teachers, there are specific strategies more critical for some teachers than others. For example, self-contained program teachers may emphasize more project-/problem-based learning and acceleration, whereas cluster teachers need to excel at using formative assessments to form flexible learning groups.

Each of the gifted teacher groups also has a PLC and ongoing training and planning meetings. This allows them to design training specific to their own programs (i.e., cluster teacher meetings, gifted specialist in-services, gifted liaison meeting, self-contained program teacher meetings). At these meetings, they share ideas, practices, and resources; lesson plan; study instructional methods; and participate in book studies. The teacher groups also participate in blogs, social media, and other digital communication forums.

WEEKLY CLUSTER TEACHERS BRIEFS

Following our last program evaluation, we determined that we needed to improve communication to gifted cluster teachers. We created a weekly gifted cluster teacher "news brief" that focuses on a specific strategy. In the newsletter, we also advertise the upcoming workshops, parent events, links to additional topics, and other resources. Lastly, we highlight a cluster teacher who is doing something exceptional. We archive these newsletters on our Gifted Resource Site. The continual snippets of pertinent information, ideas, and teaching tips serves as a constant reminder to teachers that the gifted students clustered in their classrooms need modifications in all areas.

Our high expectations for teachers necessitate that we support them by providing resources, guidance, and communication tools. We created our Gifted Resource Site (GRS; see Figure 11) to support all PV teachers with an emphasis on those who teach our gifted and talented students. This rich digital repository provides a wealth of differentiated curriculum, tools to help teachers document achievement for students working at and above grade level, and numerous teacher training resources.

The site includes:

- **Web-based training:** Links to online trainings that support our programs.
- **Differentiated lesson plans:** Organized by grade level (K–12) and by content area with a folder for each subject in each grade level.
- **Videos of classroom demonstrations:** Videos of our own gifted teachers demonstrating strategies we teach in our workshops.
- **Student work products:** Student samples and exemplars with examples of student-created and produced technology-infused schoolwork.
- **Program videos:** Our district's gifted programming options so teachers know what options to suggest to parents.
- **Training materials:** Presentations and lesson planning materials.
- **Achievement documentation:** Procedures for teachers to use ongoing diagnostic, formative, and summative assessments in their classrooms. Achievement data from state assessment for gifted students at every school.
- **Program administration:** Procedures, sample schedules, sample meeting agendas, forms, etc.
- **Communication tools:** Forums where teachers within each program communicate to share ideas, lessons, and resources. (Teachers utilize these communication tools frequently!)

The resources housed on the site support the district's adopted curriculum and initiatives and align with grade-level standards. An important feature of the resource site is its ability to provide ongoing training and resources to teachers who can access the site at their convenience. Broadly speaking, teachers are able to participate in workshops, collaborate, study archived presentations, lesson plan, and learn from others' contributions (Brulles & Brown, 2013).

Using free Google tools, the gifted program mentor and I developed and maintain this effective and cost-efficient system for providing training and access to resources from within and outside the district. The repository incorporates existing district resources and contributions from district teachers to help staff address the diverse learning needs of their gifted, talented, and general education students. We update the site constantly as many new resources become available daily. Goals of the Gifted Resource Site are to:

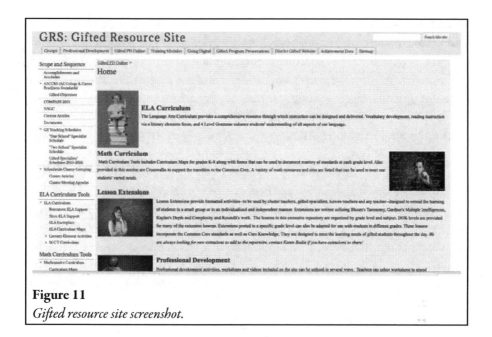

Figure 11
Gifted resource site screenshot.

- expose teachers to instructional strategies that engage, challenge, and enrich high-ability and high-achieving students;
- provide professional development in gifted education based on theory, pedagogy, and current best practices for teachers of gifted students;
- align teacher support for gifted education with the district's mission of developing and promoting digital-age literacies;
- provide all district teachers with access to innovative instructional methods, advanced and differentiated curriculum, systems for communication and collaborative learning, and achievement data;
- encourage collaboration, communication, critical thinking, and creativity throughout the district;
- motivate all district teachers to incorporate gifted education instructional objectives and strategies into everyday teaching for all students; and
- overcome the obstacles of finding time to learn and plan new strategies that our teachers face when attempting to differentiate curriculum and instruction.

DESIGNING PROFESSIONAL DEVELOPMENT

The gifted program mentor and I determine the areas where professional development is needed and then develop the schedule accordingly. Training decisions are based on gifted student achievement data, input from gifted specialists and self-contained teachers, recommendations from cluster teachers, and requests from principals. We also design workshops to help the gifted teachers integrate district initiatives when needed. For example, how to modify the newly adopted science curriculum for advanced learners and how integrate coding into the curriculum.

The gifted education department offers numerous workshops each fall, spring, and summer. We provide workshops on general topics in gifted education, such as gifted testing and identification, learning needs, addressing social and emotional needs, teaching the nonverbally identified gifted student, etc. We also offer numerous workshops on instructional strategies for teaching high-ability and high-achieving students in any setting.

The gifted education workshops take place face-to-face and also online through the Gifted Resource Site, which teachers can take anytime outside of school hours for credit that applies toward advancement on the salary schedule. Teachers can receive additional credit hours for contributing a resource to the GRS following an online workshop. These resources might include a lesson plan, a rubric, a parent letter, etc. We also assist district teachers in obtaining the state gifted endorsement by running university cohorts at school sites, with classes meeting after school. Sample workshop topics include the following:

- Teaching in the Cluster Grouping Model
- Understanding Giftedness: How the Identification Relates to Teaching and Learning
- Interactive and Fun Vocabulary Activities That Engage Gifted Students
- Using Socratic Questioning and Critical Thinking Skills in Language Arts
- Advancing Differentiation: Thinking and Learning in the 21st Century
- Divergent Thinking Through Junior Great Books
- It's Not About More, It's About Different! Teaching Middle School Honors Classes
- Pop Culture in the Classroom?
- Developing Tiered Assignments and Extensions Menus to Increase Challenge Levels
- Understanding the Twice-Exceptional Student
- Unlock the Strategies to Teaching the Nonverbal Identified Gifted Student
- Nonverbal Identification of Giftedness: Using the Test Results to Guide Instruction
- Reaching All Learners: Making Differentiation Work for Gifted Students
- Using Khan Academy to Differentiate Math
- Are You Ready for Some Football? (Using math stats)
- Project-Based Learning
- Nonfiction Here We Come: Higher Order Thinking Through Document-Based Questions
- Where's the Rigor in Social Studies and Science?
- Arts Integration in the Content Areas

Teachers can register for the individual workshops of their interest. They can also complete modules that are designed to provide a full range of training. Upon completing four workshops in each of the four modules, teachers receive a PV gifted certification, a district designation recognizing that the teacher has participated in a balanced blend of professional development in gifted education aligned to the district's needs.

GIFTED TEACHER COLLABORATION

We do our best to build in time to collaborate, learn from each other, and plan lessons together. Providing time for this collaboration is well worth the scheduling challenge. The gifted education department arranges the following collaboration opportunities:

- **Gifted specialists and self-contained program teachers:** The gifted program mentor and I meet with these groups for six planning and training days throughout the school year and one additional day before the school year begins. We meet for professional development in the mornings and PLCs in the afternoons. Additionally, the teachers meet regularly at their sites.
- **Gifted cluster teachers:** Gifted cluster teachers meet monthly at their sites with their gifted specialists to plan, problem solve, participate in book studies, share strategies and ideas, review and discuss articles from the field, etc.
- **Gifted liaisons:** The gifted liaisons, one from each middle and high school, meet with the gifted program mentor and myself after school 6 times a year. They then share information at their sites with their honors and AP teachers.

Gifted teachers in the other specialty programs, such as the Digital Learning Center, Digital Academy of AP Scholars, Nonverbal Core, and Uniquely Gifted Program, create their own schedules for meeting and training along with support from the gifted program mentor and myself. Most of these meetings are collaborative planning time for the specific program. The gifted education department arranges for the teachers to receive professional growth credit through the professional development department. All of the gifted education teachers are invited to participate in technology pilots, book studies, blogs, and chat rooms geared around gifted education pedagogy and practices. Additional collaboration occurs throughout the year in informal ways.

All teachers in Paradise Valley participate in PLCs. Teachers in the different programs work in PLCs with their program model grade level counterparts: self-contained, content replacement, and cluster model teachers. Self-contained teachers work in grade levels across the district and also plan vertically within each self-contained program site. Gifted specialists form their own PLCs, as their curriculum and achievement data differ from that of other grade-level teachers. However, because the gifted specialists also share students with grade-level cluster teachers, they also work with grade-level teams at their sites to review and provide input to the classroom teacher.

Gifted cluster teachers work in PLCs with their grade-level team and discuss methods for differentiating instruction and implementing interventions based on the grade-level data. Some schools use the RtI model to plan specific content intervention during the PLC times. This collaboration time supports the teachers and builds consistency of services throughout the district. During the PLCs, the teachers develop SMART goals[3], study data, design interventions, share lessons that align to the standards, etc.

PARTICIPATION IN RESEARCH STUDIES, PILOTS, AND DEMONSTRATION SITES

Participation in research studies and pilots, taking part in demonstration sites, and scheduling tours serves several purposes. These practices promote the district programs, and develop instructional practices and leadership. A few examples of this type of involvement in which we have participated include the following:

- The PV Gifted Department participated in a series of research studies with doctoral students from Arizona State University for the Devareuax Student Strength Assessment (DESSA). The doctoral students examined data from gifted students in the various gifted programs by comparing the students' areas of gifted identification, academic achievement, and the results from the DESSA scales. The scales were donated to the district. Participation yielded data we used for program revision, curriculum design, and teacher training.

- PV participated in the standardization studies of NNAT2 (in 2007) and NNAT3 (in 2014). In so doing, we were able to blanket test all students in several grades levels from Title I schools at no cost. We then received a quantity of free tests for future use.

- Participation in a prototypical Depth and Complexity Program Evaluation method with a researcher from Purdue University.

- Field-tested The School Imagination, Creativity, and Innovation (ICI) Index with University of Connecticut.

- Participated in a William & Mary curriculum validation study.

- Participated in a Screening Assessment for Gifted Elementary Students (SAGES) validation study from Baylor University.

---

3   The acronym SMART has several slightly different variations, which can be used to provide a more comprehensive definition of goal setting: **S**–specific, significant, stretching; **M**– measurable, meaningful, motivational; **A**–agreed upon, attainable, achievable, acceptable, action-oriented; **R**–realistic, relevant, reasonable, rewarding, results-oriented; **T**–time-based, time-bound, timely, tangible, trackable.

Participation in activities such as these helps us evaluate our programs and explore emerging curriculum, instruction, and assessment methods. Involvement such as this also allows us to obtain free resources and training and provide attention to educational trends and initiatives.

Tours are provided for educators from school districts within the state and nationally who are seeking to strengthen their gifted programs. Requests for tours from other schools are scheduled throughout the year based on the visitors' schedules. These tours highlight the efforts and skills of the teachers. Tours for parents are scheduled quarterly at each of the self-contained program sites at the elementary and middle school levels. These tours promote our programs and increase gifted student enrollment.

CONCLUSION

As alluded to earlier, this range of gifted services represents our efforts to provide for the needs of all of our gifted students. The varying needs of our gifted students requires a varied approach to serving them. Curriculum and instructional approaches also vary for each program depending on the program design, purpose, and the need it is intended to serve. Teachers in each program model plan together regularly. We schedule workshops, trainings, and planning meetings wherein teachers from the different programs can collaborate and learn from each other. The Gifted Resource Site provides additional opportunities for teachers in the different programs to participate in PD together.

Throughout the school year we continue to accept gifted students into gifted cluster classes. We also continue to enroll students into honors classes for content replacement. However, the self-contained gifted program has a limited number of space in each school that houses the program. Our office maintains waiting lists for the self-contained program and moves students into the program when space becomes available. When we consistently fill the self-contained program classes at one location, we expand the program to a new site.

Contracts are used in the self-contained gifted programs due to the unique structure of these programs. The self-contained gifted programs, which include programs at the kindergarten, elementary, middle, and high school levels, are reserved for students who require a much more rigorous and accelerated pace than provided in the districts' regular gifted programs. Students in the self-contained programs must have the motivation, discipline, and ability to learn at these levels. Without these attributes, students fall behind and miss critical elements of their instruction. In these cases, the student, parents, and teacher convene to determine what interventions might help the student succeed in the program(s). They sometimes decide that the regular gifted program better suits the students' needs.

I was humbled by the praise of leading education expert Dr. James Delisle in his 2014 book, *Dumbing Down America: The War On Our Nation's Brightest Young Minds (And What We Can Do to Fight Back)* in which he discusses designing educational services for gifted children. He wrote, "Why not start with the best?: the gifted services provided by the Paradise Valley Unified School District (PVUSD) in Phoenix, AZ . . . If you are looking for a 'complete package' on how to serve gifted children, PVUSD is the Holy Grail you seek" (pp. 148, 150). Despite this praise, I recognize that providing gifted services in my district is an ongoing process that continues to evolve as we encounter areas of need.

All aspects of the gifted program are now continually modified based on evolving needs of the district, its students, current initiatives, and constantly changing resources. District administration has supported this program development in large part due to the efforts to align gifted services to the district's goals and long-term plans.

Chapter 6 Appendix

Description of the Gifted Programs and Services at PVUSD

The programs and services and their curricula are described in more detail below.

For Early Childhood

Gifted Preschool Program. PVUSD features a Gifted Preschool Program for 4-year-old children who score 90% or higher on the Stanford Binet Early Childhood Intelligence Scales. This tuition-based program is open to gifted and talented preschool students throughout the Valley. The program is offered at four elementary schools. The teachers are early childhood certified and hold a gifted endorsement (or are working toward acquiring one). Maximum class size is 22 students. Classes employ one teacher and two teacher's aides. The Gifted Preschool Program follows the district calendar. Transportation is not provided for preschool students.

The program features:
- emphasis on critical and creative thinking,
- accelerated curriculum,

- integrated technology,
- individualization,
- core content, and
- enrichment.

Self-Contained Kindergarten Program. In this program, gifted identified students work beyond grade level with intellectual peers and are taught by teachers who are early childhood certified and hold a gifted endorsement. Students in this specialized kindergarten also participate in the school's special areas and are included in all grade-level activities and field trips. This program is offered at four elementary schools.

To qualify for the self-contained gifted program, students must have an IQ of 128+ or gifted test scores of 97+ in at least one of the three areas: verbal, quantitative, and/or nonverbal. The program is offered at four locations. Transportation is not provided.

The program features:

- accelerated curriculum,
- shared inquiry/Socratic questioning,
- problem-based learning,
- elements of reasoning,
- technology integration,
- emphasis on critical and creative thinking,
- individualization, and
- core content/enrichment.

(Gifted kindergartners are also served in the gifted cluster classes. See below.)

FOR ELEMENTARY SCHOOL LEVEL

Placement into gifted services at the elementary level is determined by need with differing qualifying criteria for each program. The more rigorous, specialized programs have higher qualifying rates. This system allows the district to provide the most optimal programming match possible. The entrance criteria and curriculum for each program is included with the program model descriptions listed below.

The schoolwide cluster grouping model. Gifted identified students are clustered into gifted cluster classrooms with teachers who have been designated as such by their school principals. Gifted cluster teachers hold a gifted endorsement issued by the state of Arizona, or are working toward acquiring one. Gifted specialists assist gifted cluster teachers with student placements, provide professional development in gifted education, and facilitate the planning and implementation of differentiated curriculum and instruction through regularly scheduled monthly gifted cluster teacher meetings. In this model, gifted students receive differentiated curriculum and instruction in all content areas on a daily basis.

Content replacement/content enrichment services. Gifted education specialists provide content replacement and/or content enrichment to gifted students in each elementary school for grades 4–6. Students receive accelerated and enriched instruction in mathematics and/or language arts, depending upon their area(s) of identification and needs. Students receive content replacement and enrichment in lieu of the regular grade-level curriculum provided in their homeroom classes. Curriculum in these content areas is accelerated to an appropriately challenging level. In language arts, students receive instruction through grammar and literature. Students move beyond the regular language arts curriculum using advanced levels of analysis and critical thinking. In math, students pursue topics such as probability, logic, statistics, algebra, and geometry at advanced levels.

Self-contained gifted program. The self-contained gifted program (grades 1–6) is designed for highly and profoundly gifted students who are also highly achieving. Students in this program work 2 or more years beyond grade level with intellectual peers. Classroom instruction expands and accelerates traditional curriculum to accommodate the unique needs and interests of highly gifted students. Students have a rigorous interdisciplinary core curriculum of language arts, social studies, science, and math. Self-contained gifted students participate in special area classes with the other grade-level classes and are included in nonacademic grade-level activities. This district program is housed at five locations.

Students qualifying for this program must have:

- Scores (on a state-approved gifted test) of 97%+ in two of the three areas: verbal, quantitative, and/or nonverbal area(s), with the third score being 90 or higher

OR

- IQ of 140+

PLUS:

- Demonstrate accelerated learning needs that are 2 years beyond grade level
- AZMerit (Arizona's state mandated achievement assessment) scores of Proficient or Highly Proficient (for grades 3–6)

Criteria for current ELLs:

1. Score of 97%+ on a state-approved nonverbal ability test (preferred NNAT2), plus a score of 97% in reading and mathematics on the Woodcock Johnson Achievement Test administered one grade level ahead of the student's current grade level

   Or: IQ of 140+ PLUS
2. Demonstrate accelerated learning needs that are 2 years beyond grade level
3. AZMERIT scores of Proficient or Highly Proficient (for grades 3–6)

Sample curriculum and instructional methods include:
- shared inquiry/Socratic questioning,
- project-based/problem-based learning,
- Latin-based vocabulary,
- elements of reasoning,
- Junior Great Books,
- William & Mary curriculum,
- Continental Math and Math Olympiad,
- acceleration in the content areas, and
- technology integration.

Digital Learning Center Middle School (DLC). The DLC serves highly gifted seventh- and eighth-grade students who are achieving beyond grade level. (Most of the students in this program participated in the self-contained program in the elementary grades and need more than the regular honors courses offered at every middle school.) The Digital Learning Center provides students with an interdisciplinary, project-based learning environment that embodies 21st-century learning. The technology-infused program involves innovative instructional practices for authentic learning. Teaching is student centered with the instructor acting as a resource and facilitator. Core academic coursework and standards are integrated through thematic relationships and dichotomies, inquiry and project-based learning for exploring themes, extensive collaboration for student-produced outcomes, and a global perspective. Students may apply if they have two qualifying scores of 97% or higher, or if they have one score of 97%+ plus the other two scores 90% or higher, plus evidence of high academic achievement, a teacher recommendation and rating scale, and a contract.

Uniquely Gifted Program. This program offered at the elementary and middle school levels is funded by the special education department. Students in the program have an IEP for special education and are gifted identified. The teachers specialize in both areas. The school psychologists refer students to this program, whose goal is to facilitate academic and social and emotional growth. With very small class sizes and specialized staffing, instructional emphasis is directed toward the areas of students' strengths while also addressing their learning challenges. By addressing students' abilities, skills that require intensive assistance in other areas can be developed.

The learning environment in the Uniquely Gifted Program is a safe place where students can pursue their strengths and increase their confidence and abilities to address areas of challenges. It should be noted that the vast majority of twice-exceptional gifted students are served in their home schools' gifted programs. This program, which is highly sought by parents, exists for those twice-exceptional students whose learning needs are not being met in a less restrictive environment;

they need more attention than can be provided in a cluster or honors class in their home schools.

Nonverbal Honors Core. This middle school program is specifically designed for culturally and linguistically diverse (CLD) gifted students identified on the NNAT2. The teachers, who hold bilingual, ELL, and gifted certifications, incorporate an interdisciplinary, thematic instructional approach in designing and implementing project-based learning founded on gifted education pedagogy, authentic practices, and arts integration. This approach provides a culturally rich, highly engaging learning environment that embraces, encourages, and empowers gifted students of underrepresented populations. Students with testing scores of 90% or higher automatically qualify for the program.

The district created this program in response to a complaint registered by the Office of Civil Rights (OCR) when it determined that our CLD students were underrepresented in our gifted programs. We needed to construct a program that embraced and enfranchised this group of students. The program was then designed based on how we believed we could best develop these students' potential for achievement.

Honors academies. The Honors Academies of Pre-Engineering and World Language are located at Desert Shadows Middle School. The Honors Academy of Pre-Engineering includes coursework designed to prepare students for engineering programs in high school. The World Languages Academy includes instruction in Spanish, French, and Mandarin. Students also take honors classes in English, science, social studies, and advanced levels of mathematics. All gifted identified students may apply.

International Baccalaureate (IB) program. PV's IB program includes the full spectrum, grades K–12: a school-wide Primary Years Program (PYP) and application programs for the Middle Years Programme (MYP) and Diploma Program (DP). The International Baccalaureate Program is an internationally recognized honors program that creates well-rounded students and rigorous learners, and lets students earn college credit. IB students join a network of their peers across the globe in search of knowledge and experiences that will continue throughout their lives. All students with a consistent record of high achievement, plus those identified as gifted, may apply to this program.

Middle school honors and exploratory classes. These classes represent the standard program model at each of the district's seven middle schools, offering honors English, science, and social studies and advanced math courses. Instruction involves content acceleration to the level needed for each student and emphasizes critical and creative thinking, problem solving, logic, and reasoning. Students qualify for placement in an honors course by meeting district requirements for placement in the gifted program or by a combination of previous success in the subject area, superior performance on related achievement tests, and/or recommendation by previous teachers of the subject. All students who demonstrate consistent record of high achievement, plus those identified as gifted, may apply to this program.

Advanced Placement courses. A full complement of Advanced Placement (AP) classes are provided at each high school and also through PVOnline. Middle school gifted students who demonstrate the need may also participate in AP courses. All students who demonstrate consistent record of high achievement, plus those identified as gifted, may apply to this program.

Digital Academy for Advanced Placement Scholars (DAAPS). This self-contained high school gifted program represents an innovative, technology-infused, project-based program emphasizing AP coursework in an integrated format. The DAAPS features student-centered learning, study that integrates coursework in core subjects showing relationships and dichotomies in major fields of study, inquiry and project-based learning, and extensive student collaboration. The course study allows students to choose between a 3- or 4-year completion track and the opportunity to earn 30 or more college credits. All gifted identified students who demonstrate consistent record of high achievement may apply to this program.

The Center for Research in Engineering, Science and Technology (CREST). CREST is a specialty program that provides high school gifted students with the opportunity to study one of three specialized disciplines: biotechnology, computer science, or engineering. CREST is a recognized leader in STEM education with instructors who continuously develop innovative and engaging ways to provide students with authentic learning experiences that enhance the curriculum. Small class sizes, academic support, laboratory experience, collaboration with university and industry professionals, and a rich campus life provide endless opportunities for academic and personal growth. All students who demonstrate a consistent record of high achievement, plus those identified as gifted, may apply to this program.

PVOnline honors courses. Online honors courses are available to students at all school levels in several subjects, AP English 7/8 Literature and Composition, AP Government, politics, world history, and more. These courses have been developed by PVUSD teachers and education consultants, and are instructed by highly qualified, appropriately certified teachers. With PVOnline, honors students can accelerate the earning of high school credits. Classes begin each semester and are also offered in the summer. All students who demonstrate consistent record of high achievement, plus those identified as gifted, may apply to this program.

CHAPTER 7

MEGA COUNTYWIDE DISTRICT IN CENTRAL FLORIDA

Lauri Kirsch

THE DISTRICT'S GIFTED PLAN: WHY, HOW, WHAT

For any successful organization, a compelling vision and mission are essential to positive change and success. In a large Florida school district, an intentionally developed vision and mission of the gifted program with laser-like focus on the goals of the program for more than a decade has resulted in increased equity, services with a basis in current research and best practices in gifted education, and quality services provided for a greater number of K–12 students.

Since the mid 1990s, the philosophy of the district's gifted program asserts the commitment to nurturing and educating gifted students by providing a climate where their talents and potentials are valued and fostered throughout the entire school day. Curriculum is significant, relevant, and rigorous, delivered by teachers who understand and value gifted students. Their teachers have been specially trained to meet the learning needs of the gifted. Although the leadership of the district's gifted program changed in 2005, the philosophy of the district's gifted program maintains relevance and has been intentionally maintained to connect the program to its roots.

When named the coordinator of the district's gifted program midway through 2005, I revised the vision, mission, and goals of the program with wording purposefully selected to support the vision and direction of the district, yet specific to gifted education. Created in July 2005, the vision, mission, and goals of the gifted program remain constant and serve as a compass for gifted educators (see Figure 12). Since

PHILOSOPHY

In the school district there is a commitment to nurturing and educating gifted students by providing a climate where the talent and potentials of gifted students are valued and fostered throughout the entire school day. The curriculum is significant, relevant, and rigorous. It is delivered by teachers who understand and value gifted students and have been specially trained to meet the learning needs of the gifted.

VISION

The vision of the gifted program is to provide a climate which values and nurtures the talents and potential of gifted students and prepares them to be contributing members of society and successful in their future careers.

MISSION

The mission of the gifted program is to open the door to potential for gifted students.

GOALS

The goals of the gifted program are to:
- identify potential giftedness, especially among the underrepresented populations (low SES/limited English proficient),
- meet the learning needs of gifted students of all ages through a differentiated curriculum designed to focus on learning strengths, and
- enhance the capacity of teachers who serve gifted students through training, support, and leadership development opportunities.

Figure 12
Mission, vision, and goals.

then, the vision of the district's gifted program has been to provide a climate that values and nurtures the talents and potential of gifted students to prepare them to be contributing members of society and successful in their future careers. The mission of the gifted program is to open the door to potential for gifted students. The three specific goals of the gifted program are to: (1) identify potential giftedness, especially among underrepresented populations (low income and limited English proficiency), (2) meet the learning needs of gifted students of all ages through a differentiated curriculum designed to focus on learning strengths, and (3) enhance the capacity of teachers who serve gifted students through training, support, and leadership development opportunities.

The philosophy, vision, and mission of the gifted program apply to more than 250 schools. The vision, mission, and goals serve as a means for maintaining the focus of experienced gifted educators and inspiring new gifted teachers within a growing and changing district. The vision and mission are a constant reminder of *why* the district's gifted program exists and energizes gifted educators to inspire their students toward a bright future. This compelling *why* speaks to teachers' minds and touches their hearts. Their daily work has become mission driven, motivating them through a tumultuous era where focus shifted to accountability and accompanying high-stakes standardized testing, where the individual needs of advance learners might be forgotten.

The three specific goals of the gifted program have become *how* the vision and mission are achieved. All actions by the gifted department are purposefully selected to achieve the goals, especially within the district's 147 elementary schools. Elementary school educators are specifically charged with identifying potential gifted students and, once identified, providing a differentiated learning experience aligned with individual students' Education Plan goals. The goal of gifted services in district middle and high schools is high-level achievement in advanced, honors, AP, and/or IB courses taught by well-trained content experts to prepare students for entry into postsecondary educational programs. Within elementary schools, grade-level courses are the norm and appropriate differentiation of the grade-level courses becomes the focus of gifted services. A rigorous differentiated curriculum is designed to address the learning strengths and needs of each individual student. Gifted teachers in the district's elementary schools provide part-time services in various subjects, creating an engaging and challenging learning experience for their students by purposeful modification of the standards-based general education curriculum to address individual student's Education Plan goals. Identification is less relevant within middle and high schools, as, other than students new to the district, all students have been considered as potentially gifted through universal screening utilizing existing data multiple times during their elementary years.

WHAT IS GIFTED EDUCATION WITHIN THE STATE?

To provide context for the district's Gifted Plan, an overview of gifted education within the state follows. The Florida Department of Education (FDOE) provides requirements and recommendations for gifted education. Details about gifted education are available at http://www.fldoe.org/academics/exceptional-student-edu/gifted-edu.stml.

Florida statutes and rules detail the definition of gifted, as well as district responsibilities for services, procedural safeguards, education plan requirements, certification requirements, and funding. Although there is a singular definition of gifted in Florida, each school district serves gifted students according to their local plan to address academic and social emotional support. Although over the past decade there has been increased emphasis on changing conceptions of giftedness with expanded definitions and eligibility based on multiple criteria and lesser emphasis on IQ, within Florida gifted eligibility and services remain tied to IQ.

Section 1003.01(3) (F.S.) defines exceptional students as any student determined eligible for special programs in accordance with rules of the State Board of Education, including both students who are gifted and students with disabilities. Rule 6A-6.03019 defines gifted as one who has superior intellectual development and is capable of high performance. Criteria for eligibility include need for program services, a majority of characteristics of gifted students according to a standard checklist, and superior intellectual development as measured by an intelligence quotient of two standard deviations or more above the mean on an individually administered standardized test of intelligence. Per the rule, a student who is a member of an underrepresented group, either limited English proficient or from a low-socioeconomic status family, may be considered under a district plan for increasing the participation of students from underrepresented groups in special instructional programs for the gifted. Often referred to as Plan B, the district's alternate plan must include a goal to increase the participation of students who are underrepresented, screening and referral procedures to increase the number of students referred for a gifted evaluation, criteria for determining eligibility, student evaluation procedures, instructional program modifications to assure successful and continued participation of students, and an evaluation design.

In addition to the state laws and regulations, FDOE provides publications and technical assistance papers to guide district gifted programs. Among the publications are the State Plan and Resource Guide for Gifted Education in Florida (http://www.fldoe.org/core/fileparse.php/7567/urlt/stategiftedplan.pdf), and Florida's Frameworks for K–12 Gifted Learners (http://www.fldoe.org/core/fileparse.php/7567/urlt/k12giftedlearners.pdf). Some technical assistance paper topics address developing education plans, assessing limited English proficient students for gifted programs, use of nonverbal tests of intelligence, and acceleration options (ACCEL).

The FDOE Bureau of Standards provides a course code directory, including specific gifted courses that may be used by districts, Florida standards, and other standards-related resources, including CPALMS, an electronic toolbox of information, resources, and interactive tools to support implementing the Florida standards. CPALMS gifted resources for advanced academics in K–5 may be accessed at http://www.cpalms.org/Public/PreviewCourse/Preview/12852.

What Is Included in the District's Gifted Plan?

Beyond an inspiring vision and mission with worthwhile goals, educators within all schools throughout the vast district require detailed procedures and processes to specifically define their expected actions, *what* they will do on a regular basis to achieve the goals. The Gifted Plan defines the expected actions and strategies for all district schools regarding gifted identification and services.

The district Gifted Plan was developed to comply with state statues and rules and align with FDOE recommendations. The approach taken was to increase the level and quality of services for students classified as gifted, as well as take an intentional and inclusive approach to identification to provide opportunities for students who were underrepresented in the gifted program. Finally, the district's gifted initiatives were intentionally designed and implemented so that opportunities would be available for high-potential students who were not classified as gifted but could benefit from the approach and strategies.

The district's Gifted Plan addresses two broad areas: identification and services. The Gifted Plan is not a single document but multiple documents that provide specific direction on identification of potential gifted students and quality services for gifted and advanced learners. Documents that comprise the Gifted Plan include the Identification Plan, the Gifted Guidelines, and the district's ACCEL Plan. With more than 223,800 students in prekindergarten through grade 12, the district is diverse in economic status, ethnicity, and language. Students come from urban, suburban, and rural settings that cover a geographic area the size of Rhode Island. Of the district's student population, more than 17,930 are classified as gifted per the state's eligibility criteria. These factors combine to create an essential need for both a detailed plan to guide equitable identification practices and specific guidelines to ensure quality gifted services throughout the district.

The Gifted Plan serves to define practices for equitable identification and define quality gifted services across the district, ensuring greater continuity across all district schools. Although a single identification plan has continually applied throughout the district, prior to the development of the Gifted Guidelines in 2010, the quality of gifted services varied greatly from elementary school to elementary school and from classroom to classroom. Gifted service decisions were often determined by school personnel, many of whom had little training in gifted education. In many instances, gifted classes were scheduled for convenience with gifted students at the same grade level receiving the same services regardless of their individual learning needs related to their giftedness. The unevenness of services across the district was exacerbated by the frequent movement of gifted teachers between schools and roles. Approximately 30% of elementary gifted teachers are new to their positions each year. The adage that "we had a good gifted program, but she moved" was a common refrain for many of the district's schools and gifted students as well-trained, experienced gifted teachers transferred to gifted positions within other schools, were promoted as administrators, or retired.

District Plan for Identification of Gifted Students

The Identification Plan is included as part of the district's board and FDOE-approved Exceptional Student Education Special Policies and Procedures (SP&Ps;http://www.fldoe.org/academics/exceptional-student-edu/monitoring/ese-policies-procedures-spp.stml). The SP&Ps detail the district's gifted identification policies and procedures, along with other ESE policies and procedures for students with disabilities. The SP&Ps are updated and reapproved every 3 years with specific metrics updated annually as a means for evaluating gifted identification activities.

The gifted identification plan includes the current status of the gifted program with regard to eligibility by various subgroups, along with goals for continued growth toward equitable representation. The gifted section of the SP&Ps details the identification process for screening, referral, and evaluation, as well as the intent for gifted services within the district. Within the appendices of the SP&Ps is the district's approved alternate plan for the identification of students defined by the state as underrepresented in the gifted program—low-SES students and students who are English language learners (ELLs). The alternate plan is referred to as Plan B, as it is located within paragraph B of the FDOE Gifted Rule.

Because research supports universal screening rather than reliance on classroom teacher nomination to initiate the gifted identification process, the district's plan specifies that each elementary school annually conduct universal screening via the review of existing data. When data suggest high potential, additional individual screening is conducted using the Kaufman Brief Intelligence Test–2. As it is recognized that the lack of opportunity associated with poverty may be linked to lower achievement on standardized tests, the plan includes a wider range of scores leading to additional individual screening for low-SES and ELL students. Beyond universal screening with existing data as a path to individual screening, any individual who suspects a student may be gifted based upon demonstration of gifted characteristics may initiate individual screening. These individuals include parents, teachers and school personnel, a student, or a community member. Following individual screening, students who are considered good candidates for an individual gifted evaluation are referred for a gifted evaluation. As the district Plan B specifies universal screening using existing data annually, a student may be considered as a candidate multiple times and go through the identification process more than once. Within the district, gifted identification is not a single time event. Based upon the increasing number of students found eligible as gifted annually, the identification plan has shown to be inclusive and effective. Additionally, because initial screening utilizes existing data rather than administration of a purchased instrument, the identification plan is affordable and sustainable. The gifted identification plan is updated annually as part of the annual revision of the district's SP&Ps and approved by the district school board and FDOE.

The District Plan for Acceleration (ACCEL)

The district's ACCEL Plan guides decisions regarding whole-grade and subject acceleration at all levels. The ACCEL Plan is required by the FDOE and is part of the district's Student Progression Plan. ACCEL options are available to gifted and nongifted students (https://info.fldoe.org/docushare/dsweb/Get/Document-6465/dps-2012-111.pdf).

The district's ACCEL Plan was developed to align with requirements set forth by FDOE and was developed after an extensive review of acceleration plans in place in other school districts around the nation and recent research on acceleration. The goal of the plan is to provide opportunities for acceleration in a single subject (math, science, ELA, social studies) or acceleration to the next grade level. Because the district offers a wide array of advanced courses beginning at the middle school level, yet at the elementary level only grade-level courses are typically provided, the ACCEL Plan resulted in increased acceleration opportunities for elementary students. An ACCEL option may be initiated by school personnel or by a parent. Because the goal is to provide acceleration options for students for whom acceleration would be a sound decision and support the successful continued academic growth of the individual student, multiple data elements are collected and analyzed leading to a recommendation regarding acceleration. The formal process for ACCEL includes screening utilizing existing data and additional assessments to ascertain above-level academic achievement, aptitude in a specific domain, general ability, and behavioral characteristics associated with talent in a specific domain. Data are analyzed to generate a recommendation regarding single-subject or grade-level acceleration. Anecdotal information from school principals regarding students with an ACCEL option supports success of the ACCEL Plan; however, at this time, there is no districtwide formal process to track acceleration options, so it is unknown how many students currently participate in an ACCEL option or the level of success students are experiencing.

GIFTED GUIDELINES FOR GIFTED SERVICES

The Gifted Guidelines is a "working" document housed within the district intranet and accessible by all district educators (see Figure 13). Gifted Guidelines specify recommend gifted service models, curriculum differentiation approaches, scheduling guidelines, suggested professional development, recommended curricular resources, and other considerations for elementary gifted students. The defined frameworks address research-supported practices with gifted learners in each subject area.

Along with defined professional development and specific curricular resources, the Gifted Guidelines resulted in a shift to a more uniform gifted program throughout all 250+ district schools, yet allowed each individual school to select options that best matched its unique characteristics. The common frameworks became a gauge against which to monitor services at each school and provide explicit suggestions for incremental improvement. As individual teachers and schools have progressed in expanding options for quality gifted services, they have been encouraged to continue their programs and set additional goals for improving gifted services at their school. The Gifted Guidelines have provided focus for the district and for schools. As opportunities and initiatives have been considered, they have been viewed through the lens of the mission, vision, and three goals of inclusivity/equity in identification, appropriateness of services for individual gifted students, and quality professional/leadership development. As potential opportunities have arisen, those initiatives and actions that aligned with movement toward achievement of the goals have been explored and pursued. No energy or resources have been directed at initiatives and activities out of alignment with the goals.

Multiple stakeholder groups were involved in the initiative to develop the guidelines. Administrators, content supervisors, gifted teachers, university personnel, and parents provided input in the development of the initial Gifted Guidelines. The Gifted Guidelines are revised annually to reflect changes initiated by the state DOE, to align with district initiatives, to consider new technologies and approaches, and to infuse new research and best practices in gifted education. The Gifted Guidelines ask school personnel to annually consider three questions: WHY will we select specific gifted service options? HOW can we assure the best gifted service options for our current gifted students? and WHAT opportunities and support will we provide to address our students' learning strengths and needs?

Subject and Course	Student Strength/ EP Goal Focus	Gifted Design Options	Description	Time/Days (Recommended)	Service Delivery Model (Grouping)	Professional Development (Recommended)	Resources (Recommended)	Comments
English Language Arts (ELA) Course # (by grade level)	*Student Strength:* • Reading • Writing *EP Goal Focus:* • Content	**Core-Plus Reading** (SEM-R)	Differentiation through SEM-R as part of Core-Plus Reading instruction during the 90-minute reading block	30–60 minutes/day (3–5 days/week)	Support Facilitation	• Language Arts Florida Standards (LAFS) • SEM-R • Socratic Seminar Teaching • GoQuest (online)	• Joyful Reading • Joyful Reading Resources Kit • Creativity X 4 • GoQuest • Access to books at multiple levels	Requires collaboration between gifted and general education teachers. Both teachers are responsible for student achievement in ELA.
	Complexity (LA) • Research • Information Management • Communication	**Core & Core-Plus Reading** (CCSS, SEM-R, and IIM)	Core Reading instruction PLUS daily differentiation through SEM-R and IIM during the entire 90-minute reading block	90 minutes daily (5 days/week)	Resource Room	• Language Arts Florida Standards (LAFS) • SEM-R • IIM • Applying Kaplan's Depth and Complexity Model • Socratic Seminar Teaching • GoQuest (online)	Joyful Reading Joyful Reading Resource Kit IIM Manual Kaplan's Curriculum Development Tools Creativity X 4 GoQuest Access to books at multiple levels	Requires collaboration between gifted and general education teachers. Both teachers are responsible for student achievement in LA.

Figure 13
Gifted Guidelines.

Subject and Course	Student Strength/ EP Goal Focus	Gifted Design Options	Description	Time/Days (Recommended)	Service Delivery Model (Grouping)	Professional Development (Recommended)	Resources (Recommended)	Comments
English Language Arts (ELA) Course # (by grade level) *continued.*	*Student Strength:* • Reading • Writing *EP Goal Focus:* • Content Complexity (LA) • Research • Information Management • Communication *continued.*	**Core & Core-Plus LA** (CCSS, SEM-R, and IIM)	Core Reading/LA instruction PLUS daily differentiation through SEM-R & IIM	120 minutes daily (5 days /week)	Resource Room	• Language Arts Florida Standards (LAFS) • Writing • SEM-R • IIM • Applying Kaplan's Depth and Complexity Model • Socratic Seminar Teaching • GoQuest (online)	• Joyful Reading • Joyful Reading Resource Kit • IIM Manual • Kaplan's Curriculum Development Tools • Creativity X 4 • GoQuest • Access to books at multiple levels	Requires collaboration between gifted and general education teachers. Gifted teacher is responsible for student achievement in LA.
		Core-Plus LA (IIM)	Differentiation through IIM as part of LA (not during 90-minute reading block)	30 minutes/day (3–5 days/week)	Resource Room OR Support Facilitation	• Language Arts Florida Standards (LAFS) • IIM • Socratic Seminar Teaching • GoQuest (online)	• IIM Manual • Kaplan's Curriculum Development Tools • Creativity X 4 • GoQuest	Requires collaboration between gifted & general education teachers. Both teachers are responsible for student achievement in LA.

Figure 13. *Continued.*

Subject and Course	Student Strength/ EP Goal Focus	Gifted Design Options	Description	Time/Days (Recommended)	Service Delivery Model (Grouping)	Professional Development (Recommended)	Resources (Recommended)	Comments
Mathematics **Course #** **(by grade level)**	*Student Strength:* • Mathematics *EP Goal Focus:* • Content complexity (mathematics) • Information management • Spatial thinking	**Core & Core-Plus Mathematics**	Core Math instruction PLUS daily differentiation through problem-based/project-based learning connected to MAFS	60 minutes/day (5 days/week)	Resource Room OR Co-Teach Important: Single grade-level group ONLY!	• Math Florida Standards (MAFS) • Minds-on projects • GoQuest (online)	• Project-based learning • Hands-On Math Projects • Creativity X 4 • GoQuest	Gifted teacher is responsible for providing a differentiated curriculum daily. Gifted teacher is responsible for student achievement in mathematics.
		Core-Plus Mathematics	Differentiation through problem-based/project-based learning connected to MAFS	30 minutes/day (5 days/week) OR 60 minutes/day (1–2 days/week)	Resource Room OR Support Facilitation	• Math Florida Standards (MAFS) • Minds-on projects • GoQuest (online	• Project-based learning • Hands-On Math Projects • Creativity X 4 • GoQuest	Requires collaboration between gifted and general education teachers. Both teachers are responsible for student achievement in mathematics.

Figure 13. *Continued.*

Subject and Course	Student Strength/ EP Goal Focus	Gifted Design Options	Description	Time/Days (Recommended)	Service Delivery Model (Grouping)	Professional Development (Recommended)	Resources (Recommended)	Comments
Science Course # (by grade level) Science	*Student Strength:* • Science • Technology *EP Goal Focus:* • Content complexity (science) • Information management • Technology • Social action	Core & Core-Plus Science	Core Science instruction PLUS daily differentiation through problem-based/ project-based learning connected to standards	60 minutes/day (5 days/week)	Resource Room OR Co-Teach Important: Single grade-level group ONLY!	• Science content training • Minds-on projects • Think Data • Applying Kaplan's Depth and Complexity Model • GoQuest (online)	• Project-based learning • Action research • Think Data Kaplan's Curriculum Development Tools • Creativity X 4 • GoQuest • *Think Data Kit (available for loan through Gifted)	Gifted teacher is responsible for providing a differentiated curriculum daily. Gifted teacher is responsible for student achievement in science.
		Core-Plus Science	Differentiation through problem-based/ project-based learning connected to standards	30 minutes/day (5 days) OR 60 minutes (1–2 days/week)	Resource Room OR Support Facilitation	• Science content training • Minds-on projects • Think Data • Applying Kaplan's Depth and Complexity Model • GoQuest (online)	• Project-based learning • Action research • Think Data • Kaplan's Curriculum Development Tools • Creativity X 4 • GoQuest • *Think Data Kit (available for loan through Gifted)	Requires collaboration between gifted and general education teachers. Both teachers are responsible for student achievement in science.

Figure 13. *Continued.*

Subject and Course	Student Strength/ EP Goal Focus	Gifted Design Options	Description	Time/Days (Recommended)	Service Delivery Model (Grouping)	Professional Development (Recommended)	Resources (Recommended)	Comments
Social Studies Course # (by grade level) Social Studies	*Student Strength:* • Social Studies *EP Goal Focus:* • Content complexity (social studies) • Research • Information management	**Core & Core-Plus Social Studies**	Core Social Studies instruction PLUS daily differentiation through problem-based/ project-based learning connected to standards	30 minutes/day (5 days/week)	Resource Room OR Co-Teach Important: Single grade-level group ONLY!	• Florida Standards Social Studies • Minds-on projects • Applying Kaplan's Depth and Complexity Model • IIM • GoQuest (Online)	• Project-based learning • Action research • Kaplan's Curriculum Development Tools • IIM Manual • Creativity X 4 • GoQuest	Requires collaboration between gifted and general education teachers. Both teachers are responsible for student achievement in social studies unless students are scheduled with the gifted teacher for both social studies (30 minutes) and RtI (27 minutes) daily.
		RtI/MTSS for Gifted	Enrichment in ELA through IIM, SEM-R, and/or Socratic seminars	27 minutes/day (3–5 days/week)	Resource Room OR Support Facilitation	• IIM • SEM-R • Socratic seminar teaching	• IIM Manual • Creativity X 4 • Action Research • GoQuest	Requires collaboration between gifted and general education teachers. Both teachers are responsible for student achievement in social studies.

Figure 13. *Continued.*

PLANNING FOR GIFTED SERVICES:

Identify the learning needs of your school's gifted students.

- Services for gifted students MUST be based upon learning strengths and needs per data and student EPs.
- Scheduling for gifted services MUST be student driven and provide for service options in multiple content areas.
- Gather data from multiple sources including: number of gifted students by grade level (targeted roster); student strengths and needs (IPT test data and EP goal focus); student interests (GoQuest Student Profile); and teacher observations and input.

Determine the amount of service time available from gifted teachers for gifted services based upon your school's gifted unit allocation.

- Full-time gifted teachers teach gifted students for 5 hours daily.
- Part-time gifted teachers teach gifted students daily for 2 hours 15 minutes (split a.m./p.m. schedule).

Determine classroom space available for gifted services including: number of resource rooms available; homeroom classrooms where gifted students have been clustered (for possible co-teach or support facilitation services); and whether class size rules apply the same for gifted classes/co-teach as for other core classes.

- Gifted Resource Room: Only eligible gifted students may be included.
- Co-Teach: A significant number of gifted students must be clustered within the general education classroom (approximately 8–10 gifted students) according to their area of learning strength; co-teaching must occur daily for the entire class period.
- Support Facilitation: Gifted students must be grouped into general education classrooms according their area of learning strengths so that the gifted teacher can spend significant time periods delivering services to small groups of gifted students within the general education classroom.

Select the most appropriate Gifted Design Options for your school's gifted students and develop a schedule of gifted services.

Figure 13. *Continued.*

The Gifted Guidelines provide a framework for all of the district's diverse schools to operationalize the district's plan for services to maximize their resources to address the learning needs of gifted students in their unique settings. The Gifted Guidelines are designed around the Schoolwide Enrichment Model (SEM), as the approach is aligned with the philosophy of the district's gifted program. Since 2006, when the district first began exploring the SEM, significant time and effort has been dedicated to building the capacity of the district to implement and support curricular options associated with the SEM. Curricular options include the Schoolwide Enrichment Model Reading Framework (SEM-R), Mentoring Mathematical Minds (M³), the Independent Investigations Method (IIM), Seminar Teaching, and Kaplan's Depth and Complexity Model.

The guidelines include both nonnegotiables and necessary flexibility. Because gifted education is a state-mandated program with associated funding, the gifted program must meet the requirements of the state DOE. Services must address the educational plan goals of each individual gifted student and be provided within parameters defined by DOE. Flexibility is built into the guidelines regarding the subject for services, the setting and grouping of gifted students, the time for services, and gifted design options. All gifted options are standards-based and integrate both core standards and the Florida Gifted Standards. The guidelines define what curricular approaches will be implemented and suggest curricular resources and professional development recommended to support the design option. Suggestions for collaboration are detailed because the gifted program must be integral to the general education program.

WHAT IS THE HISTORY OF GIFTED EDUCATION IN THE DISTRICT?

Since 1977, the FDOE has provided rules that define gifted and detail criteria for eligibility. According to the state, gifted students are defined as "students who have superior intellectual development and are capable of high performance" (FDOE, n.d., para. 1). Criteria established by the state for eligibility in the gifted program include (a) a demonstrated need for a special program, (b) a majority of characteristics of gifted students according to a standard scale or checklist, and (c) superior intellectual development as measured by an intelligence quotient of two standard deviations above the mean on an individually administered standardized test of intelligence. Additionally, per state Board Rule, a district may elect to develop an alternate identification plan for the purpose of increasing participation in gifted programs for students who are typically underrepresented in gifted programs. Since 1992, the district has a state-approved districtwide plan to increase participation of underrepresented groups in programs for gifted students defined by the state as those who are limited English proficient, or who are from a low-socioeconomic status family. As the alternate identification plan is included in paragraph B of the state Board Rule, it is referred to as Plan B.

In 1992, the state added rules that require the gifted endorsement consisting of the completion of five 60-hour in-service gifted endorsement courses, the equivalent of five 3-credit hour courses in gifted education, for teachers who provide gifted services. The district provides gifted endorsement training to teachers who must earn the gifted endorsement through in-service training funded through Title II professional development. Beginning in 1999, the district began offering the five gifted endorsement courses online. Teachers embraced the new model, as they could tap into the interactive online courses from their own homes and no longer needed to leave their families behind to travel across the district for required training.

During 2004, the state created additional rules to guide gifted education in districts. The new FDOE rules provide requirements for gifted Education Plans (EPs) and Procedural Safeguards for Exceptional Students who are Gifted. The EP rule specified the content and duration of gifted education plans focused on student learning strengths. The Procedural Safeguards rule designated required procedures relevant to gifted identification and services within districts and defined the rights of parents of gifted students.

At the end of June 2005, the district Supervisor of Gifted, in the position since the late 1980s, retired. The current Supervisor of Gifted assumed the role and, building upon the foundation created by her predecessor, revised the vision, mission, and goals of the district's gifted program. Surveys were developed for gifted teachers and school principals as a needs assessment for the gifted program in determining future directions and initiatives.

In late 2005, the district introduced an electronic instructional planning tool (IPT) that includes demographic and test data on all district students. Analytics included within the tool provide the capability to easily sort and analyze individual, school, and districtwide data. Through use of the IPT, school personnel could easily examine "live" data regarding their students as well as analyze and compare subgroups, including gifted students.

Beginning in 2006, gifted teachers were taught in their gifted endorsement training how to use the IPT tool to analyze their school's data regarding their gifted population. The endorsement training also taught teachers to target their identification efforts so that their gifted student population would more closely mirror their school's population by gender, ethnicity, meal status, and ELL status. Armed with a commitment to the vision and mission of the district's gifted program and their school's live data, gifted teachers were tasked with developing an "action plan" to target identification efforts so that their school's gifted population would be more aligned with their school's population. As school counselors serve as the school's

Child Study Team Chair and are integral to the gifted identification process at schools within the district, training in use of the IPT was also provided for counselors. Prior to the availability of the IPT, schools were encouraged to identify gifted students to increase the number of identified gifted students, yet they had no way of knowing who to target as potentially gifted and were dependent only on nominations from classroom teachers. With use of the IPT tool, gifted identification efforts shifted away from passive activity dependent upon nomination by classroom teachers who may or may not have had any training in recognizing gifted characteristics, to an active process of universal screening. Through this process, school personnel were empowered to target their identification efforts toward finding potential gifted students within underrepresented subgroups in their school. Use of the IPT created the opportunity for cost-effective universal screening throughout the district.

Along with empowering individual educators and schools to find hidden gifted students within their own schools, it was important to assure that the district's individual screening and referral parameters were designed to cast a wide net and that potential gifted students were not being routinely screened out of the referral and evaluation process. Research on individual screening procedures was conducted in 2006–2007 in collaboration with gifted educators from the University of South Florida. Extensive data analysis resulted in a recommendation for new individual screening parameters, as findings of the research project suggested that the previous screening parameters leading to referral for a gifted evaluation may have been set too high, resulting in underidentification of potential gifted students. Meetings between researchers and district personnel in the departments of psychological services, guidance, and gifted resulted in new guidelines for screening and referral. The new parameters were put in place during 2007–2008. Consequently, more potential gifted students are being referred for individual gifted evaluations, resulting in an increased number of eligible gifted students, including students from state-defined underrepresented groups.

Since 2008, the district's identification plan for groups defined by FDOE as underrepresented in gifted programs has included the requirement to district elementary schools for annual universal screening using existing data in the elementary grades and the elimination of the requirement for formal nomination before a student may be considered as a potential gifted student. This change in the district's identification policy and procedures was a direct result of the availability of access to the IPT for data analysis, training for teachers during the gifted endorsement courses on use of the data tool, and research findings with the local university that resulted in revised individual screening parameters.

In 2008, with the introduction of the Response to Intervention (RtI) approach and changing conceptions of giftedness, it was necessary to reexamine the district's gifted program services. To guide development of a plan for improving services, a working document was created that identified and listed essential considerations (see Figure 14).

In 2009, a federal stimulus-funded district project, *Developing Model Schools for RtI With Gifted & Talent Students,* resulted in the implementation of research-supported curricular strategies and resources at nine district elementary schools as a working model for the future implementation of districtwide RtI for gifted and talented students (see Figure 15). Components of the project included teacher training for gifted and general education teachers, research-based curricular resources to support Florida standards, and problem-based learning activities to provide enrichment and develop skills in critical thinking. Additional training focused on strategies to support underachieving and twice-exceptional gifted students.

In 2011, the state initiated Florida's Plan for K–12 Gifted Education (http://www.fldoe.org/core/fileparse.php/7567/urlt/stategiftedplan.pdf) to guide districts in the design of their gifted programs regarding identification, services, and evaluation. Districts are encouraged to develop a district plan for gifted education, however there is currently no mechanism in place for submission of district Gifted Plans to the state DOE. The state DOE continues to require each district school board submit proposed procedures (SP&P) for the provision of special instruction and services for exceptional students. Approval of the SP&P document by DOE is required by state board rule as a prerequisite for the district's use of weighted cost factors under the state finance program. The SP&P document serves as the basis for the identification, evaluation, eligibility determination, and placement of students to receive exceptional education services.

Students served in the gifted program have an Educational Plan (EP) developed to address their learning strengths and needs related to their giftedness with goals to guide gifted services to support the continued academic growth of the student. Sample gifted SMART goals were developed and are provided to gifted teachers as a guideline for developing appropriate strength-based EP goals (see Figure 16). Suggested language is provided so that goals are succinct, measurable, achievable, results-oriented, and time-bound.

Since 2014, the state has provided gifted standards (http://www.cpalms.org/Public/Search/Standard) to guide curricular modifications to create an appropriate level of challenge for gifted students. The state mandates identification and services for K–12 gifted students. Partial funding for gifted programs is provided to districts by the state in the form of a "guaranteed allocation" that also supports services for some students with disabilities.

Mission: To nurture the development of giftedness among district elementary students.

Rationale: The interaction of current social, economic, and political forces may drive the need to reexamine and realign practices for identification and services for high-ability students.

Forces include, but are not limited to:
- Changing conception of giftedness: From a categorical perspective toward a developmental perspective
- Pending draft Florida State Gifted Rule
- Florida's RtI Plan
- Potential funding changes
- Other (CIM, etc.)

Guiding questions:
1. What advanced learning options are available to support district students including those who are: (a) excellent students/high achievers, (b) passionately interested in some dimensions of a school-related subject (e.g., leadership), or (c) passionately interested in talent areas outside of school?
2. What subject-specific programming options are being implemented in district schools to meet advanced learning needs?
3. What types of acceleration (subject-specific, grade-skipping, advanced courses, etc.) are being implemented in district schools?
4. What options are being implemented to develop domain-specific strengths (music, language, chess, art, etc.)?
5. What is the level of implementation of best-practice strategies among teachers of gifted and talented students? (See NAGC-CEC Standards in appendix.)
6. What teacher education opportunities relevant to gifted and talent development are available to district teachers?
7. How is the gifted program representative of the student population at the district and school level with regard to ethnicity, SES, language, and other demographics?

Figure 14
Considerations for improving gifted services.

8. How is grouping currently being used in elementary schools?
9. How may grouping be used to address the developmental needs of students who are currently more advanced than their peers and the needs of those whose talents may emerge with exposure to more challenging instruction?
10. What assessment date is currently available and how is it being used to address planning and instruction for advanced learners?
11. With regard to gifted and advanced learners, who are the stakeholders and how might they be involved in the process of examining and improving services?

GOAL 1:

To examine current services and opportunities available for district students relevant to the development of giftedness.

GOAL 2:

To use research-based best-practices to plan for improving services and opportunities to develop giftedness.

GOAL 3:

To examine level of implementation of research-based best practices among teachers who teach advanced learners.

GOAL 4:

To improve the level of implementation of research-based best practices relevant to developing giftedness among district teachers.

Figure 14. *Continued.*

RtI & High-End Learners Model Schools Project (2009–2010)

Summer 2009 Training

RtI & High-End Learners Training will prepare district administrators, classroom teachers, gifted teachers, guidance counselors, school psychologists, and others in essential components of the Response to Intervention (RtI) approach for high-end learners. RtI is a multitiered approach to providing high-quality instruction and intervention matched to student needs and includes multiple tiers of evidence-based instructional service delivery, a problem-solving method design to inform development of intervention, and an integrated data-collection/assessment system to inform instructional decisions.

Course Descriptions

RtI & High-End Learners: Introduction & Overview will introduce administrators, teachers, psychologists, and guidance counselors to the district's Response to Intervention (RtI) plan for high-end learners. RtI is the Florida Department of Education's multitiered approach to providing high-quality instruction and intervention matched to student needs in order to improve learning for all students. (Target audience: administrators, classroom teachers, gifted teachers, guidance counselors, school psychologists)

RtI & High-End Learners: Research-Based Grouping Strategies will introduce administrators and teachers to research-based grouping strategies. Research from the National Research Center on Gifted and Talented at the University of Connecticut indicates that implementation of these grouping strategies increases the number of high-achieving students and decreases the number of low-achieving students within a school. (Target audience: administrators, classroom teachers, gifted teachers, guidance counselors, school psychologists)

RtI & High-End Learners: Strategies for Differentiating Instruction will train teachers in specific DI strategies to accompany Total School Cluster Grouping, including compacting, tiered lessons, and anchor activities. (Target audience: classroom teachers, gifted teachers, administrators)

Figure 15
RtI Academy 2009 course descriptions.

RtI & High-End Learners: Maximizing Motivation will train teachers in specific strategies to enhance student motivation and increase the quality of student work. (Target audience: classroom teachers, gifted teachers, guidance counselors, administrators)

RtI & High-End Learners: Problem-Based Learning in Science and Social Studies will train teachers in inquiry-based instructional strategies to increase challenge and rigor in the curriculum and prepare learners for the real world. (Target audience: classroom teachers, gifted teachers, administrators)

RtI & High-End Learners: SEM-R Framework will train teachers to serve as facilitators for the Schoolwide Enrichment Model Reading Framework, a research-based approach to reading instruction developed at the National Research Center on the Gifted and Talented at the University of Connecticut. Research indicates that use of the SEM-R model increases reading comprehension and oral fluency and improves attitudes toward reading. Training will include group training, coaching, observation, and other strategies. (Target audience: classroom teachers, gifted teachers, reading coaches, administrators)

RtI & High-End Learners: Progress Monitoring and Performance Pitfalls will train teachers, guidance counselors, psychologists, and administrators in using preassessments to determine individual student needs linked to specific interventions and using progress monitoring strategies to measure and record student progress during interventions. Attendees will learn to use observations, checklists, rating scales, and other performance measures to monitor student performance. Training will also include a focus on empowering students to become achievers and specific strategies for addressing underachievement. (Target audience: administrators, classroom teachers, gifted teachers, guidance counselors, school psychologists)

RtI & High-End Learners: Mentoring Mathematical Minds will train teachers to implement Mentoring Mathematical Minds (M³), research-based curriculum units based on NCTM Standards developed at the National Research Center on the Gifted and Talented at the University of Connecticut. Research indicates that use of M³ increases math achievement and attitudes toward math in talented and diverse students. Teachers will learn specific strategies to address critical and creative thinking through advanced mathematical content. (Target audience: classroom teachers, gifted teachers, administrators)

Figure 15. *Continued.*

RtI & High-End Learners: Independent Investigations Model (IIM) for Research in the Real World will train teachers to teach students to do real-world research using a seven-step process. Teachers will learn to use the IIM template to turn existing curriculum units into research units and empower students to become successful researchers. (Target audience: classroom teachers, gifted teachers, administrators)

RtI & High-End Learners: Differentiation With Britannica Online will train teachers to use the districtwide technology resource, Britannica Online, to differentiate instruction for high-end learners. The focus of this session will include a brief introduction to Britannica Online and specific strategies for creating personal workspaces for both teacher and student use. (Target audience: classroom teachers, gifted teachers, administrators)

Figure 15. *Continued.*

2012 SMARTer EP Goal Guidelines and Samples

Goal	Suggested Grade Level			Suggested Content Area(s) of Strength/Interest/Service				Goal Focus	2012 Sample SMARTer Goal Language
	Elem	Mid	High	Read/LA	Math	Science	Other		
1	No	Yes	Yes	☒	☒	☒	☒	Acceleration	By (indicate end of EP period), (indicate name of student) will successfully complete above level / advanced course work in (name content area).
2	Yes	Yes	Yes	☒	☒	☒	☒	Content Complexity	By (indicate end of EP period), (indicate name of student) will successfully demonstrate the use of complex thought and processing in (indicate content area &/or areas).
3	Yes	Yes	No	☒	☐	☒	☒	Creative Thinking	By (indicate end of EP period), (indicate name of student) will successfully demonstrate creative thinking and personal expression.
4	Yes	Yes	No	☒	☒	☒	☒	Research	By (indicate end of EP period), (indicate name of student) will successfully demonstrate advanced research skills.
5	Yes	Yes	No	☒	☒	☒	☒	Information Management	By (indicate end of EP period), (indicate name of student) will successfully demonstrate advanced skills in accessing, organizing, & sharing information.
6	Yes	Yes	No	☒	☒	☒	☒	Communication	By (indicate end of EP period), (indicate name of student) will successfully demonstrate advanced communications skills.
7	Yes	Yes	No	☒	☒	☒	☒	Self-Directed Learner	By (indicate end of EP period), (indicate name of student) will successfully demonstrate effective self-directed learning.
8	Yes	No	No	☐	☐	☐	☒	Leadership Development	By (indicate end of EP period), (indicate name of student) will successfully demonstrate advanced leadership skills.
9	Yes	No	No	☒	☐	☒	☒	Social Action	By (indicate end of EP period), (indicate name of student) will successfully demonstrate advanced skills in implementation of the social action process.
10	Yes	Yes	No	☐	☒	☒	☒	Spatial Thinking	By (indicate end of EP period), (indicate name of student) will successfully demonstrate advanced skills in spatial relationships.
11	Yes	Yes	No	☒	☒	☒	☒	Technology	By (indicate end of EP period), (indicate name of student) will successfully demonstrate advanced skills in the use of technology.
12	Yes	Yes	No	☐	☐	☒	☐	Scientific Thinking	By (indicate end of EP period), (indicate name of student) will successfully demonstrate advanced skills in scientific thinking.

Guidelines for use:

☐ Consider multiple factors including: the student's grade level, strengths & interests, and service design options available in the grade-level/school

☐ Do NOT consider SMARTer goals for a student that are indicated as "NO" for the grade level and/or are NOT marked as recommended (X) based upon the strength/interest/services.

☐ When writing the goal using the sample SMARTer goal language, wherever the section is underlined, SELECT & WRITE the appropriate words (examples: date of EP expiration and name of student

☐ Keep in mind that these are only SAMPLE goals and are NOT intended to be a limited menu of choices for writing EP goals

Figure 16
Sample SMARTer goals.

THE DISTRICT GIFTED GUIDELINES: A CLOSER LOOK

The intent of the Elementary Gifted Guidelines is to guide school personnel in designing a continuum of services matched to the current needs of individual gifted students attending the school. These guidelines are designed as an at-a-glance planner for designing and implementing quality student-centered gifted services. Additional support documents include: Planning for Gifted Services Overview PowerPoint, Gifted Services Planning FAQs, Gifted Service Delivery Models, and Middle School Course Code FAQs. A link to a recorded webinar overview is also provided. All documents are available at a conference with the district intranet. Other documents within the Elementary Gifted Guidelines conference include: Student Summary Planning Template, Decision Making for Elementary Gifted Services PowerPoint, Gifted Fast Facts, Scheduling Clarification Memo, and a Florida Gifted Standards Overview.

The Elementary Gifted Guidelines are intended to provide the information necessary for each district school with K–5 students to plan, schedule, and deliver student-centered gifted services. The Elementary Gifted Guidelines include the following sections:

- **Subject and course:** Subjects for elementary gifted students may include ELA, math, science, or social studies. The FDOE provides a course code, description, and state standards for each general education course. Elementary gifted courses provide differentiation of the general education course through integration of the Florida Gifted Standards and individualization via the students' EP goals.

- **Student strength/EP goal focus:** Because gifted services occur in subject-specific courses, yet gifted goals may not be subject-specific, it is the responsibility of the gifted teacher to address each student's individual gifted goals within the learning experiences. The Elementary Gifted Guidelines include suggested gifted goal foci to best align with subject-specific content and standards. For example, a student with learning strengths in reading or writing and EP goals in research or communication is well-suited for services in ELA. A student who has demonstrated talent in science and has goals in scientific thinking, research, or technology may be best suited to services in the gifted science course.

- **Gifted design option:** Design options have been developed in the subjects of ELA, math, science, and social studies. Design options have been categorized as Core-Plus or Core & Core-Plus in the subject. Core-Plus options are the provision of learning opportunities designed to extend and enrich the core standards. The focus of the gifted teacher during Core-Plus services is differentiation beyond the core standards that integrates students' individual EP goals. In Core & Core-Plus options, the gifted teacher is responsible for addressing the core standards for the course as well as providing differentiation to extend the core and addressing gifted students' EP goals. In a Core & Core-Plus option, the gifted teacher is the student's only teacher for that subject/course.

- **Description:** The description provides additional information regarding the focus of the gifted instruction for the design option. In ELA, the guidelines specify that instruction is to utilize the Schoolwide Enrichment Model Reading Framework (SEM-R) to provide challenge for gifted readers and provide research opportunities using the 7-step Independent Investigations Model. In Core-Plus Mathematics and Core-Plus Science, instruction should provide problem-based learning and project-based learning connected to core standards. The description also provides guidance to align with Florida-specific and district-specific requirements. For example, because state statute requires that K–5 students have 90 minutes of uninterrupted reading instruction daily, the description specifies that a teacher who provides Core-Plus services in ELA may not remove students from classroom during the 90-minute reading period, rather he or she may provide the Core-Plus instruction within the general education setting.

- **Time/Days (recommended):** The suggestions for time are intended to encourage schools to schedule services for significant time periods either daily or weekly. As the number of gifted students and number of gifted teachers varies greatly between schools across the district, there is flexibility in scheduling. A single teacher responsible for services for 20 K–5 gifted students in her school must distribute her time differently to address the needs of her students than a teacher who is one of four gifted teachers at a school with 150 K–5 gifted students who may responsible for just a single subject or grade level. It is recognized that the needs of each gifted student are unique, and the services scheduled for each student should address the individual's learning needs beyond the general education curriculum. The approach to flexibility in the use of time moves the approach to gifted services beyond a time and place to an array of services designed to the individual learning needs of the individual student.

- **Service delivery model (grouping):** The FDOE lists and defines gifted service delivery models within Florida's K–12 Plan for Gifted Education. The service delivery models specify who may be included in the instructional group for gifted services. As the state accountability system has moved toward connecting students to teachers via assessments that impact the teacher's evaluation, clarity in the service delivery model has become essential. The service delivery model is part of the biannual FTE reporting process. Of the service delivery models listed as acceptable by the state, for K–5 students the district utilizes the resource/pull-out model, coteaching, support-facilitation, gifted-virtual, and full-time services. The resource/pull-out model requires that all students within the group are eligible as gifted. Coteaching is defined as a group of students including both gifted and nongifted students, taught daily for the entire class period by two teachers who are both responsible for planning, instruction, and assessment of all of the students. Within a support-facilitation group, the gifted teacher provides instruction for a group of gifted students in the general education setting for a portion of a class period or a few times each week. Students served through the virtual model receive gifted services from a gifted teacher in a virtual course. Gifted students receiving full-time gifted services receive daily instruction in all core subjects from a gifted teacher in a class of gifted peers.

- **Professional development (recommended):** Quality gifted services require teachers with adequate skills to implement the differentiated strategies and gifted approaches defined in the Elementary Gifted Guidelines. Although all teachers who serve gifted students in the state are required to have or earn the gifted endorsement, the PD recommended within the guidelines prepares teachers with the necessary skills to support the specific design options listed within the guidelines. By defining specific PD to support implementation of the design options, PD and services are aligned and the likelihood that design options will be implemented with fidelity is increased.

- **Resources (recommended):** Although multiple opportunities for flexibility are built into the guidelines, it is necessary that there is fidelity in implementation of the options. Each of the resources included in the list of recommended resources has been specifically selected to support the successful implementation of the design options. Many of the resources listed support elements of the Schoolwide Enrichment Model approach. Some resources listed in the guidelines have been provided to gifted teachers at the annual Elementary Gifted Training Day over the past 6 years, some resources are provided when teachers attend district gifted workshops, and other resources are available to all teachers via the gifted conference located on the district intranet.

- **Comments:** The comments section of the Elementary Gifted Guidelines includes additional information schools must consider as they select and implement the gifted service options. Updates to the comments are made annually as general education initiatives and requirements change. Comments are important, both for gifted teachers who provide gifted services and for general education teachers who have gifted students in their classrooms.

PLANNING FOR GIFTED
SERVICES: THE PROCESS

The Elementary Gifted Guidelines detail the recommended process for annually determining the needs of elementary gifted students and planning for appropriate student-centered services. The goal is that each K–5 gifted student will receive services for a minimum of 5 hours a week in subjects aligned to the individual student's gifted leaning needs. Schools are encouraged to begin the annual planning process by looking at the individual learning needs of their gifted students, considering current learning strengths and needs based upon data and student EP goals. School personnel are encouraged to gather data from multiple sources, including the gifted student roster, indicating the number of gifted students by grade level, the IPT to examine standardized test data, students' individual EP goals, and student interests based upon the Renzulli Learning System's Profiler. An Elementary Gifted Planner is available to guide the decision making for individual gifted students (see Figure 17).

Rather than scheduling all students for a single subject, schools are encouraged to provide gifted instruction in multiple subjects. Other considerations for planning services include classroom space available, how students have been grouped in general education classrooms, and the amount of time available in the gifted teacher's day. Full-time gifted teaches are expected to provide gifted services for 5 hours a day, while part-time gifted teachers are to provide services for 2.5 hours a day. Once all data have been collected and analyzed, gifted design options are selected and a schedule of gifted services is developed. (See Figure 18.)

WHAT MAJOR CHANGES HAVE
HAPPENED AND WHEN?

There have been a number of significant events and changes impacting the district's gifted program. So much of the attention within a large diverse school district must be on supporting struggling students and closing the achievement gap that little energy is left among district personnel and school-level administrators for attending to improving gifted programming. In gifted education, there is rarely the opportunity for a funded "top-down" initiative to drive positive change in gifted programming. Therefore, it has been essential to look for opportunities and dollars to improve gifted programming as a part of other initiatives, involving stakeholders at the district and school levels by showing how improved gifted education supports whole school improvement. In reflecting upon changes to the district's gifted pro-

Elementary Gifted Student Services Planner

Name: **Grade:**

Completed By: **Date:**

Most Recent Standardized Test Scores:

Reading: Math: Other:

Other Assessment Data:

EP Goal Focus:

☐ Acceleration in _____   ☐ Leadership Development

☐ Content Complexity in _____   ☐ Social Action

☐ Creative Thinking   ☐ Spatial Thinking

☐ Research   ☐ Technology

☐ Information Management   ☐ Scientific Thinking

☐ Communication   ☐ Other:

☐ Self-Directed Learner

In which of the following subject areas does the student display behaviors of strength?

Reading

http://projectguts.org/files/Fileshare_Area493/Teacher_Resources/NSFAYS/Scales_for_Rating_Gifted_Students.pdf

☐ Eagerly engages in reading related activities

☐ Applies previously learned literary concepts to new reading experiences

☐ Focuses on reading for an extended period of time

☐ Pursues advanced reading material

☐ Demonstrates tenacity when posed with challenging reading

☐ Shows interest in reading other types of interest-based reading material

☐ Demonstrates advanced language skills

☐ Other:

STRONG   MODERATE   NOT INDICATED

Language Arts

☐ Possesses a storehouse of information about a variety of topics

☐ Has an unusually advanced vocabulary for his/her age

☐ Recalls information quickly and accurately

☐ Quick to make connections

☐ Is intense when truly involved in an activity

☐ Questions everything; favorite question is "Why?"

☐ Displays original thinking

☐ Is highly verbal

☐ Has a great imagination

☐ Enjoys reading & writing

☐ Likes to tell stories and play word games

☐ Likes listening to stories or to other people talk

☐ Enjoys language, word play, and verbal communication

☐ Has unique ideas in their writing and speaking

☐ Uses drama and humor to engage an audience in imaginative ways through writing and drama

☐ Above level performance on multiple ELA assessments

☐ Other:

STRONG   MODERATE   NOT INDICATED

Figure 17
Elementary gifted planner.

Elementary Gifted Student Services Planner

<u>**Science**</u>

http://projectguts.org/files/Fileshare_Area493/Teacher_Resources/NSFAYS/Scales_for_Rating_Gifted_Students.pdf

- ☐ Demonstrates curiosity about scientific processes
- ☐ Demonstrates creative thinking about scientific debates or issues
- ☐ Self-selects reading material about science-related topics

- ☐ Is curious about why things are as they are
- ☐ Clearly articulates data interpretation
- ☐ Demonstrates enthusiasm in discussion of scientific topics
- ☐ Is interested in research &/or science projects
- ☐ Other:

| STRONG | MODERATE | NOT INDICATED |

<u>**Math**</u>

http://projectguts.org/files/Fileshare_Area493/Teacher_Resources/NSFAYS/Scales_for_Rating_Gifted_Students.pdf

- ☐ Standardized tests indicate high achievement in mathematics (85th Percentile or Higher)
- ☐ Eager to solve challenging math problems
- ☐ Organizes data & information to discover mathematical patterns
- ☐ Enjoys challenging math puzzles, games, & logic problems
- ☐ Understands new math concepts & processes more easily than other students
- ☐ Has creative (unusual & divergent) ways of solving math problems
- ☐ Displays a strong number sense; makes sense of large numbers, estimates easily & appropriately

- ☐ Frequently solves math problems abstractly without need for manipulatives or concrete materials
- ☐ Has in interest in analyzing the mathematical structure of a problem
- ☐ Can switch strategies easily when solving a problem
- ☐ Regularly uses a variety of representations to explain math concepts (written explanation, pictorial, graphic, equations)
- ☐ Other:

| STRONG | MODERATE | NOT INDICATED |

<u>**Social Studies**</u>

- ☐ Intense interest in world events
- ☐ Interest in history, geography, economics
- ☐ Able to view multiple perspectives
- ☐ Enjoys service to others

- ☐ Prefers self-selected problems
- ☐ Likes to solve real-world problems
- ☐ Enjoys research
- ☐ Other:

| STRONG | MODERATE | NOT INDICATED |

<u>**Summary of Subject-Area Recommendations**</u>

	STRONG	MODERATE	NOT INDICATED
<u>Reading</u>	STRONG	MODERATE	NOT INDICATED
<u>Language Arts</u>	STRONG	MODERATE	NOT INDICATED
<u>Science</u>	STRONG	MODERATE	NOT INDICATED
<u>Math</u>	STRONG	MODERATE	NOT INDICATED

Figure 17
Continued.

Elementary Gifted Design Options (See Gifted Guidelines for Details)	2016–2017 Recommended Gifted Service Delivery (Grouping Models)								
	.5 Unit	1.0 Unit	1.5 Units	2.0 Units	2.5 Units	3.0 Units	3.5 Units	4.0 Units	5.0 Units
Core Plus Reading	Support Facilitation	Support Facilitation	Support Facilitation	Support Facilitation	Support Facilitation	Support Facilitation	Support Facilitation	Support Facilitation	Support Facilitation
Core AND Core-Plus Reading				Resource	Resource	Resource	Resource	Resource	Resource
Core AND Core-Plus LA					Resource	Resource	Resource	Resource	Resource
Core-Plus LA	Resource	Resource	Resource	Resource	Resource	Resource	Resource	Resource	Resource
	Support Facilitation	Support Facilitation	Support Facilitation	Support Facilitation	Support Facilitation	Support Facilitation	Support Facilitation	Support Facilitation	Support Facilitation
Core AND Core-Plus Mathematics			Resource	Resource	Resource	Resource	Resource	Resource	Resource
			Co-Teach	Co-Teach	Co-Teach	Co-Teach	Co-Teach	Co-Teach	Co-Teach
Core-Plus Mathematics	Resource	Resource	Resource	Resource	Resource	Resource	Resource	Resource	Resource
	Support Facilitation	Support Facilitation	Support Facilitation	Support Facilitation	Support Facilitation	Support Facilitation	Support Facilitation	Support Facilitation	Support Facilitation
Core AND Core-Plus Science			Resource	Resource	Resource	Resource	Resource	Resource	Resource
			Co-Teach	Co-Teach	Co-Teach	Co-Teach	Co-Teach	Co-Teach	Co-Teach

Figure 18
Gifted service delivery models.

2016–2017

Recommended Gifted Service Delivery (Grouping Models)

Core-Plus Science	Resource / Support Facilitation	Resource / Support Facilitation	Resource / Support Facilitation	Resource / Support Facilitation	Resource / Support Facilitation	Resource / Support Facilitation	Resource / Support Facilitation	Resource / Support Facilitation	Resource / Support Facilitation	Resource / Support Facilitation
Core AND Core-Plus Social Studies	Resource / Co-Teach	Resource / Co-Teach	Resource / Co-Teach	Resource / Co-Teach	Resource / Co-Teach	Resource / Co-Teach	Resource / Co-Teach	Resource / Co-Teach	Resource / Co-Teach	Resource / Co-Teach
RtI/M TSS for Gifted	Resource / Support Facilitation	Resource / Support Facilitation	Resource / Support Facilitation	Resource / Support Facilitation	Resource / Support Facilitation	Resource / Support Facilitation	Resource / Support Facilitation	Resource / Support Facilitation	Resource / Support Facilitation	Resource / Support Facilitation

Reminders

Carefully consider all factors when selecting service options and service delivery models including the learning strengths and needs of the gifted students, number of gifted teacher units, number of gifted students in the grade-level group, level of training of the gifted teachers, and class space available. Matrix colors represent the recommended delivery models (groupings) for service options based upon units allocated: Red (NOT recommended); Yellow (Proced with caution); Green (Recommended). Refer to the 2016–2017 Elementary Gifted Service Guidelines for detailed descriptions of service options.

Figure 18. *Continued.*

gram over the course of the past decade, it is evident that key drivers for change have included state DOE rules, advanced technologies, new research in gifted education, ongoing targeted professional development, and general education initiatives.

DEPARTMENT OF EDUCATION RULES AS A DRIVER OF CHANGE

As the state has a mandate for gifted identification and services and provides partial funding for gifted programs through the state's Exceptional Student Education Guaranteed Allocation, the district is subject to state audits of the gifted program, as funding is collected to support gifted programs. Regular full-time equivalent (FTE) audits are implemented by the state to assure funding for gifted program services for individual gifted students is in alignment with identification criteria and EP requirements. The state DOE has also actively monitored gifted identification in districts. Until 2007, the state DOE LEA Profile included gifted in the annual report. Information reported in the profile included not only the total number of identified gifted students but also demographic data disaggregated according to SES, ELL status, and ethnicity. Additionally, some districts were selected by the DOE for further monitoring regarding gifted identification. The target district was among the districts selected for additional monitoring, and as result, semiannual reports were required to be submitted detailing district initiatives to target and remedy underrepresentation in gifted programs. Also, prior to 2006, the state DOE periodically selected districts for compliance audits whereby the state would not only review student records, but also interview school personnel at select schools to ascertain compliance with gifted service requirements. A compliance audit in the district was done in 2005 with findings that guided the direction of the gifted program in subsequent years. Specifically, compliance audit findings indicated there was little evidence of gifted service beyond math and science, and differentiation of gifted instruction in classes was not evident. Addressing these findings became a key driver of the direction and initiatives of the gifted program beginning during the 2005–2006 school year.

Over the past decade, the state appears to have shifted the responsibility for programming to the local districts and reduced the monitoring of district gifted programming beyond identification data collected as part of FTE reporting. Gifted data is no longer reported as part of the LEA Profile. Although the state publishes gifted standards and Florida's Plan for K–12 Gifted Education, decisions regarding what the program will look like is up to the local district. Although increased flexibility may be a positive, the need for change is often initiated by the identification of what is relative to what should be. An external report, even when unfavorable, may be the spark that ignites positive change.

When the FDOE released Florida's Plan for K–12 Gifted Education, the external document provided the compelling *why* for the need to reexamine and change some gifted practices within district schools. Goal II within Florida's Plan specifies, "Programs for students who are gifted encompass instructional and related services that provide significant adaptations in curriculum, methodology, materials, equipment, and/or the learning environment," with specific references to Rule 6A-6.0311, FAC. Although my goals and initiatives as the district gifted coordinator had been aligned with the goals of the Florida Plan since 2005, the existence of an external document from FDOE provided the muscle needed to move forward with improving gifted practices in elementary schools throughout the district. No longer could resistors to change attribute efforts to change to a single individual (the gifted coordinator); rather, the state was requiring change.

TECHNOLOGY AS A DRIVER OF CHANGE

Since the mid-1990s, much of the focus of the gifted program had been on identification of students from underrepresented groups. In 2002, the state refined who may be considered a member of an underrepresented group as those who are Limited English Proficient (LEP) or from a low-socioeconomic status family. Gifted teachers in elementary schools were charged with finding these students in their schools, yet were provided little guidance and no specific tools to do so. Beginning in 2005 with the district's provision of the electronic instructional planning tool (IPT), gifted teachers and other school personnel were provided with specific strategies for targeting underrepresented groups and empowered to use data to find and serve these students. With purposeful, targeted identification strategies, over the past 10 years, schools throughout the district have both increased the number of gifted students who are eligible to receive program services and increased equity in their gifted program to include more students from low-SES and ELL populations. By utilizing the IPT, schools can clearly see identification gaps and intentionally target their identification efforts so that their gifted population closely mirrors the school's population with regard to ethnicity, ELL category, SES, and gender.

Improved technology has been essential for examining and understanding identification practices across the district's many schools. In mid-2009, a small but significant change occurred that required schools to report how a student qualified as gifted, whether under Plan A or Plan B. Prior to this time, the individual student's file maintained at the school included how a student was identified; however, plan-type data were not collected or reported to the district. Without these data, districts were unable to accurately determine or report the number of students found eligible as gifted under their state-approved alternate plan for identification of low-SES and ELL gifted students. Consequently, the state could not determine whether a district's Plan B was successful in increasing the number of low-SES and ELL students in the gifted program because it could not be ascertained which plan had been used to identify the students. In July 2009, a new data-field was required that captured the plan-type at the time of gifted eligibility determination.

In 2016, after 8 years of collecting plan-type data, sufficient data are now available for analysis, although they still exclude the data for any K–4 student who was found eligible as gifted from 2004 to 2008, prior to the plan-type requirement. Analysis of district identification data by plan-type reveals that at the start of the 2016 academic year, 34% of the district's K–12 gifted students are from state-defined underrepresented populations and were found eligible as gifted under the district's alternate identification plan, Plan B. The district's identification plan is clearly effective in identifying gifted students who are ELLs or from a low-SES family.

Technological advances have also impacted service opportunities for gifted students. Beginning in 2013, the district added a gifted-virtual service model for elementary gifted students. With the gifted-virtual model, students can receive gifted services through a virtual course in ELA, math, science, or social studies taught by a gifted teacher at the district's Virtual School. Gifted students attending schools throughout the district may receive gifted services from a single gifted teacher in an online course. The gifted-virtual model has allowed a cost-effective way to expand gifted services in schools with a gifted teacher on staff and provide gifted services to students in schools with a vacancy in their school's gifted teacher position.

ONGOING TARGETED PROFESSIONAL DEVELOPMENT AS A DRIVER OF CHANGE

Quality, ongoing professional development (PD) is a priority of the district gifted department. Professional development experiences are available for new and experienced gifted teachers through both workshops and distance learning options. Among the PD opportunities are the state's required gifted endorsement courses, multiple workshops designed to train teachers in implementing curriculum options that are part of the district Gifted Plan, an annual day-long Gifted Training Day for elementary gifted teachers, monthly online professional learning communities (PLCs), and self-paced, prerecorded online training. As the goal of all PD is to change teachers' classroom practices to result in improved student learning outcomes, the approach to PD provided by the district gifted department begins with looking at the *why* for the specific strategies or approaches. Through intentionally designed PD that includes *why*, *how*, and *what*, teachers are prepared with the will, the skill, and resources to successfully implement the strategies and positively impact gifted learners.

Within Florida, teachers who serve gifted students are required to earn the gifted endorsement by completing five courses in gifted education. Teachers may take the endorsement courses through an accredited university (15 semester hours) or through a district's FDOE-approved add-on program. In the target district, the five endorsement courses, each the equivalent of 60 in-service hours, are available to teachers at no charge. Since 2005, between 13 and 25 courses have been offered annually with an average of 30 teachers completing each course. Since 2000, the district has offered the endorsement courses via a distance learning format. The 7-week online courses are facilitated by instructors with a master's degree (or higher), experience as a teacher of gifted students, and training as an online instructor. The courses include a blend of individual learning activities, collaborative opportunities, and facilitated learning experiences. Prior to 2011, the district also offered the endorsement courses in a "live" format; however, as more teachers preferred the online format, the live-course option was discontinued. The courses are built and maintained by the Supervisor of Gifted. In 2006, a formal evaluation of the online endorsement program supported the effectiveness of the online program in achieving the objectives of the endorsement program. A cost-analysis of the online endorsement courses supports the distance-learning program as a cost-effective PD option.

To support the curricular options included within the district Gifted Plan, workshops are offered during the summer for teachers of gifted students. Although priority for enrollment is for gifted teachers, general education teachers may attend on a space-available basis. The goal of each workshop is to provide teachers with knowledge and understanding of specific instructional strategies for each of the K–5 gifted design options included in the Elementary Gifted Guidelines. Additionally, teachers who complete training are provided with the resource materials to implement the strategies within their classrooms. Training follow-up activities include online support through prerecorded webinars, collaborative lesson planning, and distance coaching. Workshops vary in length from 3–9 hours and are facilitated by instructors who have successfully implemented the strategies within their own gifted classrooms and have gone through a train-the-trainer program within the district and/or attended training at Confratute at the University of Connecticut.

Workshop titles and training focuses include:

- **Schoolwide Enrichment Model Reading Framework (SEM-R; 9 hours):** The training prepares teachers to serve as facilitators for the Schoolwide Enrichment Model Reading Framework, a research-based approach to reading instruction developed at The National Research Center on the Gifted and Talented at the University of Connecticut. Research indicates that use of the SEM-R model increases reading comprehension and oral fluency and improves attitudes toward reading.
- **Minds-On Projects: Project-Based Learning for Gifted Students (6 hours):** Teachers learn how to use project-based learning to take learning beyond the core standards and empower application of student learning. Teachers will learn strategies for creating and implementing cross-curricular projects to motivate learners to engage in relevant and rigorous learning.

- **Think Data: Cool Tools for Inquiry (3 hours):** Teachers learn to spark student inquiry and initiate real-world problem solving using data collection instruments.
- **Independent Investigations Model for Research (6 hours):** Teachers learn to facilitate students in doing real-world research using the 7-step IIM process. Included are strategies for turning existing curriculum units into research units that empower students to become successful researchers.
- **Introduction to Kaplan's Depth and Complexity Model (6 hours):** Teachers receive tools and learn strategies for using Kaplan's model to differentiate core content for gifted learners using the elements of depth and complexity.

Annual training for all elementary gifted teachers includes an Elementary Gifted Training Day and monthly online PLCs. Elementary gifted teachers are released from their classrooms in early August for a full day of training focused on gifted strategies and innovative instructional practices. The content of the training is designed to build upon previous training. During the training, teachers collaborate with their peers and develop a plan for integrating the strategies into their classroom practices during the upcoming academic year. Follow-up support occurs throughout the year as topics are revisited during the monthly online PLCs and peers share examples of their classroom practices. Sample training topics have included: Empowering Gifted Learners: Passion, Persistence, and Personalization Through Research-Supported Strategies; Joyful Teaching and Learning in the Gifted Classroom; The Common Core State Standards and Gifted: The Creativity Connection; and Empowering Gifted Students Through Action Research.

As a strategy for providing embedded ongoing training, monthly online PLCs are held on the first Wednesday of each month. During the hour-long sessions facilitated by the gifted supervisor, teachers receive important updates and share instructional strategies and teaching tools to support current gifted initiatives. The session also highlights one or more teachers who share their innovative practices on camera and field questions from the teachers in attendance. Handouts to support the session are available for download by participants. Typically, more than 100 teachers attend the PLC each month. The interactive sessions use the web-based Adobe Connect platform that allows teachers to log in from their classrooms or remotely via the Adobe Connect AP. All sessions are recorded for future viewing by teachers unable to attend the PLC and others who wish to review the session. The online PLCs provide up to 10 hours of collaborative training and support for teachers each year.

Additional self-paced training on gifted strategies and topics is available for teachers on the district's intranet. Some topics of self-paced training include: Socratic Questioning, Implementing the Schoolwide Enrichment Model Reading Framework (SEM-R), Advancing Mathematics Performance (AMP), and Advancing

Mathematics Performance 2 (AMP2). Self-paced training supports the professional development of new and experienced teachers in expanding their knowledge and skills in gifted instructional practices.

RESEARCH AS A DRIVER OF CHANGE

Because research into best practices in gifted education is essential as the foundation for decisions regarding directions for the gifted program, solutions were sought to address the needs of the district regarding identification and services beyond the walls of the district. The district actively sought information from individuals conducting research at universities with respected gifted programs and those involved in Javits Grant-funded initiatives. Research findings have led to changes in district policy and practices.

Like other districts nationwide, the district continues to strive for equity in gifted identification. Continual review of recent research into successful practices in identification has been ongoing, and the district's identification plan has been modified as new findings have emerged. As a result of a research initiative with the University of South Florida, screening practices for potential gifted students were realigned, leading to an increase in the number of students being referred for a gifted evaluation.

Due to findings from a FDOE compliance audit in 2005, it was essential to increase services for gifted elementary students to include services in reading. Around this time, research was being conducted at The National Research Center for Gifted and Talented in the SEM-R. After attending a presentation by Dr. Sally Reis at the 2005 NAGC Annual Conference, the district gifted coordinator recognized the potential of SEM-R to address the needs of gifted students in reading and actively worked to bring SEM-R to the district. The evaluation of a pilot of SEM-R in a group of six district schools during 2006 resulted in recommendations for district-wide use of the model for gifted students. SEM-R is now a key differentiation strategy included in the district's Gifted Guidelines.

Intentionally connecting with researchers at gifted conferences has been invaluable to the district. All elements of the district Gifted Plan, the Identification Plan, the ACCEL Plan, and the Gifted Guidelines have been influenced by researchers in gifted education. Presentations by researchers at the annual NAGC convention and the University of Connecticut's Confratute have influenced the development of the approaches included in the district's Gifted Plan. The district's full-time gifted program at the Center for Gifted Studies is modeled on the Renzulli Academy in Hartford, CT, and incorporates curriculum approaches and resources developed through research at the University of Connecticut.

GENERAL EDUCATION INITIATIVES AS A DRIVER OF CHANGE

Within the district, gifted education has been intentionally approached as part of the continuum of educational opportunities for students rather than as a stand-alone program. When gifted education initiatives are perceived as providing opportunities that will positively impact academic outcomes for students throughout the district, the initiatives gain buy-in from all stakeholders.

As gifted strategies are often viewed as good for increasing the achievement of all students, professional development in gifted education for general education teachers has been a strategy that has improved outcomes for gifted students who receive only part-time gifted services. Including general education teachers from both public and private schools in gifted training has been a strategy for tapping into Title II professional development funding and has resulted in an increase in both gifted educators and general education teachers who are better prepared to address the learning needs of gifted students.

When the Response to Intervention (RtI) movement began in 2008 and RtI was specifically named by the state DOE as applicable to all students, including those identified as gifted, the district's gifted coordinator recognized an opportunity to shift additional focus to the needs of gifted students. By promoting an RtI approach and providing training for general education teachers in gifted strategies, we have significantly increased the number of teachers within the district with training in specific strategies for differentiation with gifted students. With the stringent class-size requirements legislated in Florida beginning in 2010, it was necessary to increasingly take an inclusive approach to gifted services. Rather than gifted education as a separate one-size-fits-all program with students removed from the general education classroom, gifted services options became more aligned with the goals of general education while allowing for enrichment and acceleration for individual gifted student needs.

The Every Student Succeeds Act (ESSA) provides a future opportunity to further influence general education practices. With the prospect of the achievement of advanced students being included in school and district grades provided by the state as part of ESSA, future opportunities exist to focus on the needs of gifted students and the necessity of training for general education teachers in approaches and strategies to meet their advanced learning needs.

LEADERSHIP AS A DRIVER OF CHANGE

In the words of Fela Durotoye, "No nation has ever been able to transform by chance. It is always a deliberate and conscious process." For a district's gifted program, leadership is a key element for driving deliberate and conscience transformation. In many districts, the gifted coordinator has little positional power, so "top-down" change is not an effective model for change. Lasting change comes from inspiring and activating individuals at all levels within the organization according to a common vision and mission, recognizing that real change doesn't happen quickly, easily, or haphazardly.

There are numerous research-supported models for leadership and change. Any district gifted coordinator seeking to create positive and sustainable change within his or her district is encouraged to explore the literature on leadership to identify a model that makes sense within the specific district and circumstances.

Figure 19 illustrates the interaction of elements necessary for creating positive, sustainable change within an organization. True change occurs at the intersection of the will, skill, resources, and environment of the organization. The role of the leader is to mobilize the organization to bring together the necessary elements to create change.

Will includes the commitment and mindset of individuals involved in the change. *Skill* is essential on the part of those who will implement the change to be prepared with the necessary competence to carry out the change. *Resources* include both the human and material resources necessary to implement the change with fidelity. The *environment* consists of the overall structure within which the entity exists.

For change within a district's gifted program, the *will* must consider all stakeholders: teachers, school administrators, district administrators, parents, and community members. Without the support of the stakeholders, a change effort may be derailed by those who have an alternate view of the future. Establishing a compelling why for the change for creating a better future for the district's gifted students as an outcome of the new Gifted Plan was key to fostering the *will* to continue with the change effort even when obstacles to change were encountered.

To move forward with the new Gifted Plan within schools required the intentional development of *skill* through PD. As the district moved from the pre-2010 model of a single schedule-driven model of services to the new model of student-centered gifted services, it was essential that gifted teachers were provided with effective ongoing PD to support implementation of the new gifted service options.

Sufficient human and material *resources* were essential to implement the new gifted service options. As it was recognized that no additional human resources would be added to support the change, it was important to consider time as a resource and reexamine the use of teachers' time as it was distributed across the day to best address the learning needs of gifted students. Material resources were necessary to support the new Core-Plus learning options. To provide resource to support options such as SEM-R, IIM, and Think Data, teachers attending PD supported by Title II funding received necessary materials to implement the models.

Within a school district, the *environment* includes both external and internal factors and is impacted by political, social, and economic forces. The role of the

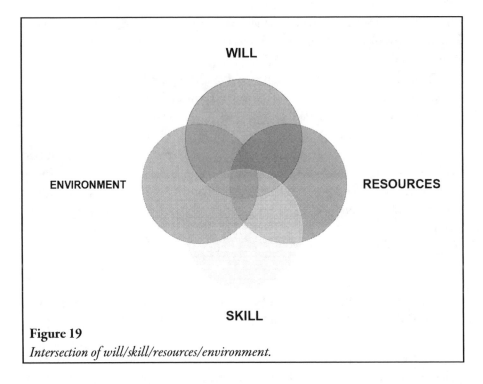

WILL

ENVIRONMENT

RESOURCES

SKILL

Figure 19
Intersection of will/skill/resources/environment.

leader is to understand the current environment and create the conditions within the environment that will be favorable to the intended change. Two major environmental factors impacting the speed and direction of the implementation of the district Gifted Plan included the Common Core State Standards initiative and the accountability movement. Implementation of the district Gifted Plan was not linear, rather a series of stops and starts as environmental factors were considered.

A good idea alone does not result in positive, sustainable change. The leader's role is to bring together the *will*, *skill*, *resources*, and *environment* leading to the intended change and to continue to monitor and address each of these elements into the future to assure that the positive change is established within the minds, policies, and practices of the district.

RECOGNIZING AND ACTING ON OPPORTUNITIES

According to author Malcolm Gladwell, successful individuals are those who recognize and act upon opportunities. Successful gifted coordinators are those who keep their eyes open for initiatives with direct or indirect connections to gifted education, and use these as opportunities to move their ideas and goals forward in efforts to improve gifted programming. Successful gifted coordinators seek opportunities to learn from experts in the field, connect gifted initiatives to existing district initiatives, and continually seek to inspire educators who directly and indirectly impact gifted students. As little dedicated funding is typically available to support gifted programs, it is essential to identify those whose goals are aligned with the gifted program and figure out how to utilize their financial resources to both drive their own program initiatives and positively impact the gifted program.

With this approach in mind, there have been a number of opportunities identified and used to move the goals of the district's gifted program forward, including (note that I have included dates for some of the past projects for clarification):

- **Magnet Schools Gifted and Talent Development Academy Programs Initiative (2005–2007):** Provided an impetus for exploring the Schoolwide Enrichment Model as an approach aligned with the district's gifted vision and mission.

- **Schoolwide Enrichment Model Reading (SEM-R) framework pilot (2006–2007):** Demonstrated the success of SEM-R in raising student achievement in reading, thus providing a solution to the district's need for a service option in ELA. The district currently includes SEM-R as a service option for elementary gifted students. Training is available annually for gifted teachers provided by a cadre of trainers who have attended Confratute and were part of a district train-the-trainer initiative. More information about SEM-R is available at http://gifted.uconn.edu/semr-about.

- **Title I-funded pilot of Mentoring Mathematical Minds (M^3) curriculum (2006–2007):** Provided an engaging standards-based alternative to the district's one-size-fits-all mathematics curriculum. For an overview of M^3, visit http://gifted.uconn.edu/projectm3.

- **Districtwide High-End RtI Model Schools Project (2009–2010):** Increased opportunities for gifted and high-achieving students in nine district schools through the development and provision of teacher training and curriculum resources to address gifted learning needs in reading, mathematics, research, project-based learning, and technology. Funded as part of a district stimulus-project, lessons learned from the RtI Model Schools Project informed the development of the district's current Gifted Plan.

- **Title II-funded gifted professional development (beginning 2010):** Title II staff development funds were utilized to provide training and training materials for gifted and general education teachers. Annual training included: Gifted Endorsement Training, required by the state for teachers who serve gifted students and subject-specific differentiation training including Schoolwide Enrichment Model Reading (SEM-R), Independent Investigations Method (IIM), project-based learning, and Think Data.

- **Other professional development (beginning 2010):**

- Annual elementary gifted training day: Elementary gifted teachers are released from their classrooms for collaborative professional development related to the district's gifted initiatives for a full day during each academic year.
- Monthly online PLCs: Gifted teachers throughout the district log in to monthly one-hour online PD sessions as ongoing training and support for district gifted initiatives. Using the interactive Adobe Connect platform, teachers attending the PLC collaborate to share best practices in gifted education. Each session is recorded and recording links are posted in the gifted conference within the district's intranet.

- **Aligning gifted services committee (2009–2010):** This was an intentionally planned process for implementing research-supported student-centered gifted services in multiple subjects across all district elementary schools. As a result of driving forces behind change in gifted education approaches including class-size requirements, compliance with the FDOE requirements, and the RtI approach, a stakeholder group was convened to examine district gifted data, survey results, current research in gifted education, and lessons learned from the High-End RtI Model Schools Project. The group included school administrators, gifted teachers, exceptional student education (ESE) personnel, district administrators, parents, and a representative from the local gifted advocacy council. The group provided feedback and recommendations for the development of the district Gifted Guidelines.
- **District Elementary Gifted Service Guidelines (initiated 2010):** Gifted services guidelines and support documents are provided to elementary gifted teachers and administrators districtwide to increase implementation of research-supported approaches within gifted classrooms and promote uniformity of learning opportunities between all district elementary schools. The guidelines are updated annually to align with other district initiatives and approaches.
- **Enrichment Summer Scholars Program (ESSP; initiated 2011):** Fee-based enrichment program for gifted and high-achieving students in grades 3, 4, and 5, providing challenging technology-infused learning opportunities beyond the school year through a problem-based learning approach. More than 1,000 students attend the ESSP program each summer. Forty gifted teachers, who serve as ESSP instructors, receive training and support for innovative technology-infused instructional practices.
- **State ACCEL legislation and District ACCEL Plan for whole-grade and single-subject acceleration:** Development of a research-supported districtwide plan for acceleration through grade-skipping or single subject acceleration for students in grades K–5 whose learning needs extend

beyond curriculum differentiation and enrichment. The district's ACCEL Plan is part of the district's Student Progression Plan as a requirement of the FDOE.

- **FDOE Challenge Grant Project: Advancing Mathematical Performance (AMP; 2014–2015):** Grant-funded project impacting approximately 600 second-grade gifted students and 40 gifted teachers through interactive online professional development and coaching for an advanced mathematics curriculum aligned with state standards resulting in increased performance of students in mathematics. Grant outcomes included the development of the AMP PD package including prerecorded training sessions, PowerPoint slides, training notes, teacher handouts, and other resources, which can be found at https://drive.google.com/drive/folders/0B9zGH1900z0tOE5RdnI5Vlc2aHc.

- **FDOE Challenge Grant Project: Advancing Mathematical Performance 2 (2015–2016):** Grant-funded project impacting approximately 785 third-grade gifted students and 50 gifted teachers with interactive online professional development and coaching for a standards-aligned mathematics curriculum resulting in improved teaching practices and improved content knowledge of students. This can be found at https://drive.google.com/drive/folders/0B9zGH1900z0tVG55ZU8zSzdkdmM.

- **Project SPARK (Scaffolding Potential Among At-Risk Kids):** A multi-year Title I-funded initiative to address underrepresentation in gifted programs in high-poverty schools. Currently being implemented within eight Title I schools, SPARK activities include gifted teacher training, the provision of specific learning experiences focused on vocabulary development, creative, and critical thinking and growth mindset, and parent involvement activities. SPARK gifted teachers involved classroom teachers in the use of a specific observation protocol to increase the number of students who are screened and referred as potentially gifted.

- **Center for Gifted Studies (opened August 2016):** Full-time gifted services infusing all elements of the district Gifted Guidelines provided for approximately 200 gifted students in grades 1–5 as a "Choice" option within an existing district elementary school. The Center for Gifted Services is modeled after the Renzulli Academy in Hartford, CT.

FUTURE DIRECTIONS

So much attention within a school district must be on supporting struggling students and closing the achievement gap that little energy and resources are left among district personnel and school-level administrators for attending to improving gifted programming. With more than a decade of focus on improving the educational experience of gifted students through research-supported strategies, the district has built capacity for supporting quality gifted services through ongoing professional development and a collective mindset supportive of gifted education.

The district's gifted program is an extension of the standards-based general education program, with additional layers of support and challenge appropriate for gifted students. As our nation shifts away from a deficit model of education focused only on raising the achievement of struggling students and toward a direction of addressing the needs of all students, the approaches of gifted education hold promise for positively impacting additional students. It is anticipated that with the roll-out of ESSA, the perceived value of gifted education will increase, resulting in the desire to spread gifted education philosophy and pedagogy to additional students to engage, enrich, and empower student achievement.

CHAPTER 8

SMALL RURAL DISRICT IN MONTANA

Tamara J. Fisher

GIFTED EDUCATION IN MONTANA

Montana's Constitution, written during our 1972 Constitutional Convention, calls for "a system of education which will develop the full educational potential of each person. Equality of educational opportunity is guaranteed to each person of the state" [Article X, Section 1(1)]. Laws supporting the goals of our 1972 Constitution were written in the following years, including the adoption in 1979 of Montana Code Annotated Title 20 Chapter 7 Part 9: Gifted and Talented Children (MCA 20-7-901 through MCA 20-7-904), which mandates the identification of gifted and talented children and the development of programs to serve them (MCA 20-7-902).

The state law regarding services for gifted children also provides for a state funding mechanism (MCA 20-7-903) through which school districts submit program proposals (i.e., District Plans) to the state superintendent in order to receive those funds (MCA 20-7-904). Additionally, MCA 20-2-121(10) says that "the board of public education shall adopt policies for the conduct of programs for gifted and talented children"—one of only 12 board of public education powers and duties listed.

Montana's gifted and talented association, AGATE, was established at about the same time, on February 28, 1980, with 62 individuals from across our vast state signing AGATE's charter document. Also in 1980, the Polson School District hired its first Gifted and Talented Specialist, Carolyn Heinz, who held the position for 15 years. The district superintendent at the time was forward thinking and believed in keeping pace with new changes in education, including Montana's new law regarding gifted students. Clearly this was a time of important steps being taken for gifted education in Montana, and my district chose to be a part of that movement.

GIFTED EDUCATION IN POLSON

In the early years, Polson's gifted program grew by one grade level each year, eventually becoming K–6, with inclusion and thinking skills for K–1 and pull-out groups for 2–6. Carolyn's time with the pull-out students (4 hours per week in two 2-hour blocks) focused on thinking skills and social-emotional needs of the gifted.

When the district wanted Carolyn to either expand to K–12 or switch to 7–12, she opted instead to return to the regular classroom, and I was hired a year later to fill the now K–12 Gifted Education Specialist position in our district. Between Carolyn and I, the Polson School District holds a sadly rare distinction in Montana of 35+ years of consistent gifted programming. Although mandated to identify and provide services for these students, most Montana schools—nearly all of which are rural—do not, and there is no consequence for them for not doing so.

There are many reasons why most districts do not provide these services, including lack of funding and other resources, lack of training in gifted education (and thus lack of teachers with expertise in the area), and quite probably a lack of understanding about the needs of gifted students (stemming from the lack of training, perhaps?). I suppose some rural districts are also small enough that they believe they can't possibly have any gifted students in their slim ranks.

The Polson School District is located on the Flathead Indian Reservation in northwestern Montana, and for the last 25 years has had a student population of roughly 1,600 students K–12. More than half of our students qualify for free and reduced lunch and around a third of them are Native American or of Native descent. Some of our students live in town, some live on ranches and farms in the areas surrounding town, some live on Tribal lands, some are homeless and bounce between relatives' couches, and others live in large, beautiful homes on the shores of Flathead Lake. The students in our gifted program come from all of these various backgrounds. Our schools are primary (K–1), intermediate (2–4), middle (5–8), and high school (9–12), so all of our 1,600 students are integrated for their full schooling experience. The only other (nonpublic) schooling options within a 40-mile radius are homeschooling and a small K–12 Christian academy.

Our District Gifted Education Plan

The impetus for creating our District Plan was so that our district could apply to receive a portion of the state gifted and talented funds. These funds are allocated as grants to districts that apply for them and have a qualifying Gifted Program Plan as well as a qualifying use for the funds. In the early years of my job, I didn't apply for the state grant funds ($200,000 for all of Montana's approximately 900 schools and 450 school districts) as it seemed like a lot of time and effort for a few hundred dollars when I already had a reasonably sufficient budget supplied by my district.

As the needs of my gifted students expanded along with my realization of the importance of having documents in place to support the program, I came to see the grant process and its supporting documentation as valuable beyond just the application process. While attending a gifted conference in Idaho one summer (http://www.edufest.org), I had the opportunity to work closely with the man who, at the time, was Idaho's Gifted Specialist at its State Department of Education. He guided me through the writing of a philosophy statement, definition, goals and objectives, etc. When it came time to apply for Montana's state GT grant the next school year, I was ready with a document that outlined our program and indicated its mission and purpose.

Our program's guiding philosophy states,

> The Polson School District recognizes that each student brings to our schools unique intellectual and creative abilities and that the abilities of some students exceed those of the general population. We are dedicated to making the necessary accommodations for these exceptional students.

Goals for the program include:

> To exercise the mind at the upper reasoning levels, to provide enrichment and pull-out opportunities for gifted students to explore and strengthen their unique talents and interests, to provide opportunities for acceptance of the unique qualities and unusual academic passions of gifted students, to aid in developing each child's strengths to their greater potential, to provide assistance to teachers for making in-classroom accommodations for gifted students, and to aid in meeting the unique emotional and social needs of gifted students.

Our District Gifted Education Plan does not cover content areas (other than mentioning advanced coursework available in content areas) because Montana does not require gifted programs to be content-area-based. Rather, our program has always focused on thinking skills and social-emotional needs of the gifted in combination with seeking and advocating for challenging accommodations in the regular classroom (whether those accommodations are classroom-based differentiation, acceleration options, or within-grade-level advanced course options).

As often happens in small and rural settings, we as individuals wear many hats and take on many roles. I am both teacher and coordinator for our gifted program in all four of our schools, K–12. This means that I am responsible for all identified gifted students K–12: I am responsible for the screening and identification of all students; I am responsible for teaching all of the gifted classes and all of the GT pull-out groups; I am responsible for collaborating with teachers and providing them with professional development so gifted students' needs are met in the regular classroom; I am responsible for parent contact and education; and I am responsible for the drafting and implementation of all gifted program documents, including our District Plan. In larger districts, these roles are split among and/or shared among a handful or more people.

So, although our District Plan has been reviewed by district-level administrators and state-level representatives, it was not a document created in collaboration with a team of stakeholders. As the "superintendent's designee" in district policy, I'm the one tasked with the job of fulfilling this and other aspects of bringing our gifted program to life. Montana does not require that a district-level team of stakeholders create the plans, but does allow for the request of "assistance from the staff of the [state] superintendent in formulating program proposals" [MCA 20-7-904(2)], and this assistance was utilized as our District Plan was revised over the years.

IDENTIFICATION

Identification of gifted students in our district consists of using multiple measures to uncover evidence that a given child is in need of more than what the regular classroom can provide. Practically speaking, this means utilizing formalized classroom teacher observations (often through the Kingore Observation Inventory), formal observations by the Gifted Education Specialist, achievement data, and cognitive ability assessments (primarily the Cognitive Abilities Test [CogAT]). The identification process begins the first month of kindergarten with inclusion thinking-skills-based activities by the Gifted Education Specialist in these classrooms. This process continues through first grade, and then all first graders are given the CogAT in the spring (any kindergartener or first grader could be tested sooner than this if needed and/or if there is a recommendation by anyone to do so). Above first grade, any referred students are observed in the classroom by the Gifted Education Specialist, then tested using the CogAT, and input is sought from all of that student's previous teachers as well as the student's achievement data.

This comprehensive collection of information is used by the Gifted Education Specialist together with any of the child's teachers to make a decision on placement. Essentially, our identification window is always open. A child can be referred at any time during any grade level by any person. Most referrals come from teachers, but some come from parents, some from already-identified students who see the signs in their classmates or new students, and some from self-referrals. I've even had referrals from the school nurse and the public librarian.

SERVICES

In grades K–6, our gifted program provides thinking skills and creativity opportunities that are bolstered with a strong focus on the social and emotional needs of the gifted. Identified K–5 students meet with the Gifted Education Specialist once a week for 45 minutes, which in the short-term doesn't seem like much contact time, but is strengthened by the long-term continuity that the Gifted Education Specialist has with the identified students over multiple consecutive years. That long-term continuity is one advantage of being the Gifted Education Specialist in a small, rural district. Activities in the K–5 pull-out groups range from discussions on social-emotional needs, to building thinking skills such as strategy and logic, to challenging tasks that help the students develop a tolerance for frustration and healthy skills for persisting and overcoming. These "struggle strategies" are spiraled into many conversations over the years for subtle yet consistent effect.

Gifted education is incorporated into general education curriculum and programming decisions by way of classroom-based differentiation, advanced course options, advanced intervention groups, subject and/or whole-grade acceleration, early entrance, dual enrollment, K–1 inclusion activities, and collaboration between the Gifted Education Specialist and classroom teachers. Many of these options also impact above-average and other advanced learners in addition to the gifted students.

Gifted students in grades 6–12 have the opportunity to meet with the Gifted Education Specialist almost every day through a scheduled class called Advanced Studies. Students pursue self-selected, self-directed independent learning projects on topics of their own choosing. Class discussions on social-emotional needs are also incorporated into the class.

Based on Renzulli's Type III's in the Enrichment Triad Model, the third stage of Feldhusen's Purdue Three-Stage Model, and the goal of Betts's Autonomous

Learner Model (the creation of lifelong autonomous learners), Advanced Studies is an open-ended, passion-based opportunity for gifted students. Whereas some project-based learning is centered around content-area topics or teacher-directed projects, our Advanced Studies class is open to topics and projects within the wide latitude of three basic criteria: The topic or project must be legal, it must be appropriate to school, and it must have academic value. Additionally, this curricular option is highly student-centered. Independent learning projects involve student-selected topics of personal interest, student-created plans of action for pursuing that topic, student choice in the final product, and student-led initiative in putting the product forth to an authentic audience. The key ingredient in all of this is the student.

In these projects, the students have a blank slate of time, space, and even a little bit of money from the GT state grant to find their passion and take it as far as they want. One student who began learning about mushing in eighth grade continued the pursuit through the acquisition of three dogs given to her, then six more she inherited, and then four more she purchased with her 4-H money. In ninth grade, she hand-built a sled and competed in Montana's Race to the Sky. Her sophomore year, she will compete in at least three races and she is taking an online Veterinary Science course with an additional focus on canine nutrition. And her dog team now includes five puppies unexpectedly conceived at last year's Race to the Sky! Needless to say, she orders dog food by the pallet.

Another student created his own web design business, including filing the legal paperwork with the State of Montana for the official designation of his business. Students have designed apps and learned programming languages, written and self-published books, designed and printed snowboard skins, designed and built an electric guitar from scratch, composed music, designed and built an operating system using a Linux kernel, and, in one case, literally learned how to fly. Gifted learners often have early and unusual interests, talents, and ambitions (such as studying coccidiosis, trying to determine a formula for time travel, training for a Spartan Race, magnetic levitation, etc.), and an independent learning project gives them the window of opportunity to pursue those aspirations within school.

STUDENT REFLECTIONS

What do gifted learners gain from self-selected, self-directed independent learning projects? Self-reliance, self-motivation, and self-efficacy, among other things. They have said:
- "The most important thing I learned is not to underestimate challenges because I will never succeed if I downplay what I must face" (eighth grader).

- "I learned that if I make a commitment, I must live up to it. I learned that sometimes ideas and plans change, and just because something isn't perfect doesn't mean it isn't GOOD" (ninth grader).

- "I now think with extreme creativity, and I'm way better at using critical and flexible thinking. I'm also much wiser than I was and more responsible. I learned to not procrastinate and to never, ever, EVER give up. I learned how to be independent, hard-working, and responsible. This is all important because in the real world, you have to learn to do things yourself" (10th grader).

- "I learned that I was underestimating myself. When I discovered the things I was capable of, I was so surprised! That inspired me to do more, which I am grateful for" (seventh grader).

CHANGES AND CHALLENGES

The first major change in Polson's gifted program was its expansion from K–6 to K–12 when I was hired in 1996. Our state accreditation standards do call for K–12 programming (ARM 10.55.804), so this move was in keeping with state requirements. Admittedly, it took a few years before the high school level of our program was as "filled out" as it is now.

The only other *major* change in our program came about in 2010 when our district adopted the use of cognitive ability assessments that I, as the Gifted Education Specialist, could administer for identification purposes (rather than relying on IQ tests which could only be administered by a school psychologist). Our school psychologist had so many special education referrals that there was no time for him to do gifted education referrals, too. This meant I had been relying on any other piece of available data on a student, which frankly, at the time, wasn't much. These new cognitive assessments made it possible for me to expand the data sets used in the identification process, as well as to expand the number of students in our identification filter.

When RtI first came on the scene, I instinctively saw how it could help districts plan for accommodating the academic needs of gifted and advanced learners. I approached an authority figure in my district and offered to be a part of our district's RtI team(s) and to talk with our schools about how RtI could also be used to meet high-end learning needs. His response was, "Oh, that's not necessary. It's pretty much just a special education thing." Undeterred, I went instead to the teachers on the teams and talked with them about creating pathways for our gifted and advanced learners. They were open and agreeable, and now most of our pathways include aspects for reaching our advanced learners, too.

However, between RtI's focus on "core for all" and an interpretation by some current and former decision-makers in my district that the new Common Core State Standards meant all children had to be exposed to the same curriculum, we have—in my opinion—gone backward in meeting diverse learning needs. Whereas we used to offer within-grade-level, flexibly leveled instructional groups for math and reading in grades K–6, now all children are on the same page on the same day for the instructional core lesson and then they receive their intervention—whether for additional support or more challenge—at a different time. At least challenge groups are included as a part of this intervention time, but this new method also means that my gifted students are part of far more grade-level instruction (well below their needs) than they ever were before. Recent district-provided professional development indicates that teachers will be afforded more small-group, in-class differentiation leeway, which I see as a very positive move toward reaching our range of learners where they all are. However, it might be at the sacrifice of some or all of the within-grade-level intervention groups, particularly the challenge ones. Some support and Title I intervention groups will, of course, be maintained.

Administrative philosophy about gifted education can vary widely, and in my 20+ years of working in this position, I've experienced the indifferent, the supportive, the subtly (and not so subtly) undermining, the curious, the passionate, the wild cards, the converts, the manipulative, and the fellow warriors. There have been times (and probably still will be in the future) when I fight internally with myself about speaking up or keeping quiet (at the classroom level, the building level, and the district level). It almost feels as if I have an unwritten quota of times that I can play that card. If I speak up too much, I worry people will start to tune me out. If I speak up too little, I worry that I will miss a critical opportunity for advocacy. I have also come to find it quite illogical that doing right by my students sometimes means having to be an incorrigible employee—or that being a model employee sometimes means having to sacrifice the needs of my students. It shouldn't be that way. But it sometimes is. I can't profess to have any answers on this. These are incredibly difficult situations fraught with complexity and emotion. Sometimes I choose one way, sometimes I choose the other (depending on the circumstance). Sometimes it turns out I chose wisely, and sometimes not. Either way, it always eats me up inside, and I've had to rebuild some bridges and apologize—and yet, try again. Being the rope in a tug-of-war is stressful. Advocacy opportunities are actually abundant. But decision makers' tolerance and willingness to hear my passion on the subject of gifted learners may not be. So I tread carefully, sometimes with expertly placed steps and sometimes sinking into quicksand.

What would my advice be to other gifted specialists regarding working with this range of administrators? Nurture and support positive working relationships with them (and with school board members). They are often the final deciders, and whether or not they have some understanding of the needs of gifted learners (and therefore how those needs are impacted by their decisions) may depend on whether or not you've made or taken advantage of opportunities to educate them about those needs. Be positive. Be proactive. Be persistent. Be subtle when necessary and blunt when necessary. But above all, put in the effort—with small and big steps over time—to communicate to them who gifted learners are and what they need in school. Never assume they already understand—because, they often don't. At least not initially. It will be up to you to help them develop understanding—by the carefully chosen or self-created or sometimes-thrust-upon-you opportunities that you capitalize.

In a small or rural district it is often just you. Whereas a larger district likely has a team of gifted specialists and coordinators who can share and tag-team these advocacy needs, particularly at the district level, in a small or rural district that burden is on two shoulders: yours. Yes, parents and students and teachers can advocate. But depending on the climate in your district, you may or may not be allowed to organize them in the mission. I have been both encouraged to do so, as well as cautioned against doing so. Yes, it's confusing. But bearing the weight of this advocacy responsibility can be both grounding and empowering.

GIFTED NATIVE AMERICAN STUDENTS

Gifted Native American students are among the underrepresented subpopulations in gifted programs across the country. This is largely because most schools with high Native student populations don't even have a gifted program. It's not so much that they aren't being identified, although that can be and is a problem, but more so that they *don't even have an opportunity to be identified* because their schools typically don't have gifted programs for them to be involved in.

Montana has seven Indian Reservations, each with multiple schools, and ours is the only one of those districts to have a gifted program (although a second is in the development stage). Ensuring proportional representation of our Native students in the gifted program here is always on my mind. Steps taken in this endeavor include screening all students in grades K and 1 through multiple inclusion thinking-skills-based activities conducted by the gifted specialist, testing all students at the end of first grade (also done by the gifted specialist), utilization of a formalized observation inventory by classroom teachers (to help teachers when making referrals to focus on gifted behaviors rather than teacher-pleasing behaviors—which may or may not indicate giftedness), and providing teachers with information about characteristics of gifted Native children specific to our local tribes (as these characteristics can vary culturally among tribes). These practices have contributed to proportional representation of Native children in our gifted program. (They have also helped to increase the number of also often underrepresented low-income children—from all ethnic backgrounds—in our gifted program, although their numbers are not as close to proportional.)

Although the programming options aren't specifically unique for the identified Native children, there are aspects that I include in the hopes of contributing to their comfort level in the program. When a newly identified Native child enters the program, I find a way to casually (and privately) mention which of their siblings, cousins, aunts, etc., have also been a part of the program because this helps them know they aren't alone. When talking with students about independent learning project opportunities, I always make sure to mention culturally relevant options, and the gifted Native students often do use their independent learning project opportunities within the program to pursue such topics (e.g., beading, Native language, Tribal history, etc.). And finally, I always make sure to express to my students that being part of the gifted program isn't about being "better," but rather it's simply about having a learning difference that at times requires some accommodation and attention.

THE FUTURE OF GIFTED EDUCATION IN POLSON AND IN MONTANA

Where do I see the district heading regarding gifted programming in the future? Every year, I vacillate between confidence that my district will continue its 35+ years of consistent support for gifted education and fearing that tightening budgets will render its demise (in spite of our state mandate—clearly the state mandate isn't compelling other districts to have a program). Broader awareness statewide is contributing to more state-level conversations about gifted education, however, which will hopefully continue to keep the needs of gifted learners on the plate rather than off the menu—in my district and in other districts.

For example, the 2015 Montana Legislature called for a School Funding Commission to meet every 10 years to discuss and make proposals about school funding issues. The first School Funding Commission met in 2016 and one of the dozen or so topics that received serious examination was gifted education (thanks in part to a couple of in-the-know legislators and a handful of dedicated parent and teacher advocates of gifted education from across the state). Although the draft bill that the Commission wrote to strengthen gifted education in our state law and accreditation standards was not put forth to the legislature, a bill proposing a six-fold increase in state funding for gifted programs will be supported by the Commission and likely voted on by our 2017 legislature. New provisions in federal law, parts of the Every Student Succeeds Act, may also contribute to my district—

and all districts—being ever more likely to keep the needs of gifted and advanced learners closer to the forefront rather than on the back burner.

Professional Development

One feature of ESSA that I'm hopeful will be embraced by my state and district is new permissions to use Title II professional development funds for gifted education training. My district does send a few of us to our state gifted conference every year (http://www.mtagate.org), but teachers' professional development needs regarding gifted learners are always broader than what that once-a-year opportunity can fulfill. If I had the funds, I would love to be able to send teachers from my district to larger, regional gifted conferences, such Edufest in Idaho or the Hormel Symposium in Minnesota. Online options, such as GT Ignite and Gifted Guild, are also worthy of consideration, but once again require more funds than I currently have access to within my district GT budget, especially if I aim to reach a large number of teachers.

My district has been mostly supportive in making sure that I, as the Gifted Specialist, have received frequent and quality gifted education professional development (although some of it, such as my master's degree in gifted education, I pursued on my own). And I have at times provided professional development for my district's teachers on my own. But with four schools and 13 grade levels, there's only so much of me to go around. One way I have tried in recent years to fill the void of gifted professional development is by the creation of what I call "5 Minute GT PD," an e-mail I send approximately once or twice a month to all of the staff in my district (plus other interested individuals outside of my district), which includes high-quality information about gifted learners that they can read or watch in 5 minutes or less. I know the teachers and administrators in my district are busy people, but I also know they have a need and a desire for more information regarding gifted learners. So "5 Minute GT PD" has been one way I have threaded that needle.

Policy and Procedure

The Montana School Boards Association (MTSBA) provides districts with templates of board policies that they can then revise (within legal parameters) to fit their district. Despite the mandate in our state law and accreditation standards that schools identify and provide services for gifted students, the MTSBA template for "Recommended Policy 2166: Gifted Program" is, first of all, a *recommended* policy and not a required one as it should be, given the mandate. It also begins with the words, "*To the extent possible within the resources available . . .*" Sadly, this wording (which doesn't appear in any other policy) allows districts a loophole written directly into their policy (if they even adopt policy 2166) by which they don't have to actually identify and provide services for these students.

I serve on our district's Policy Committee, and when Policy 2166 was up for adoption (it had previously never been adopted by my district), those words were my first and primary priority to change. Most on the committee agreed to strike them from the language, but a couple of individuals in positions of power did not want to do so. The phrase "pick your battles" comes to mind. I had to give up on a couple of other parts of the policy that I wanted to see implemented or changed in order to make sure that this most egregious segment was eliminated. Of the few districts in Montana who have chosen to adopt Policy 2166, most have *not* removed this language from their policy.

STUDENT SELF-REFLECTIONS

Documented effects of the District Plan come in the form of the reflections of the gifted program provided to me by my current and former students. Perhaps most poignant is this comment:

> I was a GATE student through most of my education. For most of my childhood, it was one of the very few places I felt I fit in. I was a scrawny 120-pound fantasy nerd who was passionate about becoming an author. I lived in a town that prized athleticism and masculinity and that had little tolerance for big dreams. I was also one of the people who did very well all around in school, but I doubt I would have done so without the program. The reality is that I may not have made it through high school without the GATE program giving me an outlet. I highly doubt I would have made it out of Polson, Montana. I suspect I would be struggling with serious drug addiction. I might not be alive.

Additional student reflections:
- "I'm thankful for GT because it has given me a way to channel my energy and creativity into something healthy and productive. Without it, I wouldn't know what to put my abilities into or the best ways to do it."— Marie, sophomore

- "Without GT, I would be so ahead in my other classes that I wouldn't even come half the time. I wouldn't have half the skills I have today [in my passion area] and I wouldn't know what 'work' really is. And I would never have met people like me."—Brad, freshman
- "I'm thankful for GT because it gives me a chance to stretch myself in ways that I wouldn't ever be able to otherwise. Without the gifted program, I wouldn't still be in public school, and I might not still be alive."—Juniper, junior
- "Without the gifted program, I wouldn't be able to sort my thoughts and understand that it's okay to be unique. I am thankful for GT because it helped me to better understand my potential and it keeps me curious."—Adam, junior
- "Being a gifted kid in a small town is . . . interesting. Not many people know what 'gifted' means; they think physical skills are the only possible 'gift' and don't understand that mental 'gifts' count, too."—MRK, sophomore
- "I'm thankful for GT because it has expanded my way of thinking and has given me the resources I will need to succeed in life. Without the gifted program, I wouldn't have my future profession. Here I have the opportunity to do/study/learn about pretty much anything. It allows me to learn about things that would never be glanced at in a normal curriculum."—MRK, sophomore
- "Without the gifted program, I would never have been challenged in my academics. Never would I have pursued the 'what-ifs' in my life or encouraged myself to try without a constant fear of failure. I never would've challenged myself, and I wouldn't be the type of 'go-getter' person that I feel I am today. GT connected me with peers who had similar learning styles as I do, that otherwise I never would've considered getting acquainted with. It made me feel like I wasn't alone in my academic challenges."—Nika, senior
- "I'm thankful for GT because it gives me an opportunity to let my mind roam and fulfill its potential."—Roger, eighth grade
- "I'm thankful for GT because it's AMAZING. It gives us a chance to do things more fit for us and what we want to do. School would be much more boring and difficult to escape without GT."—Loki, sixth grade
- "Without the gifted program, I wouldn't be as creative as I am today, and I wouldn't be as motivated to try hard in school. I'm thankful for GT because elsewhere I do not have an opportunity to learn about what I want."—Odell, eighth grade
- "I'm thankful for GT because it makes me feel much better about my thinking because now I know I'm not the only one who thinks other classes are easy. Also, I like it because it's such a safe environment to share ideas and troubles. I don't think I would feel comfortable with sharing my ideas

in other classes because I feel different in that kind of environment. Also, I would feel very outnumbered by everyone else."—CJ, sixth grade

- "I am happy that we even have a gifted program because our town isn't even that big. Without the gifted program, school is depressing and boring to me because it's just repeat after repeat after repeat."—Josh, seventh grade

The district documents included online are partially state-created by the Montana School Boards Association and based off of state law and accreditation standards and partially district-created by our District's Policy Committee. The Montana School Boards Association creates templates of all policies and then districts can modify them to suit their own needs.

CHAPTER 9

MEDIUM-SIZED SUBURBAN DISTRICT IN WISCONSIN

Jane McMahon and Lori M. Mueller

DISTRICT HISTORY OF GIFTED AND TALENTED EDUCATION

Prior to 2011, Baraboo School District's gifted and talented education was virtually nonexistent. By nonexistent, I mean that the district did not have a written document to guide teachers, parents, and staff on providing necessary services. The district did not have a staff member assigned as a Gifted and Talented Coordinator. For more than a decade, an administrative assistant was responsible for collecting the identification data the district reported to the state. Every year, she would put a form in teachers' mailboxes and request that they identify students who were advanced in general intellectual ability, specific academic ability, creative thinking, artistic ability, and leadership. A mini candy bar attached to the form served as an enticement for teachers to complete this task. These were the names that were then gathered and submitted as the district's gifted and talented student population.

Despite these compliance efforts for identification, there was no consistency in numbers of students identified, who was identified, and services provided to identified students. This was a source of frustration to many who recognized the unmet needs of our advanced learners—students, parents, and teachers alike. Additionally, the district was not immune to federal legislation that dictated allocation of resources to meet the individual needs of students. With the passing of No Child Left Behind in 2001, district resources, like those in many school districts across the state and nation, were allocated in a way that primarily supported students who were not at proficiency to meet identified proficiency benchmarks by 2014. For example, district federal funds were directed to hiring full-time literacy coaches who also served as reading interventionists.

The district purchased evidence-based literacy curriculum and intervention instructional materials. Professional development funds targeted literacy and intervention efforts. The district did not specifically set aside or allocate funds for gifted and talented education.

CREATING A STRUCTURE

In 2011, our district hired a new Director of Curriculum and Instruction. Anecdotally, this new coordinator had heard stories of families who elected to homeschool or open enroll their children in another school district in frustration of the lack of services for the district's gifted and talented student population. The new Director of Curriculum and Instruction met with parents of homeschooled children to determine needs that were not sufficiently provided in the district. Parents were sharing concerns that the curriculum and instruction was not challenging enough for their children. Additionally, a neighboring district created an elementary charter school that drew advanced learners away at that level.

Teachers had also expressed concerns over the inability to address the learning needs of these students. The director had an unwavering determination that all students deserved at least a year's worth of growth in a year's worth of time. When she arrived in this role in 2011, the district had math coaches in every building who were using a professional learning community (PLC) structure to ensure consistency across buildings with curriculum implementation, pacing, and data analysis and also providing instructional support to peers. With this as a model and the realization that gifted and talented advocates were needed in each school building, the director worked with the Board of Education to develop a gifted and talented coach job description parallel to the role of math coach and secured district professional development funds as annual stipends for teachers to serve as district gifted and talented coaches in every building.

The Board of Education at that time was also highly supportive of change for the benefit of advanced learners due to their own personal experiences with their children in the district. Dollars were also prioritized to send teachers to professional development opportunities to grow capacity as leaders in gifted and talented education. In the new role of gifted and talented coach, the expectations identified were to work with peers to analyze assessment data to differentiate instruction, provide resources and strategies to differentiate instruction, act as a liaison between parents and educators to guarantee properly aligned services, offer enrichment opportunities, and collaborate with school counselors to ensure socioemotional supports.

The new director established a Gifted and Talented Advisory Council that met 3 times a year and included students, parents, teachers, coaches, and board members. There were many teachers and community members who were passionate about meeting the needs of advanced learners. It was the creation of these structures that then gave these advocates voice as well as channels for their enthusiasm and passion. It also gave the district's gifted and talented work some much-needed momentum.

The key to jump starting the district's journey was an administrative leader who had the vision to put pieces in place to create the structures, build the capacity, and establish a culture where the needs of *all* learners were tantamount. For such a sea change to occur, it was critical that an administrator took the lead in the district's efforts to improve gifted and talented education. Without that leadership, it would have been difficult to have a united vision that became sustainable with the system.

CREATING A PLAN

With structures in place, the district then needed a substantive plan. The creation of a plan seemed like a natural first step in creating a common understanding or foundation for the district to begin to address these concerns and needs. Gifted and talented education became a district priority. Not only did the evolving local needs create urgency, but the Wisconsin State Statute ("Standard t") demanded at the very least compliance with outlined requirements, such as a district-identified gifted and talented coordinator and a plan that ensured identification processes for different areas of giftedness and matched services.

Prior to the creation of this plan, the district experienced a number of "false starts" in creating a plan that involved primarily parent stakeholders and one administrator. With the administrative shift in 2011, urgency led to drafting a plan to serve as a visionary document for district administration and staff to better deliver needed services. On the outset, however, the district needed to consider its guiding philosophy for gifted and talented education.

The Baraboo School District believes that all children are entitled to an education commensurate with their particular needs. Although all students have personal strengths, some have abilities and talents that go beyond the core curriculum. Such students often require access to differentiated or advanced curriculum in order to realize their potential contribution to themselves and society. All children learn and experience success given time and opportunity, but the degree to which academic content standards are met and the time it takes to reach the standards will vary from student to student. The Baraboo School District believes that all students, including advanced learners, should be challenged and supported to reach their full potential.

The district's purpose and goals for the gifted and talented services are outlined in our "Advanced-Learner Services Core Beliefs." The Baraboo School District utilizes the Response to Intervention (RtI) framework for its continuous school improvement process. Service delivery for advanced learners needs to be an essential component of our RtI process.

The Baraboo School District formally adopted the Common Core State Standards (CCSS) in 2013 for its curriculum development and delivery. At the same time, the district was also aggressively working on creating a common understanding and approach to using the RtI framework for the district's continuous school improvement model. With the CCSS as a foundation for curriculum and instructional delivery, students demonstrating mastery of content and skills on universal screeners could receive targeted enrichment by teachers looking at the next level of the CCSS to guide their instruction.

With the districtwide implementation of the RtI framework, each building structured its schedule to provide additional instructional minutes for students needing intervention or enrichment. The district relied and continues to rely on early release PLCs for teachers to collaborate on assessment data analysis and lesson/intervention/enrichment planning. Building-level gifted and talented coaches advocate for student needs in the PLCs and provide instructional supports for peers to better meet the needs of our advanced learners. Additionally, with the cohort of gifted and talented certified staff in the district, effort is made to match certified teachers with our most advanced students for intervention and enrichment time.

The district's gifted and talented plan drafted in 2012 was truly a synthesis of work from a number of pioneers in gifted and talented education and collaborative efforts with other Wisconsin school districts. It was tailored to the context of the Baraboo School District. The district's context was important in this development because the plan needed to demonstrate to disenfranchised families that gifted and talented education was moving to a top priority. Additionally, the work and beliefs outlined in the plan are heavily influenced by research and teachings by Dr. Colleen Capper at the University of Wisconsin–Madison and focused on social equity and service delivery models.

Dr. Capper advocates for service delivery and full inclusion versus separate or pull-out programs for traditionally labeled subgroups of students to better meet individual needs. The director produced a draft plan based on these tenants for the district's newly formed Gifted and Talented Advisory Council and teachers to review. Based on feedback from stakeholders, the draft was finalized and taken to the Board of Education for approval.

Over the past few years, the plan has evolved with tweaks and additions from input from the district's Gifted and Talented Advisory Council, district gifted and talented coaches, and a group of 18 teachers who received their Wisconsin Gifted and Talented certification through a collaborative process between the district, the

University of Wisconsin–Whitewater, and the University of Wisconsin–Stevens Point. The most recent revision, in fact, stemmed from an assignment that educators in the gifted and talented cohort completed as part of their coursework—a careful analysis of the existing plan.

CAPACITY BUILDING

Between the creation of the original plan and its most recent revision, however, there was a great deal of capacity building. The director recognized that she alone could not facilitate high-quality gifted and talented services in a district of 3,000 students and 250 teachers. Additionally, she realized that this effort could not be sustained with administrative leadership alone. In 2013, the director sent three of the district gifted and talented coaches to the National Association for Gifted Children (NAGC) convention in Indianapolis. In 2014, she sent two teams of Baraboo presenters to the NAGC convention in Baltimore. She also provided release time for district gifted and talented coaches to attend regional gifted and talented meetings and the annual Wisconsin Association of Talented and Gifted Conference—encouraging teams to present as well as attend.

Jonathan Plucker's work inspired the district to remove barriers to subject-level acceleration—in particular at the middle school where many students now are receiving high school credit for math and language arts as a result of subject-level acceleration. Plucker's work on *Equal Talents, Unequal Opportunities* (Plucker, Giancola, Healey, Arndt, & Wang, 2015) spelled out that removing barriers to subject-level acceleration is key to serving academically talented low-income students—a population that our data indicated was not being served well. Dr. Scott Peters's various work on identification also inspired the district to make dramatic revisions to identification guidelines (broadening the scope) and spurred the district to strive for more proportional representation.

A presentation by Dr. Tonya Moon that included an example from Illinois schools working to certify large groups of teachers in gifted education ultimately inspired the collaboration between the director and Dr. Peters that afforded 18 of Baraboo's educators an opportunity to pursue a gifted and talented licensure. In 2013 and 2014, the director sent teams of teachers to University of Wisconsin's Challenging Advanced Learners Academy over the summer. It was over lunch at one of these academies that the director and Peters collaborated to create a unique opportunity for our Baraboo educators—a chance to pursue a gifted and talented licensure during our PLC structure that would entail the professors coming to our campus rather than our educators going to theirs. Placing this opportunity into the district's existing PLC structure ensured that teachers would not miss time in front of students and that they could use hours already built into the school day. This partnership signaled the start of our district's efforts to personalize the professional development that is offered to our staff during this time. It was a win-win proposition.

The benefits of sending such a large group through this program are too numerous to mention. There are a few, however, that need to be shared. In education, the magic is in the classroom. Eighteen educators in the Baraboo district now have a breadth and depth of understanding regarding how to meet the needs of advanced learners. This is significant when considering teacher capacity. These educators serve in each of the district's seven school buildings where they influence peers and administrators with knowledge and expertise to serve advanced learners that simply did not exist before this rich professional development opportunity (not to mention their influence on their students!). Also noteworthy is that regardless of potential administrative turnover, the advanced learners in our school district will have a throng of advocates! This web of professional development that was cast for many stakeholders was the impetus for the revision of our original plan.

THE REVISION PROCESS

When the director transitioned into the role of District Administrator, the middle school gifted and talented coach (who holds an administrative degree) took the reigns as Gifted and Talented (GT) Coordinator. As a member of the district's GT cohort she had both insights and a cadre of colleagues with whom to embark on the revision process.

With recommendations from the GT cohort and the GT advisory council, the gifted coordinator, along with a district literacy coach, an art teacher, and a fourth-grade teacher began the process. The underlying philosophy of gifted and talented education in the district had not changed. There were, however, several changes that needed to be made that stemmed from 3 years of learning and growing as a team of gifted and talented educators.

The district is presently in its first phase of this revision process. The revision group met for two mornings over the summer to get the work started. The first challenge, spurred by a recommendation of the GT cohort, was determining whether or not to shift from "gifted and talented" to "advanced learner" throughout. With the district's initial plan, the term *gifted* was used intentionally with a clear goal of communicating to our disenfranchised stakeholders that the district was working to meet the needs of this student population. Now, having established a better reputation for serving this population, the revision group felt like the term *advanced learner* was less of a label and generally a more fluid term than gifted.

The group also felt that with ongoing community outreach this shift would not hinder our goals of serving these students and their families. The switch wasn't made without some expressed reservations, however. For example, the group felt that the term advanced learner was appropriate for general and subject area giftedness, but that it was a poor fit for other areas like creativity or leadership.

When presented to the Gifted and Talented Advisory Council, one long-standing parent member pointed out, "The term 'advanced learner' feels like a name d'jour—something that will probably change in a few years, but it might allow us to break free of some of the negative stereotypes that are associated with the 'gifted' label." After weighing the pros and cons, the team opted to switch to advanced learner terminology throughout the new plan.

Identification proved to be the trickiest component to update. In part, this stems from our district's philosophy that our goal is to ensure that every student is challenged appropriately. Identification seemed like a fluid construct, and one where, frankly, we didn't want to focus our collective energies. The team was more intent on ensuring students that had access to appropriately challenging learning environments. The question this team grappled with was, "If the structures the district has in place and efforts at personalization and differentiation are ensuring a challenging environment for all, then is there a need to label students?" And yet, the team recognized that without a more formal identification process, we might not be providing equitable access to opportunities. We also struggled with the fact that we did not have a very good system for recognizing students who were advanced in the areas of creativity, leadership, and the arts.

Two major changes to our plan resulted from these struggles. First, we addressed the need to be more inclusive, another recommendation by the GT cohort. Originally, the district plan recognized gifted and talented students as those performing at the 97th percentile and above on standardized tests. The team recognized the need to use multiple measures and to ensure that the district was casting a much broader net. Thankfully, tools like eduCLIMBER, an educational data warehouse, make the district's data analysis much easier than it used to be.

With the RtI framework in mind, the team determined that any student scoring at or above the 80th percentile would be on our watch list, while students scoring at the 95th percentile and above would be students with whom coaches would touch base to ensure they were being challenged appropriately. The building gifted and talented coaches share with staff and administration the students who are on the watch list. Gifted and talented coaches also work with school counselors to ensure they recognize that these individuals might have unique counseling needs, including, but not limited to, college and career planning and social and emotional issues.

Secondly, we recognized a gaping void in our identification of those gifted in leadership, creativity, and the arts—three of the state-required areas of identification. After a fruitless search for suitable screeners, the team decided to create its own modeled off of a creativity screener from the Bangor School District in Maine. An elementary art teacher and the GT coordinator created screeners for creativity, performing arts, leadership, and music. The district's emphasis is on service delivery rather than identification. And yet, there was room to develop more services for these identified areas of giftedness within the walls of the district schools.

Presently, services are primarily pull-out options sponsored through our state's gifted and talented organizations. Examples include a Fine Arts Weekend for high school students at a Shakespearean theater, a gifted Teen Conference sponsored by the Wisconsin Association of Talented and Gifted, and a leadership conference sponsored by the state Student Council Association. Internally, we have art clubs, a gifted choir at the middle school that meets during an enrichment period, and several club opportunities to serve these students.

Given in both the third and seventh grades, these screeners will allow the district coaches to identify students with a strong interest or predilection in these arenas and, consequently, to offer them supports to foster and develop these high-interest areas. The team also plans on including the HOPE Teacher Rating Scale (Gentry, Peters, Pereira, McIntosh, & Fugate, 2015) as a screener in hopes of better identifying advanced learners who are economically disadvantaged, a growing population in Baraboo. In the past 15 years, the percentage of students identified as economically disadvantaged has gone from 15%–50%. One elementary school in the district is nearing 75%. Because the district recognizes that identification means little without programs and services, gifted and talented leaders will continue to work to remove barriers to learning for all students. Certainly, there will be modifications that need to be made to the screening process, but it is a start!

Moving Forward

We know our work will never be finished when it comes to meeting the needs of our advanced learners. For example, our district is in the second year of a 3-year study with Dr. Marcia Gentry of Purdue University on the impact of clustering at the elementary level. This will provide insight into the effectiveness of our district's total schoolwide clustering efforts.

The revised Advanced Learner Plan has been rolled out to gifted and talented coaches as well as to our Advisory Council for feedback. Both groups have been given copies of the original plan and the newly revised plan. They have been asked to review the changes and bring recommendations to the next Gifted and Talented Advisory Council meeting. At that point, we will make possible revisions and move forward to secure board approval.

Additionally, we hope to enroll more teachers in the gifted and talented licensure program starting this spring. Although the need for administrative support is critical in meeting the needs of advanced learners, teacher capacity is also critical.

In Baraboo, for example, administrators come and go more often that teachers do. The more teachers in the Baraboo School District with a strong foundation in gifted and talented education, the less likely the chance that this population will ever be underserved in our district again!

Our advisory board continues to meet 3 times a year, and our focus this year will be on fine-tuning our new Advanced Learner Planning Guide, bolstering the identification and services we offer in the areas of leadership and creativity, and continued community outreach. In previous years, the district has sponsored speakers to present to our staff, parents, and community members about the unique needs of gifted students. With the capacity that now exists in our district, these presentations will be conducted by district staff.

The Baraboo School District recently engaged community stakeholders in creating the 2015–2018 District Strategic Plan. The plan has four strategic directions: community partnerships, maximizing the potential of all learners and educators, modernized community campuses, and personalized learning. One of the first tasks with the personalized learning strategic plan direction was to define for all stakeholders what it really means to personalize learning (in doing so, we found ourselves referencing research and work from Carol Ann Tomlinson on differentiation). As we continue to determine what personalized learning looks like in the district, we see the value of our focus for our gifted and talented population in structuring voice and choice for their learning.

REFERENCES

Berger, S. L. (1991). *Developing programs for students of high ability*. Reston, VA: Council for Exceptional Children.

Brulles, D. (2014, Winter). Identifying, serving and supporting gifted students and their teachers: Paradise Valley's comprehensive approach. *IAGC Journal*, 54–58.

Brulles, D., & Brown, K. L. (2013, July/August). Teacher support is just a click away! *Educational Technology*, 25–32.

Brulles, D., & Winebrenner, S. (2011). The schoolwide cluster grouping model: Restructuring gifted education services for the 21st century. *Gifted Child Today*, *34*(4), 35–46.

Callahan, C. M., Moon, T. R., & Oh, S. (2014). *National surveys of gifted programs: Executive summary, 2014*. Charlottesville: University of Virginia, National Research Center on the Gifted and Talented. Retrieved from http://www.nagc.org/sites/default/files/key%20reports/2014%20Survey%20of%20GT%20programs%20Exec%20Summ.pdf

Card, D., & Giuliano, L. (2015). *Can universal screening increase the representation of low income and minority students in gifted education?* (National Bureau of Economic Research Working Paper No. 21519). Retrieved from http://www.nber.org/papers/w21519

Clark, B. (2012). *Growing up gifted: Developing the potential of children at home and at school (8th ed.)*. New York, NY: Pearson Education.

Delisle, J. (2014). *Dumbing down America: The war on our nation's brightest young minds (And what we can do to fight back)*. Waco, TX: Prufrock Press.

Florida Department of Education. (n.d.). *Gifted education*. Retrieved from http://www.fldoe.org/academics/exceptional-student-edu/gifted-edu.stml

Gentry, M., Pereira, N., Peters, S. J., McIntosh, J. S., & Fugate, C. M. (2015). *HOPE teacher rating scale: Involving teachers in equitable identification of gifted and talented students in K–12: Administration manual*. Waco, TX: Prufrock Press.

Grissom, J. A., & Redding, C. (2016). Discretion and disproportionality: Explaining the underrepresentation of high-achieving student of color in gifted programs. *AERA Open*, *2*(1), 1–25. doi:10.1177/2332858415622175

Idaho Department of Education. (n.d.). *Gifted and talented rules and regulations* (IDAPA 08.02.03.999). Retrieved from https://sde.idaho.gov/academic/gifted-talented/files/general/Gifted-and-Talented-Rules-and-Regulations.pdf

Iowa Department of Education. (2016). *District gifted and talented program plan requirements*. Retrieved from https://www.educateiowa.gov/documents/advanced-learning-opportunities/2016/05/district-gifted-and-talented-program-plan

Kuncel, N. R., & Hezlett, S. A. (2010). Fact and fiction in cognitive ability testing for admissions and hiring decisions. *Current Directions in Psychological Science, 19,* 339–345. doi:10.1177/0963721410389459

Landrum, M., Callahan, C., & Shaklee, B. (Eds.). (2001). *Aiming for excellence: Gifted program standards: Annotations to the NAGC Pre-K–Grade 12 Gifted Programming Standards.* Waco, TX: Prufrock Press.

Lohman, D. F. (2006). *Identifying academically talented minority students* (RM05216). Storrs: The National Research Center on the Gifted and Talented, University of Connecticut.

McBee, M. T., Peters, S. J., & Miller, E. M. (2016). The impact of the nomination stage on gifted program identification: A comprehensive psychometric analysis. *Gifted Child Quarterly, 60,* 258–278. doi:10.1177/0016986216656256.

McBee, M. T., Peters, S. J., & Waterman, C. (2014). Combining scores in multiple-criteria assessment systems: The impact of combination rules. *Gifted Child Quarterly, 58,* 69–89. doi:10.1177/0016986213513794.

Naglieri, J., Brulles, D., & Lansdowne, K. (2008). *Helping all gifted students learn: A teacher's guide to using Naglieri Nonverbal Assessments.* San Antonio, TX: Pearson.

National Association for Gifted Children. (2010). *NAGC Pre-K–grade 12 gifted programming standards: A blueprint for quality gifted education programs.* Retrieved from http://www.nagc.org/sites/default/files/standards/K-12%20 standards%20booklet.pdf

National Association for Gifted Children. (2015). *State of the states in gifted education: 2014–2015.* Washington, DC: Author.

National Association for Gifted Children. (n.d.). *Gifted education practices.* Retrieved from https://www.nagc.org/resources-publications/gifted-education-practices

Peters, S. J., Matthews, M., McBee, M., & McCoach, D. B. (2014). *Beyond gifted education: Designing and implementing advanced academic programs.* Waco, TX: Prufrock Press.

Peters, S. J., Rambo-Hernandez, K., Makel, M., Matthews, M. S., & Plucker, J. A. (2017). Should millions of students take a gap year? Large numbers of students start the school year above grade level. *Gifted Child Quarterly, 61,* 229–238. doi:10.1177/0016986217701834

Plucker, J., Giancola, J., Healey, G., Arndt, D., & Wang, C. (2015). *Equal talents, unequal opportunities: A report card on state support for academically talented low-income students.* Landsdowne, VA: Jack Kent Cooke Foundation. Retrieved from http://www.jkcf.org/assets/1/7/JKCF_ETUO_Executive_Final.pdf

Rogers, K. B. (2002). *Re-forming gifted education: How parents and teachers can match the program to the child.* Tucson, AZ: Great Potential Press.

Seagoe, M. (1974). Some learning characteristics of gifted children. In R. Martinson (Ed.), *The identification of the gifted and talented* (pp. 20–21). Ventura, CA: Office of the Ventura County Superintendent of Schools.

Steenbergen-Hu, S., Makel, M. C., & Olszewski-Kubilius, P. (2016). What one hundred years of research says about the effects of ability grouping and acceleration on K–12 students' academic achievement: Findings of two second-order meta-analyses. *Review of Educational Research, 86,* 849–899.

Tennessee Department of Education. (2010). *Tennessee state plan for the education of intellectually gifted students.* Retrieved from https://www.tn.gov/assets/entities/education/attachments/se_eligibility_gifted_manual.pdf

United States Department of Education. (1993). *National excellence: The case for developing America's talent.* Washington, DC: U.S. Government Printing Office.

Winebrenner, S., & Brulles, D. (2008). *The cluster grouping handbook: How to challenge gifted students and improve achievement for all.* Minneapolis, MN: Free Spirit.

Wis. Stat. § 121.02(1)(t). Retrieved from https://docs.legis.wisconsin.gov/statutes/statutes/121/II/02/1/t

Wis. Admin. Code 8.01(2)(t)2. Retrieved from https://docs.legis.wisconsin.gov/code/admin_code/pi/8/01/2/t/2

Wyner, J., Bridgeland, J. M., & DiIulio, J. J. (2009). *Achievement trap: How America is failing millions of high-achieving students from lower-income families.* Landsdowne, VA: Jack Kent Cooke Foundation. Retrieved from: http://www.jkcf.org/assets/1/7/Achievement_Trap.pdf

Xiang, Y., Dahlin, M., Cronin, J., Theaker, R., & Durant, S. (2011). *Do high flyers maintain their altitude? Performance trends of top students.* Retrieved from http://edex.s3-us-west-2.amazonaws.com/publication/pdfs/Do_High_Flyers_Maintain_Their_Altitude_FINAL_8.pdf

APPENDIX A

NAGC PRE-K–GRADE 12 GIFTED PROGRAMMING STANDARDS[1]

NAGC Pre-K-Grade 12 Gifted Programming Standards

A Blueprint for Quality Gifted Education Programs

NATIONAL ASSOCIATION FOR
Gifted Children

November 2010

---

1   Copyright 2010 by National Association for Gifted Children. Reprinted with permission from NAGC.

Table of Contents

November 1, 2010

Dear Gifted Education Supporter:

On behalf of NAGC, I am extremely pleased to present the *2010 Pre-K-Grade 12 Gifted Programming Standards*. The revised programming standards update the initial program standards developed in 1998.

Program standards provide a structure for defining important benchmarks and for identifying practices that are the most effective, in this case, for students with gifts and talents. A common set of standards helps to ensure consistency among schools and school districts so that all students who require advanced services receive **quality** services. Standards can guide our continual progress toward excellence and equity.

The 2010 programming standards have been developed with input from a variety of stakeholders over the past two years and integrate principles and concepts from the initial program standards and the national NAGC-CEC/TAG teacher preparation standards. You will note an increased focus on diversity and collaboration – two powerful principles that guide high quality programs and services. The new standards use student outcomes, rather than teacher practices, as goals. Both revisions create stronger standards and align them with current thinking in education standards generally.

With new standards come numerous questions from concerned gifted education professionals. This booklet addresses many of the frequently asked questions about the new programming standards to give us all a running start. In addition, NAGC will be delivering online and print resources in the coming year to assist school districts in implementing the new standards. We welcome your suggestions on the resources that will be most helpful.

My deepest thanks go to Susan Johnsen of Baylor University, chair of the standards revision workgroup, for her leadership and commitment. Thank you, also to the Pre-K-Grade 12 workgroup members: Alicia Cotabish, University of Arkansas at Little Rock; Todd Kettler, Coppell (TX) ISD; Margie Kitano, San Diego State University; Sally Krisel, Hall County (GA) Public Schools; Wayne Lord, Augusta State University; Michael S. Matthews, University of North Carolina at Charlotte; Chrystyna Mursky, Wisconsin Department of Public Instruction; Christine Nobbe, Center for Creative Learning (MO); Elizabeth Shaunessy, University of South Florida; and Joyce VanTassel-Baska, College of William and Mary who gave both their expertise and time to producing the new standards. The group continues its work as they make presentations and develop resources to accompany the standards.

NAGC looks forward to working with educators across the country in using these standards to improve services for our most able learners. In advance, I thank you for your commitment to serving students with gifts and talents with the best possible programs and services.

Sincerely,

Ann Robinson, Ph.D.
Center for Gifted Education
University of Arkansas at Little Rock
President

An Introduction to the Gifted Programming Standards

Why does gifted education need standards?
Standards provide a basis for policies, rules, and procedures that are essential for providing systematic programs and services to any special population. While standards may be addressed and implemented in a variety of ways, they provide important direction and focus to the endeavor of program development. They also help define the comprehensiveness necessary in designing and developing options for gifted learners at the local level. Because these standards are grounded in theory, research, and practice paradigms, they provide an important base for all efforts on behalf of gifted learners at all stages of development.

How may the standards be used?
There are a variety of ways in which the *2010 Pre-K-Grade 12 Gifted Programming Standards* may be used in schools and districts across the country. The uses fall into six categories:
- Assess, evaluate, and improve local plans and programming
- Plan curriculum
- Provide professional development
- Advocate
- Develop, improve, and evaluate state standards
- Approve gifted plans and programs and monitor for compliance with state regulations

How were these standards developed?
In 2007, the NAGC Board created the Professional Standards Committee to align the 1998 Gifted Program Standards with the NAGC-CEC Teacher Preparation Standards. After an initial alignment, a Pre-K-Grade 12 Gifted Program Standards Revision Workgroup was formed to undertake the revision. In revising the standards, the workgroup was guided by these principles:
1. Giftedness is dynamic and is constantly developing; therefore, students are defined as those with gifts and talents rather than those with stable traits.
2. Giftedness is found among students from a variety of backgrounds; therefore, a deliberate effort was made to ensure that diversity was included across all standards. Diversity was defined as differences among groups of people and individuals based on ethnicity, race, socioeconomic status, gender, exceptionalities, language, religion, sexual orientation, and geographical area.
3. Standards should focus on student outcomes rather than practices. The number of practices used or how they are used is not as important as whether or not the practice is effective with students. Consequently, the workgroup decided not to identify acceptable vs. exemplary standards. Moreover, such a distinction would be difficult to support with the research.
4. Because all educators are responsible for the education of students with gifts and talents, educators were broadly defined as administrators, teachers, counselors, and other instructional support staff from a variety of professional backgrounds (e.g., general education, special education, and gifted education).
5. Students with gifts and talents should receive services throughout the day and in all environments based on their abilities, needs, and interests. Therefore, the Workgroup decided to use the word "programming" rather than the word "program," which might connote a one-dimensional approach (e.g., a once-a-week type of program option).

How are these standards different from the 1998 Program Standards?
The major differences between the 1998 Gifted Program Standards and the *2010 Pre-K-Grade 12 Gifted Programming Standards* center on the following areas:
1. The revised programming standards focus on student outcomes.
2. The revised programming standards reflect a stronger emphasis on diversity.
3. The revised programming standards emphasize stronger relationships between gifted education, general education, and special education and integrate cognitive science research.
4. The revised programming standards emphasize evidence-based practices that are based on research.
(See: Matthews & Shaunessy, 2010)

How do the programming standards relate to other professional standards?
The 2010 programming standards adhere very closely to the language in the NAGC-CEC/TAG Teacher Preparation Standards and the 1998 Gifted Program Standards and integrate the two sets of standards within evidence-based practices. The 2010 Programming Standards include areas from the NAGC-CEC/TAG teacher preparation standards that were minimally addressed or were omitted in the 1998 Gifted Program Standards, such as language and communication, learning environments and social interaction, diversity, collaboration between gifted education and special education, and ongoing assessment. Moreover, the 2010 Programming

Standards retain criteria that were not addressed in the NAGC-CEC/TAG teacher preparation standards such as program evaluation and professional development.

(NOTE: See the NAGC website for tables illustrating the relationship and alignment among the 2010 Pre-K-Grade 12 Gifted Programming Standards, the 1998 Gifted Program Standards, and the NAGC-CEC/TAG Teacher Preparation Standards.)

How are the standards supported by research and current effective practices?

The field of gifted education has evolved since the original gifted program standards were developed in 1998. The 2010 standards include only evidence-based practices that support the corresponding student outcomes. This support falls into three categories: (a) research-based, (b) practice-based, and (c) literature-based.

Research-based studies provide the most compelling evidence and are peer-reviewed, use qualitative or quantitative methodologies to address questions of cause and effect, and have been independently replicated and found to be effective. Practice-based strategies are practices that have been used widely with success, so there is a professional assumption that the practice is effective. Practice-based studies also include strategies that class-room teachers use and validate through some degree of action research. Literature-based studies are those that are based on theories or philosophical reasoning.

(NOTE: See the NAGC website for the research citations and references for all of the recommended practices.)

My school/district doesn't have a formal gifted education program, although we do offer services in several grades to advanced students. How can we use these standards? My school/district's gifted education program is just being launched. How do you recommend we get started with these standards?

The early stages of program planning and development are ideal times to study and use the 2010 Programming Standards. Before you get too far along in a journey that, without careful planning, may not serve gifted and talented students well or, in the worst-case scenario, may actually diminish support for gifted education in your school or district, use the 2010 Programming Standards to conduct an internal analysis of the comprehensiveness and defensibility of your plans/program at this point in time. If a school doesn't have a gifted education program or is just getting started, the stan-

GAP ANALYSIS CHART

Standard	Evidence-Based Practices	What We Do To Support This Practice	Desired Student Outcomes	What Evidence do We Have that Current Practices are Leading to Desired Student Outcomes?	What Additional Evidence do We Need? (Gaps)

dards will help document the need for the program and/or justify the case for a particular programming approach. As the program grows, the standards will help identify program strengths and weaknesses, focus on potential trouble spots, determine new directions or new components, or provide support to maintain current programs and services. Schools may continue to use the standards as a roadmap for evaluation or to set goals and plan strategically for meeting those goals.

My school district uses the 1998 Program Standards. How might we transition to the new standards?

The 1998 *Gifted Program Standards* have been aligned with the *2010 NAGC Pre-K-Grade 12 Gifted Programming Standards*, and this alignment demonstrates that all of the 1998 standards are represented in the 2010 document. The revised standards, however, are framed as student outcomes instead of best practices. So all the work school districts have done with the 1998 standards is not wasted; rather it will serve as the foundation for continuous improvement. The revised standards will elucidate the next steps toward excellence in gifted programming by helping school districts move beyond the focus on practices alone to the relationship between cer-

tain practices and desired student outcomes. The 2010 standards invite educators to address these important questions related to student outcomes in each area:
• What is it that individuals with gifts and talents need other than the excellent core curriculum we want all students to have in school?
• If these unique needs are met, how is school and life better for students with gifts and talents?
• What do those changes look like in terms of student behavior?

In other words, what difference does gifted education programming make in the lives of participating students?

To summarize the progress districts have already made using the 1998 standards and chart a course for continued program improvement, program personnel might elect to use a gap analysis chart and the related action planning chart below. These two tools will help planners acknowledge specific strategies/activities already used for each evidence-based practice, identify gaps, and develop an action plan to address those gaps.

The decision to focus on student growth mirrors current practice in most schools, so the 2010 standards should connect without difficulty to state and local ini-

ACTION PLAN CHART

Standard	Evidence-Based Practices	Desired Student Outcomes	Identified Gaps	Information To Be Collected	Person(s) Responsible	Timeline

tiatives. This approach is the key to using the *2010 Pre-K-Grade 12 Gifted Programming Standards*.

How can my school/district use these standards for program evaluation purposes?

The student outcomes and evidence-based practices in the programming standards serve as criteria on which to collect data to make informed judgments about the quality and effectiveness of their programming for learners with gifts and talents. Once the data is in hand, school leaders may establish benchmarks or set goals and timelines to ensure that they are on track to achieving the desired student outcomes.

How do we know that the student outcomes are being met?

The task of assessing the standards' student outcomes becomes a major part of program design and development annually through the use of appropriate and varied measures. In general, use off-level measures to assess the achievement level of gifted students. To assess deeper and more complex learning behaviors, more tailored performance-based or product-based instruments should be employed. To assess critical and creative thinking, the use of tests that focus on these higher skills would be recommended. Finally, if one wants to assess affective behavioral change, the use of products (i.e. journals, written essays, talent development plans), examined over time in a pre-post or portfolio model may be most desirable. Assessing gifted student learning also requires matching the desired outcome to the student's knowledge and skills and level of interest. Exams like AP and IB are carefully crafted performance-based assessments that tap into advanced learning in traditional and free response modes. They may be used as models for thinking about appropriate approaches at earlier stages of development in a gifted program as would other examples of Performance-Based Assessments (e. g., see the College of William and Mary Units of study).

What resources does NAGC have and will develop to assist in implementing the 2010 standards?

A new publication to accompany the 2010 Programming Standards is underway. However, NAGC has resources available now to assist school leaders in implementing the new standards.

- The NAGC website contains the full glossary of terms used with the 2010 Programming Standards as well as tables that show the relationship and alignment among the 2010 programming standards, the previous gifted program standards, and the NAGC-CEC/TAG Teacher Preparation Standards. See the "Standards in Gifted Education" section of the website at www.nagc.org.

- The NAGC website also contains information and links to references for many of the strategies recommended in the 2010 programming standards. The online bookstore includes publications that address special populations of gifted students, best practices in gifted education, designing services in P-12, and assessments of gifted learners, among other key topics.

- A guidebook for P-12 educators that was developed to implement the teacher education standards is available in the online bookstore. See Kitano, M., Montgomery, D., VanTassel-Baska, J., & Johnsen, S. (2008). *Using the national gifted education standards for PreK-12 professional development.* Thousand Oaks, CA: Corwin Press.

- A publication on CD is available in the online store that addresses critical state policies in gifted education, such as identification, personnel preparation, and programs and curriculum, and includes links to actual state policies in each key area. See Clinkenbeard, P. R., Kolloff, P. B., & Lord, E. W. (2007). *A guide to state policies in gifted education.* Washington, DC: National Association for Gifted Children.

- NAGC plans a series of webinars in 2011 that will focus on each of the standards to provide additional support for implementation.

NAGC Pre-K-Grade 12 Gifted Programming Standards

Gifted Education Programming Standard 1:
Learning and Development

Introduction

To be effective in working with learners with gifts and talents, teachers and other educators in PreK-12 settings must understand the characteristics and needs of the population for whom they are planning curriculum, instruction, assess-ment, programs, and services. These characteristics provide the rationale for differentiation in programs, grouping, and services for this population and are translated into appropriate differentiation choices made at curricular and pro-gram levels in schools and school districts. While cognitive growth is important in such programs, affective development is also necessary. Thus many of the characteristics addressed in this standard emphasize affective development linked to self-understanding and social awareness.

STANDARD 1: LEARNING AND DEVELOPMENT

Description: *Educators, recognizing the learning and developmental differences of students with gifts and talents, promote ongoing self-understanding, awareness of their needs, and cognitive and affective growth of these students in school, home, and community settings to ensure specific student outcomes.*

STUDENT OUTCOMES	EVIDENCE-BASED PRACTICES
1.1. Self-Understanding. Students with gifts and talents demon-strate self-knowledge with respect to their interests, strengths, iden-tities, and needs in socio-emotional development and in intellectual, academic, creative, leadership, and artistic domains.	1.1.1. Educators engage students with gifts and talents in identifying interests, strengths, and gifts. 1.1.2. Educators assist students with gifts and talents in developing identities supportive of achievement.
1.2. Self-Understanding. Students with gifts and talents possess a developmentally appropriate understanding of how they learn and grow; they recognize the influences of their beliefs, traditions, and values on their learning and behavior.	1.2.1. Educators develop activities that match each student's developmental level and culture-based learning needs.
1.3. Self-Understanding. Students with gifts and talents demon-strate understanding of and respect for similarities and differences between themselves and their peer group and others in the general population.	1.3.1. Educators provide a variety of research-based grouping practices for students with gifts and talents that allow them to interact with individuals of various gifts, talents, abilities, and strengths. 1.3.2. Educators model respect for individuals with diverse abilities, strengths, and goals.
1.4. Awareness of Needs. Students with gifts and talents access resources from the community to support cognitive and affective needs, including social interactions with others having similar in-terests and abilities or experiences, including same-age peers and mentors or experts.	1.4.1. Educators provide role models (e.g., through mentors, bibliotherapy) for students with gifts and talents that match their abilities and interests. 1.4.2. Educators identify out-of-school learning opportunities that match students' abilities and interests.
1.5. Awareness of Needs. Students' families and communities understand similarities and differences with respect to the develop-ment and characteristics of advanced and typical learners and sup-port students with gifts and talents' needs.	1.5.1. Educators collaborate with families in accessing resources to develop their child's talents.
1.6. Cognitive and Affective Growth. Students with gifts and tal-ents benefit from meaningful and challenging learning activities ad-dressing their unique characteristics and needs.	1.6.1. Educators design interventions for students to develop cognitive and affective growth that is based on research of effective practices. 1.6.2. Educators develop specialized intervention services for students with gifts and talents who are underachieving and are now learning and developing their talents.
1.7. Cognitive and Affective Growth. Students with gifts and talents recognize their preferred approaches to learning and ex-pand their repertoire.	1.7.1 Teachers enable students to identify their preferred approaches to learning, accommodate these preferences, and expand them.
1.8. Cognitive and Affective Growth. Students with gifts and tal-ents identify future career goals that match their talents and abilities and resources needed to meet those goals (e.g., higher education opportunities, mentors, financial support).	1.8.1. Educators provide students with college and career guidance that is consistent with their strengths. 1.8.2. Teachers and counselors implement a curriculum scope and sequence that contains per-son/social awareness and adjustment, academic planning, and vocational and career awareness.

Gifted Education Programming Standard 2: Assessment

Introduction

Knowledge about all forms of assessment is essential for educators of students with gifts and talents. It is integral to identification, assessing each student's learning progress, and evaluation of programming. Educators need to establish a challenging environment and collect multiple types of assessment information so that all students are able to demonstrate their gifts and talents. Educators' understanding of non-biased, technically adequate, and equitable approaches enables them to identify students who represent diverse backgrounds. They also differentiate their curriculum and instruction by using pre- and post-, performance-based, product-based, and out-of-level assessments. As a result of each educator's use of ongoing assessments, students with gifts and talents demonstrate advanced and complex learning. Using these student progress data, educators then evaluate services and make adjustments to one or more of the school's programming components so that student performance is improved.

STANDARD 2: ASSESSMENT

Description: *Assessments provide information about identification, learning progress and outcomes, and evaluation of programming for students with gifts and talents in all domains.*

STUDENT OUTCOMES	EVIDENCE-BASED PRACTICES
2.1. *Identification.* All students in grades PK-12 have equal access to a comprehensive assessment system that allows them to demonstrate diverse characteristics and behaviors that are associated with giftedness.	2.1.1. Educators develop environments and instructional activities that encourage students to express diverse characteristics and behaviors that are associated with giftedness. 2.1.2. Educators provide parents/guardians with information regarding diverse characteristics and behaviors that are associated with giftedness.
2.2. *Identification.* Each student reveals his or her exceptionalities or potential through assessment evidence so that appropriate instructional accommodations and modifications can be provided.	2.2.1. Educators establish comprehensive, cohesive, and ongoing procedures for identifying and serving students with gifts and talents. These provisions include informed consent, committee review, student retention, student reassessment, student exiting, and appeals procedures for both entry and exit from gifted program services. 2.2.2. Educators select and use multiple assessments that measure diverse abilities, talents, and strengths that are based on current theories, models, and research. 2.2.3 Assessments provide qualitative and quantitative information from a variety of sources, including off-level testing, are nonbiased and equitable, and are technically adequate for the purpose. 2.2.4. Educators have knowledge of student exceptionalities and collect assessment data while adjusting curriculum and instruction to learn about each student's developmental level and aptitude for learning. 2.2.5. Educators interpret multiple assessments in different domains and understand the uses and limitations of the assessments in identifying the needs of students with gifts and talents. 2.2.6. Educators inform all parents/guardians about the identification process. Teachers obtain parental/guardian permission for assessments, use culturally sensitive checklists, and elicit evidence regarding the child's interests and potential outside of the classroom setting.
2.3. *Identification.* Students with identified needs represent diverse backgrounds and reflect the total student population of the district.	2.3.1. Educators select and use non-biased and equitable approaches for identifying students with gifts and talents, which may include using locally developed norms or assessment tools in the child's native language or in nonverbal formats. 2.3.2. Educators understand and implement district and state policies designed to foster equity in gifted programming and services. 2.3.3. Educators provide parents/guardians with information in their native language regarding diverse behaviors and characteristics that are associated with giftedness and with information that explains the nature and purpose of gifted programming options.
2.4. *Learning Progress and Outcomes.* Students with gifts and talents demonstrate advanced and complex learning as a result of using multiple, appropriate, and ongoing assessments.	2.4.1. Educators use differentiated pre- and post-performance-based assessments to measure the progress of students with gifts and talents. 2.4.2. Educators use differentiated product-based assessments to measure the progress of students with gifts and talents. 2.4.3. Educators use off-level standardized assessments to measure the progress of students with gifts and talents. 2.4.4. Educators use and interpret qualitative and quantitative assessment information to develop a profile of the strengths and weaknesses of each student with gifts and talents to plan appropriate intervention. 2.4.5. Educators communicate and interpret assessment information to students with gifts and talents and their parents/guardians.
2.5. *Evaluation of Programming.* Students identified with gifts and talents demonstrate important learning progress as a result of programming and services.	2.5.1. Educators ensure that the assessments used in the identification and evaluation processes are reliable and valid for each instrument's purpose, allow for above-grade-level performance, and allow for diverse perspectives. 2.5.2. Educators ensure that the assessment of the progress of students with gifts and talents uses multiple indicators that measure mastery of content, higher level thinking skills, achievement in specific program areas, and affective growth. 2.5.3. Educators assess the quantity, quality, and appropriateness of the programming and services provided for students with gifts and talents by disaggregating assessment data and yearly progress data and making the results public.
2.6. *Evaluation of Programming.* Students identified with gifts and talents have increased access and they show significant learning progress as a result of improving components of gifted education programming.	2.6.1. Administrators provide the necessary time and resources to implement an annual evaluation plan developed by persons with expertise in program evaluation and gifted education. 2.6.2. The evaluation plan is purposeful and evaluates how student-level outcomes are influenced by one or more of the following components of gifted education programming: (a) identification, (b) curriculum, (c) instructional programming and services, (d) ongoing assessment of student learning, (e) counseling and guidance programs, (f) teacher qualifications and professional development, (g) parent/guardian and community involvement, (h) programming resources, and (i) programming design, management, and delivery. 2.6.3. Educators disseminate the results of the evaluation, orally and in written form, and explain how they will use the results.

A Blueprint for Quality Gifted Education Programs **9**

Gifted Education Programming Standard 3: Curriculum Planning and Instruction

Introduction

Assessment is an integral component of the curriculum planning process. The information obtained from multiple types of assessments informs decisions about curriculum content, instructional strategies, and resources that will support the growth of students with gifts and talents. Educators develop and use a comprehensive and sequenced core curriculum that is aligned with local, state, and national standards, then differentiate and expand it. In order to meet the unique needs of students with gifts and talents, this curriculum must emphasize advanced, conceptually challenging, in-depth, distinctive, and complex content within cognitive, affective, aesthetic, social, and leadership domains. Educators must possess a repertoire of evidence-based instructional strategies in delivering the curriculum (a) to develop talent, enhance learning, and provide students with the knowledge and skills to become independent, self-aware learners, and (b) to give students the tools to contribute to a multicultural, diverse society. The curriculum, instructional strategies, and materials and resources must engage a variety of learners using culturally responsive practices.

STANDARD 3: CURRICULUM PLANNING AND INSTRUCTION

Description: *Educators apply the theory and research-based models of curriculum and instruction related to students with gifts and talents and respond to their needs by planning, selecting, adapting, and creating culturally relevant curriculum and by using a repertoire of evidence-based instructional strategies to ensure specific student outcomes.*

STUDENT OUTCOMES	EVIDENCE-BASED PRACTICES
3.1. Curriculum Planning. Students with gifts and talents demonstrate growth commensurate with aptitude during the school year.	3.1.1. Educators use local, state, and national standards to align and expand curriculum and instructional plans. 3.1.2. Educators design and use a comprehensive and continuous scope and sequence to develop differentiated plans for PK-12 students with gifts and talents. 3.1.3. Educators adapt, modify, or replace the core or standard curriculum to meet the needs of students with gifts and talents and those with special needs such as twice-exceptional, highly gifted, and English language learners. 3.1.4. Educators design differentiated curricula that incorporate advanced, conceptually challenging, in-depth, distinctive, and complex content for students with gifts and talents. 3.1.5. Educators use a balanced assessment system, including pre-assessment and formative assessment, to identify students' needs, develop differentiated education plans, and adjust plans based on continual progress monitoring. 3.1.6. Educators use pre-assessments and pace instruction based on the learning rates of students with gifts and talents and accelerate and compact learning as appropriate. 3.1.7. Educators use information and technologies, including assistive technologies, to individualize for students with gifts and talents, including those who are twice-exceptional.
3.2. Talent Development. Students with gifts and talents become more competent in multiple talent areas and across dimensions of learning.	3.2.1. Educators design curricula in cognitive, affective, aesthetic, social, and leadership domains that are challenging and effective for students with gifts and talents. 3.2.2. Educators use metacognitive models to meet the needs of students with gifts and talents.
3.3. Talent Development. Students with gifts and talents develop their abilities in their domain of talent and/or area of interest.	3.3.1. Educators select, adapt, and use a repertoire of instructional strategies and materials that differentiate for students with gifts and talents and that respond to diversity. 3.3.2. Educators use school and community resources that support differentiation. 3.3.3. Educators provide opportunities for students with gifts and talents to explore, develop, or research their areas of interest and/or talent.
3.4. Instructional Strategies. Students with gifts and talents become independent investigators.	3.4.1. Educators use critical-thinking strategies to meet the needs of students with gifts and talents. 3.4.2. Educators use creative-thinking strategies to meet the needs of students with gifts and talents. 3.4.3. Educators use problem-solving model strategies to meet the needs of students with gifts and talents. 3.4.4. Educators use inquiry models to meet the needs of students with gifts and talents.
3.5. Culturally Relevant Curriculum. Students with gifts and talents develop knowledge and skills for living and being productive in a multicultural, diverse, and global society.	3.5.1. Educators develop and use challenging, culturally responsive curriculum to engage all students with gifts and talents. 3.5.2. Educators integrate career exploration experiences into learning opportunities for students with gifts and talents, e.g. biography study or speakers. 3.5.3. Educators use curriculum for deep explorations of cultures, languages, and social issues related to diversity.
3.6. Resources. Students with gifts and talents benefit from gifted education programming that provides a variety of high quality resources and materials.	3.6.1. Teachers and administrators demonstrate familiarity with sources for high quality resources and materials that are appropriate for learners with gifts and talents.

Gifted Education Programming Standard 4: Learning Environments

Introduction

Effective educators of students with gifts and talents create safe learning environments that foster emotional well-being, positive social interaction, leadership for social change, and cultural understanding for success in a diverse society. Knowledge of the impact of giftedness and diversity on social-emotional development enables educators of students with gifts and talents to design environments that encourage independence, motivation, and self-efficacy of individuals from all backgrounds. They understand the role of language and communication in talent development and the ways in which culture affects communication and behavior. They use relevant strategies and technologies to enhance oral, written, and artistic communication of learners whose needs vary based on exceptionality, language proficiency, and cultural and linguistic differences. They recognize the value of multilingualism in today's global community.

STANDARD 4: LEARNING ENVIRONMENTS

Description: *Learning environments foster personal and social responsibility, multicultural competence, and interpersonal and technical communication skills for leadership in the 21st century to ensure specific student outcomes.*

STUDENT OUTCOMES	EVIDENCE-BASED PRACTICES
4.1. Personal Competence. Students with gifts and talents demonstrate growth in personal competence and dispositions for exceptional academic and creative productivity. These include self-awareness, self-advocacy, self-efficacy, confidence, motivation, resilience, independence, curiosity, and risk taking.	4.1.1. Educators maintain high expectations for all students with gifts and talents as evidenced in meaningful and challenging activities. 4.1.2. Educators provide opportunities for self-exploration, development and pursuit of interests, and development of identities supportive of achievement, e.g., through mentors and role models. 4.1.3. Educators create environments that support trust among diverse learners. 4.1.4. Educators provide feedback that focuses on effort, on evidence of potential to meet high standards, and on mistakes as learning opportunities. 4.1.5. Educators provide examples of positive coping skills and opportunities to apply them.
4.2. Social Competence. Students with gifts and talents develop social competence manifested in positive peer relationships and social interactions.	4.2.1. Educators understand the needs of students with gifts and talents for both solitude and social interaction. 4.2.2. Educators provide opportunities for interaction with intellectual and artistic/creative peers as well as with chronological-age peers. 4.2.3. Educators assess and provide instruction on social skills needed for school, community, and the world of work.
4.3. Leadership. Students with gifts and talents demonstrate personal and social responsibility and leadership skills.	4.3.1. Educators establish a safe and welcoming climate for addressing social issues and developing personal responsibility. 4.3.2. Educators provide environments for developing many forms of leadership and leadership skills. 4.3.3. Educators promote opportunities for leadership in community settings to effect positive change.
4.4. Cultural Competence. Students with gifts and talents value their own and others' language, heritage, and circumstance. They possess skills in communicating, teaming, and collaborating with diverse individuals and across diverse groups[1]. They use positive strategies to address social issues, including discrimination and stereotyping.	4.4.1. Educators model appreciation for and sensitivity to students' diverse backgrounds and languages. 4.4.2. Educators censure discriminatory language and behavior and model appropriate strategies. 4.4.3. Educators provide structured opportunities to collaborate with diverse peers on a common goal.
4.5. Communication Competence. Students with gifts and talents develop competence in interpersonal and technical communication skills. They demonstrate advanced oral and written skills, balanced biliteracy or multiliteracy, and creative expression. They display fluency with technologies that support effective communication.	4.5.1. Educators provide opportunities for advanced development and maintenance of first and second language(s). 4.5.2. Educators provide resources to enhance oral, written, and artistic forms of communication, recognizing students' cultural context. 4.5.3. Educators ensure access to advanced communication tools, including assistive technologies, and use of these tools for expressing higher-level thinking and creative productivity.

[1] *Differences among groups of people and individuals based on ethnicity, race, socioeconomic status, gender, exceptionalities, language, religion, sexual orientation, and geographical area.*

Gifted Education Programming Standard 5: Programming

Introduction

The term programming refers to a continuum of services that address students with gifts and talents' needs in all settings. Educators develop policies and procedures to guide and sustain all components of comprehensive and aligned programming and services for PreK-12 students with gifts and talents. Educators use a variety of programming options such as acceleration and enrichment in varied grouping arrangements (cluster grouping, resource rooms, special classes, special schools) and within individualized learning options (independent study, mentorships, online courses, internships) to enhance students' performance in cognitive and affective areas and to assist them in identifying future career goals. They augment and integrate current technologies within these learning opportunities to increase access to high level programming such as distance learning courses and to increase connections to resources outside of the school walls. In implementing services, educators in gifted, general, special education programs, and related professional services collaborate with one another and parents/guardians and community members to ensure that students' diverse learning needs are met. Administrators demonstrate their support of these programming options by allocating sufficient resources so that all students within gifts and talents receive appropriate educational services.

STANDARD 5: PROGRAMMING

Description: *Educators are aware of empirical evidence regarding (a) the cognitive, creative, and affective development of learners with gifts and talents, and (b) programming that meets their concomitant needs. Educators use this expertise systematically and collaboratively to develop, implement, and effectively manage comprehensive services for students with a variety of gifts and talents to ensure specific student outcomes.*

STUDENT OUTCOMES	EVIDENCE-BASED PRACTICES
5.1. *Variety of Programming.* Students with gifts and talents participate in a variety of evidence-based programming options that enhance performance in cognitive and affective areas.	5.1.1. Educators regularly use multiple alternative approaches to accelerate learning. 5.1.2. Educators regularly use enrichment options to extend and deepen learning opportunities within and outside of the school setting. 5.1.3. Educators regularly use multiple forms of grouping, including clusters, resource rooms, special classes, or special schools. 5.1.4. Educators regularly use individualized learning options such as mentorships, internships, online courses, and independent study. 5.1.5. Educators regularly use current technologies, including online learning options and assistive technologies to enhance access to high-level programming. 5.1.6. Administrators demonstrate support for gifted programs through equitable allocation of resources and demonstrated willingness to ensure that learners with gifts and talents receive appropriate educational services.
5.2. *Coordinated Services.* Students with gifts and talents demonstrate progress as a result of the shared commitment and coordinated services of gifted education, general education, special education, and related professional services, such as school counselors, school psychologists, and social workers.	5.2.1. Educators in gifted, general, and special education programs, as well as those in specialized areas, collaboratively plan, develop, and implement services for learners with gifts and talents.
5.3. *Collaboration.* Students with gifts and talents' learning is enhanced by regular collaboration among families, community, and the school.	5.3.1. Educators regularly engage families and community members for planning, programming, evaluating, and advocating.
5.4. *Resources.* Students with gifts and talents participate in gifted education programming that is adequately funded to meet student needs and program goals.	5.4.1. Administrators track expenditures at the school level to verify appropriate and sufficient funding for gifted programming and services.
5.5. *Comprehensiveness.* Students with gifts and talents develop their potential through comprehensive, aligned programming and services.	5.5.1. Educators develop thoughtful, multi-year program plans in relevant student talent areas, PK-12.
5.6. *Policies and Procedures.* Students with gifts and talents participate in regular and gifted education programs that are guided by clear policies and procedures that provide for their advanced learning needs (e.g., early entrance, acceleration, credit in lieu of enrollment).	5.6.1. Educators create policies and procedures to guide and sustain all components of the program, including assessment, identification, acceleration practices, and grouping practices, that is built on an evidence-based foundation in gifted education.
5.7. *Career Pathways.* Students with gifts and talents identify future career goals and the talent development pathways to reach those goals.	5.7.1. Educators provide professional guidance and counseling for individual student strengths, interests, and values. 5.7.2. Educators facilitate mentorships, internships, and vocational programming experiences that match student interests and aptitudes.

Gifted Education Programming Standard 6: Professional Development

Introduction

Professional development is essential for all educators involved in the development and implementation of gifted programs and services. Professional development is the intentional development of professional expertise as outlined by the NAGC–CEC teacher preparation standards and is an ongoing part of gifted educators' professional and ethical practice. Professional development may take many forms ranging from district-sponsored workshops and courses, university courses, professional conferences, independent studies, and presentations by external consultants and should be based on systematic needs assessments and professional

reflection. Students participating in gifted education programs and services are taught by teachers with developed expertise in gifted education. Gifted education program services are developed and supported by administrators, coordinators, curriculum specialists, general education, special education, and gifted education teachers who have developed expertise in gifted education. Since students with gifts and talents spend much of their time within general education classrooms, general education teachers need to receive professional development in gifted education that enables them to recognize the characteristics of giftedness in diverse populations, understand the school or district referral and identification process, and possess an array of high quality, research-based differentiation strategies that challenge students. Services for students with gifts and talents are enhanced by guidance and counseling professionals with expertise in gifted education.

STANDARD 6: PROFESSIONAL DEVELOPMENT

Description: *All educators (administrators, teachers, counselors, and other instructional support staff) build their knowledge and skills using the NAGC-CEC Teacher Standards for Gifted and Talented Education and the National Staff Development Standards. They formally assess professional development needs related to the standards, develop and monitor plans, systematically engage in training to meet the identified needs, and demonstrate mastery of standard. They access resources to provide for release time, funding for continuing education, and substitute support. These practices are judged through the assessment of relevant student outcomes.*

STUDENT OUTCOMES	EVIDENCE-BASED PRACTICES
6.1. Talent Development. Students develop their talents and gifts as a result of interacting with educators who meet the national teacher preparation standards in gifted education.	6.1.1. Educators systematically participate in ongoing, research-supported professional development that addresses the foundations of gifted education, characteristics of students with gifts and talents, assessment, curriculum planning and instruction, learning environments, and programming. 6.1.2. The school district provides professional development for teachers that models how to develop environments and instructional activities that encourage students to express diverse characteristics and behaviors that are associated with giftedness. 6.1.3. Educators participate in ongoing professional development addressing key issues such as anti-intellectualism and trends in gifted education such as equity and access. 6.1.4. Administrators provide human and material resources needed for professional development in gifted education (e.g. release time, funding for continuing education, substitute support, webinars, or mentors). 6.1.5. Educators use their awareness of organizations and publications relevant to gifted education to promote learning for students with gifts and talents.
6.2. Socio-emotional Development. Students with gifts and talents develop socially and emotionally as a result of educators who have participated in professional development aligned with national standards in gifted education and National Staff Development Standards.	6.2.1. Educators participate in ongoing professional development to support the social and emotional needs of students with gifts and talents.
6.3. Lifelong Learners. Students develop their gifts and talents as a result of educators who are life-long learners, participating in ongoing professional development and continuing education opportunities.	6.3.1. Educators assess their instructional practices and continue their education in school district staff development, professional organizations, and higher education settings based on these assessments. 6.3.2. Educators participate in professional development that is sustained over time, that includes regular follow-up, and that seeks evidence of impact on teacher practice and on student learning. 6.3.3. Educators use multiple modes of professional development delivery including online courses, online and electronic communities, face-to-face workshops, professional learning communities, and book talks. 6.3.4. Educators identify and address areas for personal growth for teaching students with gifts and talents in their professional development plans.
6.4. Ethics. Students develop their gifts and talents as a result of educators who are ethical in their practices.	6.4.1. Educators respond to cultural and personal frames of reference when teaching students with gifts and talents. 6.4.2. Educators comply with rules, policies, and standards of ethical practice.

Glossary of Terms

An abridged version of the glossary used in the NAGC Pre-K-Grade 12 Gifted Programming Standards

(Note: a full glossary is available at www.nagc.org)

Ability. Capacity to develop competence in an area of human endeavor; also referred to as 'potential'. Abilities can be developed through appropriate formal and informal education experiences and typically are assessed by measures such as intelligence tests, though environmental factors such as schooling, self-concept, and trust can lead to inaccurate results.

Aptitude. Ability to learn material at advanced rates and levels of understanding in a specific area (e.g., humanities, mathematics, science). Measured by tests of knowledge, speed and accuracy in reasoning, and information retrieval in the content area (Reis & Housand, 2008).

Assessment. Process of gathering data or using instruments for this purpose, typically to determine an individual's status with respect to a characteristic or behavior. Strictly speaking, assessment refers to the data that are collected or the collection process, while evaluation refers to making a judgment of some kind based on the assessment data.

Cognitive and affective growth. Cognitive growth refers to the development of concepts and thinking skills, while affective growth relates to the development of social-emotional needs.

Collaboration. Stakeholders purposefully working together and sharing responsibility for achieving a common goal; reaching out to engage others in responding to needs (e.g., educators responsible for G/T and bilingual education together planning instruction for English language learners with gifts and talents).

Coordinated services. Instruction and resources within and outside of programming specifically for students with gifts and talents (e.g., general, special, bilingual, or arts education) that are intentionally connected and articulated with each other to effectively support learners with gifts and talents.

Cultural competence. Skills and dispositions for establishing and maintaining positive relationships and working effectively with individuals and communities from diverse backgrounds. Includes an open mind, willingness to accept alternative perspectives, critical self-examination, and acquisition and use of information (Shaunessy & Matthews, 2009).

Culturally relevant. Describes elements (e.g., curriculum, materials) within culturally responsive classrooms that are rigorous and multicultural, engage culturally different students and have meaning for them, and enable them to connect new learning with their interests (Ford, 2010).

Differentiated assessment. The practice of varying assessment in such a way that it reflects differentiation in the curriculum and/or the instruction. Differentiated assessment implies that as students experience differences in their learning, they should experience differences in their assessment. For example, students with gifts and talents may require off level/above grade-level tests to accurately assess their level of ability or achievement.

Differentiated curriculum. Adaptation of content, process, and concepts to meet a higher level of expectation appropriate for advanced learners. Curriculum can be differentiated through acceleration, complexity, depth, challenge, and creativity (VanTassel-Baska & Wood, 2008).

Differentiated instruction. Multiple ways to structure a lesson so that each student is challenged at an appropriate level. Differentiated instruction may include such features as learner centeredness; planned assignments and lessons based on pre-assessment; and flexible grouping, materials, resources, and pacing (Tomlinson & Hockett, 2008).

Diversity. Differences among groups of people and individuals based on ethnicity, race, socioeconomic status, gender, exceptionalities, language, religion, sexual orientation, and geographical area (Matthews & Shaunessy, 2008; NCATE, 2010).

Identification. A needs assessment whose primary purpose is the placement of students into educational programs designed to develop their intellectual, emotional, and social potential (Richert, 2003). The identification process moves from screening to placement (Matthews & Shaunessy, 2010) and involves use of multiple measures to assess high-level ability, aptitude, achievement, or other constructs of interest in one or more areas of learning (Johnsen, 2008).

Individual learning options. Specific and unique academic plans developed for a student to include a range of possibilities such as grade acceleration, advanced study of a particular academic area, off-campus instruction, or resource programs. Individualized learning options may be called IEPs in some states; they generally include goals, outcomes, and assessments for each student with gifts and talents and are reviewed and revised annually.

Off-level/above-grade level. Tests normed for students at a higher grade level than the students who are being tested. Widely used in talent search testing (Matthews, 2008) to provide an accurate picture of the relative ability level of students whose abilities exceed those that can be measured using on-grade level instruments. Individually administered assessments such as IQ tests often can also provide this information.

Programs/programming. Formally structured, regularly scheduled, ongoing services provided to students with gifts and talents in school or community settings (e.g., museum, laboratory, or university). Programming includes goals, student outcomes, strategies to accomplish them, and procedures for assessing and evaluating these over time. The Committee prefers the term "programming" because it indicates the ongoing nature of these services, while "program" could refer to a one-time event.

Qualitative instruments. Measures that use primarily words rather than numbers to describe or investigate student, teacher, parent, or other stakeholders' reactions to or perceptions of strengths or weaknesses of gifted programming and related phenomena. Interviews and portfolios (Johnsen, 2008) are two commonly used types of qualitative instruments.

Quantitative instruments. Measures that use numerical data (Johnsen, 2008) to describe performance in relation to others (e.g., norm referenced intelligence tests) or in relation to a standard of performance (e.g., criterion referenced achievement tests).

Services/servicing. Educational and related interventions that are provided to students in or outside of the regular school setting. A given service may be one-time-only, annual, or ongoing, and may be provided even in the absence of formal gifted programming. Examples may include counseling, tutoring, and mentoring.

Social competence. The ability to interact effectively with others. Component skills include creating and maintaining positive interpersonal relationships, communicating, listening, and feeling empathy. Related dispositions include appreciation of human diversity, commitment to social justice, and holding high ethical standards (Moon, 2008).

Socio-emotional development. Those factors from a psychological perspective that assert an affective influence on an individual's self-image, behavior, and motivation; issues such as but not limited to peer relationships, emotional adjustment, stress management, perfectionism, and sensitivity (Moon, 2003).

Special Educator. In a handful of states, gifted education is included within special education (NAGC, 2009) and teachers of students with gifts and talents in these states are special educators. In other locations, state law does not consider gifted education to be a part of special education and teachers of students with gifts and talents are not considered special education staff.

Students with gifts and talents. This phrasing is currently preferred over "gifted and talented students" because it emphasizes the person rather than the exceptionality and is consistent with usage in the field of special education. It includes those students whose abilities are latent as well as students whose abilities already are manifest. Individuals with gifts and talents also includes 'gifted and talented students,' 'high-ability students,' 'academically advanced students,' 'gifted students with potential,' and so on.

Technical adequacy. This term refers to the psychometric properties of an assessment instrument. Instruments with technical adequacy demonstrate validity for the identified purpose, reliability in providing consistent results, and minimal bias, and have been normed on a population matching the census data (Johnsen, 2008).

Twice exceptional. A learner who evidences high performance or potential in a gift, talent, or ability area combined with one or more disabilities that may affect achievement (e.g., learning disability, attention deficit hyperactive disorder, Asperger's syndrome, or a physical or sensory disability).

Underachieving. This term refers to students who demonstrate a discrepancy between ability and performance (Reis & Housand, 2008). Underachieving students exhibit a severe discrepancy between expected achievement as measured by standardized assessments and actual achievement as measured by class grades or teacher evaluations (McCoach & Siegle, 2003). The discrepancy must persist over time and must not be the direct result of a diagnosed learning disability.

Glossary References

Ford, D. Y. (2010). Culturally responsive classrooms: Affirming culturally different gifted students. *Gifted Child Today, 33*(1), 50-53.

Johnsen, S. K. (2008). Identifying gifted and talented learners. In F. A. Karnes & K. R. Stephens (Eds.), *Achieving excellence: Educating the gifted and talented* (pp. 135-153). Upper Saddle River, NJ: Pearson.

Matthews, M. S. (2008). Talent search programs. In J. A. Plucker & C. M. Callahan (Eds.), *Critical issues and practices in gifted education: What the research says* (pp. 641-654). Waco, TX: Prufrock Press.

Matthews, M. S., & Shaunessy, E. (2008). Culturally, linguistically, and economically diverse gifted students. In F. A. Karnes & K. R. Stephens (Eds.), *Achieving excellence: Educating the gifted and talented* (pp. 99-115). Upper Saddle River, NJ: Pearson.

Matthews, M. S., & Shaunessy, E. (2010). Putting standards into practice: Evaluating the utility of the NAGC Pre-K—Grade 12 Gifted Program Standards. *Gifted Child Quarterly, 54*, 159-167.

McCoach, D. B., & Siegle, D. (2003). Factors that differentiate underachieving gifted students from high-achieving gifted students. *Gifted Child Quarterly, 47*, 144-154.

Moon, S. M. (2003). Counseling families. In N. Colangelo & G. A. Davis (Eds.), *Handbook of gifted education* (3rd ed., pp. 388-402). Boston, MA: Allyn & Bacon.

Moon, S. (2008). Personal and social development. In F. A. Karnes & K. R. Stephens (Eds.), *Achieving excellence: Educating the gifted and talented* (pp. 83-98). Upper Saddle River, NJ: Pearson.

National Association for Gifted Children & Council of State Directors of Programs for the Gifted. (2009). *2008-2009 State of the States in Gifted Education* [CD]. Washington, DC: Author.

National Council for Accreditation of Teacher Education (2010). Unit Standards Glossary downloaded 8/22/10 from http://www.ncate.org/public/glossary.asp?ch=155.

Reis, S. M., & Housand, A. M. (2008). Characteristics of gifted and talented learners: Similarities and differences across domains. In F. A. Karnes & K. R. Stephens (Eds.), *Achieving excellence: Educating the gifted and talented* (pp. 62-81). Upper Saddle River, NJ: Pearson.

Richert, E. S. (2003). Excellence and justice in identification and programming. In N. Colangelo & G. A. Davis (Eds.) *Handbook of gifted education* (3rd ed., pp. 146-158). Boston, MA: Allyn & Bacon.

Shaunessy, E., & Matthews, M. S. (2009). Preparing culturally competent teachers of the gifted: The role of racial consciousness. In Castellano, J.A. (Ed.), *Perspectives in Gifted Education: Diverse Gifted Learners* [monograph series], *4*, 5-26. Denver, CO: University of Denver, Institute for the Development of Gifted Education.

Tomlinson, C. A., & Hockett, J. A. (2008). Instructional strategies and programming models for gifted learners. In F. A. Karnes & K. R. Stephens (Eds.), *Achieving excellence: Educating the gifted and talented* (pp. 154-169). Upper Saddle River, NJ: Pearson.

VanTassel-Baska, J., & Wood, S. (2008). Curriculum development in gifted education: A challenge to provide optimal learning experiences. In F. A. Karnes & K. R. Stephens (Eds.), *Achieving excellence: Educating the gifted and talented* (pp. 209-229). Upper Saddle River, NJ: Pearson.

A Blueprint for Quality Gifted Education Programs **15**

NATIONAL ASSOCIATION FOR

1331 H St., NW, Suite 1001, Washington, DC 20005
202-785-4268 | www.nagc.org

About the Authors

Scott J. Peters, Ph.D., is an Associate Professor of Educational Foundations and the Richard and Veronica Telfer Endowed Faculty Fellow at the University of Wisconsin–Whitewater, where he teaches courses related to educational measurement, research methods, and gifted and talented education. His primary research area involves gifted and talented student identification and talent development with a focus on students from underrepresented populations. His scholarly work has appeared in *Teaching for High Potential, Gifted Child Quarterly,* the *Journal of Advanced Academics, Gifted and Talented International,* the *Journal of Career and Technical Education Research, Ed Leadership, Gifted Child Today,* and *Pedagogies.* He is the first author of *Beyond Gifted Education: Designing and Implementing Advanced Academic Programs* and *Designing Gifted Education Programs and Services: From Purpose to Implementation,* both from Prufrock Press, and the coauthor (along with Jonathan Plucker) of *Excellence Gaps in Education: Expanding Opportunities for Talented Students,* published by Harvard Education Press.

Dina Brulles, Ph.D., is the Director of Gifted Education at Paradise Valley Unified School District, is Gifted Program Coordinator at Arizona State University, and serves on the National Association for Gifted Children (NAGC) Board of Directors. She received the inaugural 2014 NAGC Gifted Coordinator Award and also the first NAGC Professional Development Network Award in 2013. Brulles coauthored the books *Differentiated Lessons for Every Learner, The Cluster Grouping Handbook: How To Challenge Gifted Students and Improve Achievement for All, Teaching Gifted Kids in Today's Classrooms,* and *Helping All Gifted Children Learn,* along with other publications and teacher training courses. Brulles assists school districts in developing, supporting, and evaluating gifted programs with an emphasis on integrating current educational initiatives. She has implemented and supervised the Schoolwide Cluster Grouping Model and has become a recognized expert in that practice.

ABOUT THE CONTRIBUTORS

Tamara Fisher is the K–12 Gifted Education Specialist for the Polson School District on the Flathead Indian Reservation in Montana. She is Past-President of the Montana Association for Gifted and Talented Education (AGATE). Fisher earned her bachelor's degree in elementary education from Montana State University-Bozeman and her master's degree in gifted education from the University of Connecticut. She coauthored, with Karen Isaacson, *Intelligent Life in the Classroom: Smart Kids and Their Teachers*, which won the 2007 Texas Association for the Gifted and Talented Legacy Book Award and a 2008 *Learning Magazine* Teacher's Choice Award. Fisher's writing also appeared for 6 years on the *Education Week* teacher website, where she wrote about gifted education in her "Unwrapping the Gifted" blog. She has presented on gifted-related topics for local, county, tribal, state, regional, national, and international audiences. She was selected as the 2001 Polson Teacher of the Year and the 2013 Montana AGATE Educator of the Year.

Lauri Kirsch, Ed.D., is the Supervisor of Gifted Programs for the nation's eighth largest school district. Since 1994, her involvement in gifted education has been through a multitude of roles, allowing her to learn and lead from a variety of perspectives. Through these experiences, Kirsch has found that leadership is the critical element for success in any organization, from the classroom, to a school district, to a state affiliate group. She is a former NAGC Board Member and was the recipient of the 2014 NAGC Coordinator Award. As the parent of two grown gifted daughters, Kirsch has navigated the unchartered waters that are integral to parenting the gifted. Her goal is to share a common sense message that may inspire and guide others in supporting the children who will be the leaders in our world's future.

Jane McMahon taught middle school English for 20 years before transitioning into her current role as Instructional Facilitator and Advanced Learner Coordinator for the Baraboo School District. She was named the 2014 Wisconsin Teacher of the Year, and in 2015, was the recipient of the University of Wisconsin–Madison Distinguished Education Alumni Award. In her free time, McMahon and her wife Lisa enjoy kayaking, fly fishing, and live music.

Lori M. Mueller, Ed.D., serves as the District Administrator for the School District of Baraboo. Mueller completed the doctoral program at Edgewood College and received her master's degree in educational administration from the University of Wisconsin-Madison and a bachelor's degree in French and health education from the University of Wisconsin-Whitewater. In her 22 years in education as a teacher, Director of Curriculum and Instruction, and now superintendent, Mueller has presented at regional, state, and national conferences on topics related to grading for communicating student learning, developing assessment literacy, gifted and talented services, implementing a Response to Intervention framework, continuous school improvement, and strategic planning.